INSIGHTS ON IMMERSIVE JOURNALISM

Bringing together theory and practice, this collection critically examines emerging conceptual, methodological and production frameworks for the study of immersive journalism.

Having first begun in academia, the practice of virtual reality/360° video immersive journalism has seen a steep rise in the professional arena in recent years. Uniting contributions from scholars and practitioners at the cutting-edge of this vibrant field, this book provides a summary of the history, development and key debates in immersive journalism and considers issues such as conceptualising and researching immersive journalism, teaching and producing immersive journalism, and situating immersive journalism in a wider theoretical and ethical context. Each chapter introduces readers to the key terms and concepts in that area and provides study questions to help them engage with the text.

Encouraging further enquiry and theorisation, and experimental design and production, *Insights on Immersive Journalism* is an invaluable resource for students and scholars interested in Immersive Journalism and Media.

Ana Luisa Sánchez Laws is Professor of Interdisciplinary Methodologies and Methods at the University of Tromsø The Arctic University of Norway. She has published extensively on uses of digital technologies in museums and in news media.

JOURNALISM INSIGHTS

The Journalism Insights series provides edited collections of theoretically grounded case study analyses on an eclectic range of journalistic areas, from peace and conflict reporting to fashion and sports reporting.

The series has a bias towards the contemporary, but each volume includes an important historical, contextualising section. Volumes offer international coverage and focus on both mainstream and 'alternative' media, always considering the impact of social media in the various fields.

The volumes are aimed at both undergraduate and postgraduate students on journalism as well as media and communication programmes who will find the texts original, interesting and inspirational.

For information on submitting a proposal for the series, please contact the Series Editor Richard Lance Keeble, of the University of Lincoln and Liverpool Hope University, at RKeeble@lincoln.ac.uk

Insights on Reporting Sports in the Digital Age
Ethical and Practical Considerations in a Changing Media Landscape
Edited by Roger Domeneghetti

Insights on Peace and Conflict Reporting
Edited by Kristin Skare Orgeret

Insights on Fashion Journalism
Edited by Rosie Findlay and Johannes Reponen

Insights on Immersive Journalism
Edited by Ana Luisa Sánchez Laws

For more information visit: www.routledge.com/Journalism-Insights/book-series/JI

INSIGHTS ON IMMERSIVE JOURNALISM

Edited by Ana Luisa Sánchez Laws

LONDON AND NEW YORK

Designed cover image: metamorworks/iStock/Getty Images Plus via Getty Images

First published 2023
by Routledge
4 Park Square, Milton Park, Abingdon, Oxon OX14 4RN

and by Routledge
605 Third Avenue, New York, NY 10158

Routledge is an imprint of the Taylor & Francis Group, an Informa business

© 2023 selection and editorial matter, Ana Luisa Sánchez Laws; individual chapters, the contributors

The right of Ana Luisa Sánchez Laws to be identified as the author of the editorial material, and of the authors for their individual chapters, has been asserted in accordance with sections 77 and 78 of the Copyright, Designs and Patents Act 1988.

All rights reserved. No part of this book may be reprinted or reproduced or utilised in any form or by any electronic, mechanical, or other means, now known or hereafter invented, including photocopying and recording, or in any information storage or retrieval ystem, without permission in writing from the publishers.

Trademark notice: Product or corporate names may be trademarks or registered trademarks, and are used only for identification and explanation without intent to infringe.

British Library Cataloguing-in-Publication Data
A catalogue record for this book is available from the British Library

Library of Congress Cataloging-in-Publication Data
Names: Sánchez Laws, Ana Luisa, editor.
Title: Insights on immersive journalism / edited by Ana Luisa Sánchez Laws.
Description: Abingdon, Oxon ; New York, NY : Routledge, 2023. |
Series: Journalism insights | Includes bibliographical references and index.
Identifiers: LCCN 2022042008 | ISBN 9781032107776 (hardback) |
ISBN 9781032107721 (paperback) | ISBN 9781003217008 (ebook)
Subjects: LCSH: Immersive journalism.
Classification: LCC PN4784.I46 I59 2023 |
DDC 070.4/3–dc23/eng/20221123
LC record available at https://lccn.loc.gov/2022042008

ISBN: 9781032107776 (hbk)
ISBN: 9781032107721 (pbk)
ISBN: 9781003217008 (ebk)

DOI: 10.4324/9781003217008

Typeset in Bembo
by Newgen Publishing UK

CONTENTS

List of figures   vii
List of tables   viii
List of contributors   ix
Preface   xiii

    Introduction   1
    Ana Luisa Sánchez Laws

PART I
Practicing and teaching immersive journalism   **15**

1   A prospective analysis of immersive journalism from the perspective of experts   17
    Susana Herrera Damas and Mª José Benítez de Gracia

2   Screenplay writing for immersive journalism   46
    Nili Steinfeld

3   Teaching immersive journalism production   60
    Tormod Utne

PART II
Researching immersive journalism 73

4 Evolution of immersive journalism research: A scientometric
   analysis 75
   Seok Kang

5 Main concepts in immersive journalism: Immersion and presence 92
   António Baía Reis, Lukas Kick and Marina Oliveto

PART III
Critical views on immersive journalism 105

6 Normative questions in immersive journalism 107
   Tanja Aitamurto

7 Promises, pitfalls and potentials of immersive journalism 124
   Holger Pötzsch

8 Journalism, technology and truth in the age of digital 143
   Robert Hassan

Index *165*

FIGURES

3.1	Pre-course survey questions	65
3.2	End of course survey results (1)	68
3.3	End of course survey results (2)	69
4.1	Number of publications on immersive journalism by year	84
4.2	Labels of keywords with different groups	85
4.3	Density view with keyword connections	85
4.4	Publication time view with keyword connections	86

TABLES

1.1 List of participants in the academics' focus group   21
1.2 List of participants in the professionals' focus group   22
4.1 List of top 20 communication journals with published articles on immersive journalism   83
4.2 Top 20 keywords with the number of occurrences and link strength   84
5.1 Number of scientific publications related to the wider conceptual categories of the term 'immersion'   97
5.2 Number of scientific publications related to the wider conceptual categories of the term 'presence'   99

CONTRIBUTORS

Tanja Aitamurto is Assistant Professor in the Department of Communication at the University of Illinois Chicago, USA. Her work examines new media technologies for informing, empowering and connecting people, addressing how new media technologies impact human behaviour and society and how these technologies can be harnessed for social good. She has attended meetings and given talks about her research at the White House, the United Nations, the Organisation for Economic Co-operation and Development (OECD), the Council of Europe and in several parliaments and governments. Tanja has worked as a journalist specialising in military and defence, reporting in countries such as Afghanistan, Angola and Uganda. She also covered technology at VentureBeat, a Silicon Valley-based tech blog.

António Baía Reis is Assistant Professor at the University of Passau, Germany. His research, teaching and creative activities are largely interdisciplinary, combining areas such as digital and emergent media, communication and performing arts. Dr Baía Reis has a strong focus on immersive media (VR, AR, MR), participatory and collaborative practices, practice and arts-based research, creativity studies, innovation in education and social impact. He is the founder of the Future Media Colab at the University of Passau and co-founder of the XR theatre collective La Cuarta Pared VR (The Fourth Wall VR).

Mª José Benítez de Gracia is Faculty member at the Department of Journalism and Audiovisual Communication, Universidad Carlos III de Madrid, Spain. Her field of research encompasses uses of 360° video in journalism. She has previous experience as Section Editor at the magazine Computer Hoy (Axel Springer). With Susana Herrera Damas, she has co-authored the manual *Cómo producir reportajes* *inmersivos con vídeo en 360°* ('How to produce immersive journalism with 360° video', Editorial UOC).

Robert Hassan is Professor of Media and Communication at the University of Melbourne, Australia. He has taught, researched and written at the intersection of politics, media, technology, time and philosophy of science for over 20 years. He has written 12 books that explore these conjunctions and have been translated into Chinese, Arabic and Korean. He is the author of *The Condition of Digitality* (University of Westminster Press), *Uncontained* (Grattan Street Press), *The Age of Distraction* (Routledge) and *Analog* (MIT Press).

Susana Herrera Damas is Journalism Professor at Universidad Carlos III de Madrid, Spain, and current head of the Innovation on Digital Media research group. Her research focuses on media innovation initiatives to improve journalism. Prof. Herrera Damas and Dr Mª José Benítez de Gracia are co-authors of the manual *Cómo producir reportajes inmersivos con vídeo en 360°* ('How to produce immersive journalism with 360° video', Editorial UOC). With Maria Luengo, Herrera Damas is co-editor of the book *News Media Innovation Reconsidered* (John Wiley & Sons).

Seok Kang is Professor in Digital Communication at the University of Texas at San Antonio, USA. His teaching and research areas focus on new communication technologies, mobile communication, m-marketing, social media, communication research methods, theory, digital journalism, artificial intelligence, augmented reality, virtual reality, big data and digital message design. Prof. Kang has published 46 refereed journal articles and 16 books and book chapters. He is the author of *Disruptive Digital Innovation*, *Digital Message Design*, *Handbook of Digital Media Production* (all with Linus Publications) and *Motivational Use of Web News* (Lambert Academic Publishing).

Lukas Kick is a PhD candidate at the Department of Media, University of Passau, Germany. His doctoral work concerns the ethics of immersive journalism.

Marina Oliveto is a Brazilian journalist, economist and PhD candidate in Communication Sciences at ULHT, Lisbon, Portugal. Her research is in the field of immersive journalism and new narratives. She is an active 360° video producer at the company 360 Film Lab. She currently also works as reporter for Deutsche Welle.

Holger Pötzsch is Professor in Media and Documentation Studies at UiT The Arctic University of Norway. His field of research includes the war film and war games, the role of art and technology in processes of bordering, the interrelation between popular culture and memory politics as well as the impact of new media technologies on perception and practices of warfare. Along with Philip Hammond,

Prof. Pötzsch is co-editor of the anthology *War Games: Memory, Militarism and the Subject of Play* (Bloomsbury Academic).

Ana Luisa Sánchez Laws is Professor in Interdisciplinary Methodologies and Methods at the Centre for Peace Research, Centre for Sami and Indigenous Studies and Centre for Women and Gender Research at UiT The Arctic University of Norway. Her work focuses on digital technologies, diversity and inclusion of minorities in museums and digital media. She is the author of *Museum Websites and Social Media* and *Panamanian Museums and Historical Memory* (both with Berghahn Books). Her work on immersive journalism is synthesised in the book *Conceptualizing Immersive Journalism* (Routledge).

Nili Steinfeld is Leader of the Digital Communication Track and Academic Director at the Institute of New Media Research, Politics and Society, The Moskowitz School of Communication, Ariel University, Israel. Her research covers a wide range of topics on the political and civic uses of the internet, where she combines various methodological approaches, among them online experiments, surveys, eye tracking and digital methods for scraping and analysing digital objects.

Tormod Utne is Associate Professor at the Media Department at Volda University College, Norway. Utne has over 20 years of experience as Head Editor of several leading national, regional and local news organisations in Norway. He is also advisor at Norsk presseforbund (Norwegian Press Association). He has published in the areas of immersive journalism and ethics and pedagogical approaches to 360° video and VR for journalists and media producers.

PREFACE

This book examines emerging conceptual, methodological, pedagogical and production frameworks for immersive journalism. In addition to providing a discussion of production practices, the book offers expert practitioner, researcher and educator perspectives of the development of immersive journalism as a field of practice-based research. It is intended primarily for an audience of scholars, early career academics and undergraduate and advanced students in journalism and communication. It is a book aimed at encouraging further theorisation, empirical research as well as experimental design and production.

The book includes contributions from Europe, North America, the Middle East and Australia. Invited contributors are scholars who have developed cutting-edge empirical and theoretical research on immersive journalism. Authors are selected for their demonstrated research rigour, the interplay between their approaches and the innovative potential of their work. Along with the conceptual, methodological, pedagogical and practical issues that these authors reflect upon, they bring to the table discussions about ethics and other overarching topics regarding new paths for journalism in a digital era. We hope the volume will serve as future reference for students, researchers and practitioners engaging with this exciting field.

The practice of virtual reality/360° video immersive journalism saw a steep rise in interest around 2015. Since then, research activity has also grown at a steady pace. The number of articles with immersive journalism as central topic continues to increase each year (see Chapter 4 in this volume). In addition to the steady increase of published articles, three scholarly books (two monographs and one edited collection) have also been published in the last years: Sánchez Laws, 2019; *Conceptualizing Immersive Journalism* (Routledge); Pavlik, 2020, *Journalism in the Age of Virtual Reality: How Experiential Media Are Transforming News* (Columbia University Press) and Uskali, Gynnild, Jones and Sirkkunen (eds.), 2020, *Immersive Journalism as Storytelling* (Routledge). The collection of articles in *Insights on Immersive Journalism* should be a good complement to these volumes, thus contributing to the growing body of literature on this topic.

This edited collection wishes to contribute to the task of gathering existing knowledge in a format that allows it to be used as a guide for students, researchers and professionals.

Any guideline for immersive journalism must consider a multiplicity of research traditions, given that research and production of immersive journalism has often involved collaboration in interdisciplinary teams, each with its own concerns regarding ethical stances and the limits of research. The authors contributing to this volume reflect this interdisciplinarity and this variety of views. We hope that our contribution can further help immersive journalism become a leading research field within media and communications, especially when it comes to exploring new interdisciplinary ethical frameworks for journalism research.

Missing from this volume, however, are contributions that discuss in more depth the technologies and design aspects of immersive journalism. Without these perspectives, the field is weakened. Researchers considering entering this field are thus invited to do so by embracing an even broader diversity of views than what has been captured by our collection. We hope then that as the field continues to evolve, ours is but one of the many volumes that students will be able to consult. We truly hope that multiple disciplinary, professional and cultural perspectives will continue to inform the core of principles of immersive journalism, as it transforms into a format that can ethically bring the news closer to the people who most need them.

INTRODUCTION

Ana Luisa Sánchez Laws

Insights on Immersive Journalism offers a broad overview of current research activity in the field of immersive journalism. The volume presents the ways in which this vibrant field of research is developing conceptually, pedagogically and methodologically. It also offers a look at the extent to which practice frameworks have become more established. By unpacking implicit assumptions, identifying gaps and reassessing current findings, the goal of the volume is to serve as a springboard for new research avenues in this field.

This introductory chapter provides a brief overview of key themes in immersive journalism covered by this collection of chapters. These themes are (a) issues for teaching and professional practice, discussed in 'Part I: Practicing and teaching immersive journalism', (b) research approaches and definitions, discussed in 'Part II: Researching immersive journalism' and (c) concerns regarding ethics and the wider impact of immersive technologies for journalism, discussed in 'Part III: Critical views on immersive journalism'.

Part I: Practicing and teaching immersive journalism

In Chapter 1, 'A prospective analysis of immersive journalism from the perspective of experts', Susana Herrera Damas and Mª José Benítez de Gracia provide a compilation of expert discussions about the status and future of immersive journalism. Expert insights are provided by 15 scholars and professionals including António Baía-Reis, Jorge Esteban Blein, Eva Domínguez Martín, Suzana Barbosa, Ana Luisa Sánchez Laws, Sara Pérez-Seijo, Pavel Sidorenko, Lucielle Lima, Javier Coloma, Nonny De la Peña, Ignacio Ferrando, Robert Hernández, Clàudia Prat, Laura Raya and Daniel Rojas Roa.

Damas and Benítez de Gracia ask these internationally renowned academics and professionals to think together about what specific issues immersive journalism

DOI: 10.4324/9781003217008-1

should be reserved for and what they see as the future of immersive journalism and metaverse in relation to immersive journalism.

Amongst the issues raised are the need to make immersive journalism more accessible as a form of production. For instance, Hernández talks about how this form of journalism should be produced not only by the rich or those with the technical capacity – immersive journalism researchers and practitioners also have the responsibility to make these tools more accessible, so that more diverse perspectives can be included. In addition, experts talk about the need to be humble, keeping an attitude of constant learning from the mistakes being made. Amongst these mistakes, some experts argue, is the idea that this kind of journalism is for mass consumption. On the contrary, one idea emerging from the expert panel is that immersive journalism could be thought of much more as a type of production that is intended for a small segment of the audience. In this, the field could promote the idea that media companies should engage with immersive journalism in a similar fashion to what is done with documentary production, departing from the view that this work requires time, resources and appropriate assumptions about the audiences sought to be reached.

Overall, experts agree upon the need for diverse strategies, which may include (a) partnering with start-ups and professionals who have the necessary capabilities, (b) reinforcing a commitment to the documentary genre, (c) creating immersive experiences in public spaces like museums, (d) enhancing and expanding university-based training and (e) compiling new knowledge in written form.

In terms of point (a) above about having the necessary capabilities, immersive journalism is an interdisciplinary practice that requires technical, conceptual and production skills in addition to knowledge and understanding of ethical journalistic norms. From the perspective of production, immersive journalists using virtual reality and 360° video must solve the conundrum of making audiences feel present in the moment while also introducing the perspective of the journalist capturing the story and the deeper issues that the story raises. One solution may be through the development of specific screenwriting techniques. This is the topic of Chapter 2, 'Screenplay writing for immersive journalism', where Nili Steinfeld discusses strategies for screenplay writing that address the above concerns.

The chapter explores the ever-evolving definitions of journalism and relates these to definitions of journalism as storytelling. This involves defining immersion in news reporting as a practice aimed at increasing audience engagement with news before and after the introduction of virtual reality to journalism practice. The chapter reviews projects which make use of screenplay for illustrating an event or phenomenon of journalistic importance. Steinfeld discusses the boundaries between art and journalism as they are formed and blurred within this practice. Ethical considerations and social implications are also raised as the chapter strives to position the use of screenplay writing with respect to immersive journalism practice.

Steinfeld departs from the point of view that the main goal of immersive journalism projects is often to allow participants to have a first-person experience in a virtually recreated scenario representing a news story (De la Peña et al., 2010).

For example, in the projects led by De la Peña, audio recorded during an event was used in an animated simulation of the event. However, as Steinfeld points out, not all news stories can be recorded in real-time. She then asks: For cases aiming at allowing participants to enter a representation of a news story which cannot be recorded, can a script written based on testimonies, simulating both the visual and audio of a representative event, still be considered journalism? To what extent should journalists allow interpretive elements, that is, reconstructions, as part of the communication of the news event? What elements help establish an objective representation of news?

To answer these questions, Steinfeld reminds us that one of journalism's basic goals is to create an affective relationship between the public and the news (Baía Reis and Coelho, 2018). This is not new and has not been invented with immersive journalism. In fact, as she tells us, storytelling forms of journalism, aimed at increasing audience immersion and engagement with the story gained prominence during the 20th century, long before virtual reality was introduced to journalism. She reminds us of both Gellhorn's 'view from the ground' coverage of World War II (Gellhorn, 1994) and Orwell's literary journalism designed to 'make political writing into an art' (Orwell and Angus, 1968, as cited in Keeble, 2020).

In immersive journalism, we are told we will be the first person – it is us, the audience, who will become the narrator, the witness and the person undergoing a transformation during immersion. We are asked to adopt the eyes and shoes of the journalist, yet in many of these projects, we do so without having the opportunity to listen to the inner struggles of the journalists trying to make sense of the situation. Since we witness only the end of the process (the final product), this kind of immersion may make us more tourists than travellers. This goes against the intended goal of bringing us closer to the events and creating more compassion and empathy via virtual reality immersion. One of the issues Walters (2015) has pointed out as a challenge for journalists when doing immersion is how to 'crack a closed culture to write about it in the truest way'. This includes the idea of being a traveller rather than a tourist, that is, spending enough time immersed with subjects and in their situation to be able to achieve a much deeper knowledge. The problem, however, is how to maintain a distance while keeping compassion for the subjects. Walters argues that being able to avoid 'going native', that is, to be able to keep a distance that enables literary journalists to mirror back events to their subjects in a new light as well as allows them to connect stories to larger topics, is one of the hallmarks of modern immersion journalism of the kind practised by Ted Conover in *Rolling Nowhere* (1984) and *Newjack* (2000) and Adrian Nicole LeBlanc in *Random Family* (2003). Immersive journalists working in the virtual reality/360° video format also face this issue: Virtual reality projects tend to be long-term investigations that require journalists to spend considerable amounts of time at a location and with their subjects. However, immersive journalists have tended to hide their persona from the narration of the event in virtual reality. For Steinfeld, a better inclusion of these aspects in immersive journalism pieces through the art of screenplay writing can help the further development of immersive storytelling forms of journalism.

Steinfeld's perspective allows the use of screenplay writing to include artistic elements that represent the complexity of voices entangled in journalistic storytelling. This is because she holds the position that the ideal of full objectivity in journalistic reporting is unattainable. Journalism scholarship provides varying, complex, sometimes contradictory definitions to journalism and of journalists. However, she argues that journalistic coverage is practically never mere reporting of events: Good journalism is expected to make complex events and issues into simple and understandable stories (Zelizer, 2005), which implies that editing and interpretation is a necessity. Her chapter is thus based on the idea that although some perceptions of journalism still aspire for it to be a strict mirroring of events, without filtering or editing, completely objective and clear of bias, many contemporary reporters as well as scholars consider this approach nonviable (Zelizer, 2005). She also agrees with Roeh's (1989) argument that journalism is and always has been a form of storytelling and that coverage always follows a narrative. There is no such thing as objective, fact-only reporting of news and anything other than that is already storytelling. Thus, instead of pushing for more objective reporting, we should use the craft of screenplay writing to define a new role for immersive journalism. In fact, screenplay writing can help overcome the seeming contradiction between immersion and accuracy in news reporting.

The chapter explores a range of immersive projects that recreate and illustrate news stories and events, from animation illustrations to development of fictitious scripts based on real events and testimonies (for example, Steinfeld, 2020; Emblematic group's various projects; BBC's *We Wait*; *The Financial Times*'s The uber game, etc.). It discusses the blurring boundaries between art and journalistic practice within immersive storytelling. It also touches upon the ethical and societal dilemmas such practices raise resulting from the persuasive power of immersive experiences and their increased potential to evoke empathy, the blurring of boundaries between fact and fiction that perhaps characterise some of these productions. Finally, Steinfeld uses the topic of screenplay writing to also pose pressing questions about the future role of immersive journalism. As Steinfeld's examples show, when looking at immersive journalism products, it is possible to identify trends in the uses of immersive technologies that correspond to two ideologically distinct positions about news communication that Schudson (2001) describes as the American ideology of news as the communication of objective facts, versus the European ideology of news as more open to interpretation. Immersive Journalism in its virtual reality/360° video form represents a new arena where these tensions resurface. She prompts us to ask whether immersive journalism (and journalism more generally) will maintain its status as an ideology consisting of the obligation for objectivity and impartial interpretation of the world (Deuze, 2004), as a tool to create affective relationship between the public and the news (Baía Reis and Coelho, 2018), or will it become a propaganda machine serving the elite (Herman and Chomsky, 2010 [1988]).

However, these tensions are also visible in the history of documentary, where one tradition sought for some time transparency and objectivity provided by the concept of 'fly on the wall', while other documentarists were more comfortable with a freer 'creative treatment of actuality'. It seems appropriate then to use documentary, more specifically web documentary, as a topic that can help students achieve a broader perspective upon the issues that surround many forms of factual storytelling, including immersive journalism. This is the topic of Chapter 3, 'Teaching immersive journalism production', where Tormod Utne describes experiences from teaching web documentary and immersive journalism to journalism, media production, animation, PR and design students at Volda University College (VUC).

Utne argues that the spheric medium of a 360° video scene gives audiences the opportunity to experience content on both traditional screens and virtual reality glasses. Placing the audience at the centre of documentaries means students must adopt new mindsets and tools for planning, filming/coding, storyboarding and building stories. The questions teachers face include how to deal with classical work methods when students apply immersion into their storytelling and how to change the way students work from idea development to user experience. The chapter covers the kinds of adjustments that must be made and how media students deal with the perspectives needed to create immersive content.

Utne tells us how implementing immersive journalism in media education at VUC has been of great value: 360° video and VR productions challenge students to rethink established practices and narratives. The newness of this technology helps students learn how to deal with technical-production challenges. Also, co-operation with technology actors such as Google News Lab has meant that students can be inspired by professionals in the field.

Amongst the factors that educators need to consider is the complexity of dealing with multiple disciplinary backgrounds. Students will come from different traditions: Some are trained more heavily in technology, some have an educational programme that emphasises ethics issues, some are more trained in aesthetics. All these backgrounds can provide strength to student teams, but they can also be the source of conflict, when leadership of the project is unclear, or when it is difficult for the students to decide which aspect should be prioritised given any time or production constraints. Utne talks about the special effort that needs to be put into creating rapport, allowing students to get to know each other beyond their disciplinary 'labels' as journalists, videographers, technologists, etc. He also discusses how the collaboration with technology companies has provided benefits both for students and for start-up owners, as they get to test together the limits of the technologies under development. These and other lessons learned form the core of this chapter, which we hope can be useful for other educators wanting to implement these technologies into their journalism and media courses.

Part II: Researching immersive journalism

Part II provides an overview of the development of the conceptual base of immersive journalism. The first part is a mapping of the entire field to assess which trends have dominated thus far. The second part then zooms in into two basic concepts, namely *immersion* and *presence*.

In Chapter 4, 'Evolution of immersive journalism research: A scientometric analysis', Seok Kang examines immersive journalism research conducted over the past several decades from its origin to the current advancement. He departs from the perspective that immersive journalism is a form of journalism production that allows audience engagement, user experience and evaluation in multimodal news media platforms. Kang also sees the emergence of immersive journalism as a culmination of the long arc of the experiential news media evolution. Based on the scientometrics of bibliometric data assessment, the chapter's meta-analysis aims at quantifying and measuring immersive journalism as experiential news media in the participatory media environment to develop accurate formal representations of the patterns and implications in the journalism field. Specifically, this chapter (a) identifies the main concepts and foci of research on immersive journalism, (b) visualises the conceptual and thematic structure of research on immersive journalism and (c) identifies key components that are revealed in the immersive journalism discipline.

The mapping of immersive journalism research in this chapter offers insights into what topics are overstudied and understudied. Kang finds that topics such as engagement, power, empathy, documentary, games and credibility are being actively researched. Future journalism research, Kang suggests, could focus more on the role of immersive journalism in technology adoption, civic engagement, emotion, information processing, intention and behavioural aspects.

Kang's findings point to the continued influence of disciplines such as psychology and computer science in shaping the field. However, it also reveals the need to reinvigorate close collaboration with these disciplines. It should be noted that these disciplines were central to the first steps taken to develop the field. The 2010 classic paper by De la Peña and colleagues is a great example of interdisciplinary collaboration between journalism scholars, computer scientists and psychologists. Thus, it should be well within reach to follow Kang's suggestions for future topics and give new impulse to the strand of research that connects ideas from psychology, computer science, game studies and journalism and media studies.

Interdisciplinary discussions involving inputs from psychology and philosophy have contributed to defining the specialised terminology for the field of immersive journalism. An example of this is the work on defining the terms *immersion* and *presence*. Building on these insights, António Baía Reis, Lukas Kick and Marina Oliveto describe in Chapter 5, 'Main concepts in immersive journalism: Immersion and presence', how more precision has been sought over the years to distinguish between immersion and presence for the specific purposes of immersive journalism. This chapter takes us through a full examination of these concepts and their entanglements. This examination includes (a) how immersion and presence have been theoretically contextualised within key immersive journalism research and (b) how immersion and presence in immersive journalism draw from rather old discussions about such phenomena from the wider fields of virtual reality and media studies. For instance, immersive journalism's goal to place the user in the middle of the news event and to augment the richness of the news format to provide a more vivid rendering of events has been a long-held desire for several previous journalistic movements, including New Journalism.

The chapter discusses approaches from Da Costa and Brasil (2017), Dominguez Martinez (2013) and Murray (1997), who talk about spatial and sensory types of immersion, where spatial immersion covers presence, simulation and plausibility and sensory immersion covers engagement, adaptation and absorption. The chapter also shows how in the early literature, immersion and presence are used interchangeably. For some authors, immersion is the actual level of sensorimotor stimulation experienced by the subject, while presence is the level of psychological response to the simulation (Bohil et al., 2011; Cummings and Bailenson, 2016; Slater and Wilbur, 1997). In what concerns presence, Metzinger (2018) argues that a sense of presence depends on three elements: (a) identification (a self), (b) self-location in a temporal frame of reference (now) and (c) self-location in space (place illusion). Presence is thus the ability to locate an egocentric (as in 'individual-centric') point of focus in an otherwise indetermined time-space field. Presence is also defined as the feeling of being in a world that exists outside the self (Waterworth et al., 2010), a fundamental component of cognition that goes beyond interacting with immersive technologies and a monitoring activity that helps delimit the self (Triberti and Riva, 2015). In the context of 360° video/VR-based immersive journalism, which seems to be adopting the direction of dealing primarily with 'sensorimotor stimulation', immersion encompasses the technologies, the psychology and the behaviours of users. From this, it can be argued that what is called immersion in the context of other forms of journalism such as literary journalism, also called immersion journalism, is in fact what is meant by presence in immersive journalism, since presence places more emphasis in aspects of augmenting 'the psychological response' to a depiction of newsworthy events.

The investigation in this chapter shows that one aspect that has not received enough attention is the individual user's characteristics. Psychology and neuroscience have begun to focus much more on the role of our internal signals (heart rate, blood pressure, signals from the visceral system, etc.) as constitutive of perceptual experiences such as the sense of presence. However, the literature on immersive journalism has yet to consider such physiological aspects in full, even though, as Kang points in Chapter 4, some studies have indeed included this aspect by monitoring physiological responses.

Further research on the individual differences that affect the sense of presence in immersive journalism is highly needed. Again, the call is for greater interdisciplinary collaboration to further expand the field. In the not-so-distant future, virtual reality biofeedback systems with immersive technologies, which are under development in other fields (for example, for psychological therapy and sports), could be used for immersive journalism research. Also, when it comes to finding new ways to assess the emotional impact that news has on audiences, the field of media psychology offers robust pointers on how these collaborations can develop (see for example the work of Slater and colleagues at the Event Lab in Barcelona and Bailenson and colleagues at Stanford University).

Part III: Critical views on immersive journalism

After a period of enthusiasm and innovative energy in building the field, as the mapping in Part II shows, it is necessary to step back and consider the outcomes of these creative efforts, including the mistakes made and the pitfalls that need to be avoided in the future. Therefore, Part III of the book takes a highly critical stance towards immersive journalism. Tanja Aitamurto starts this critical work in Chapter 6, 'Normative questions in immersive journalism', where she discusses the issues of accuracy and objectivity in visual journalism. She tells us that these aspirational norms serve as the fundamental building blocks for journalistic credibility and authority and that immersive journalism could hold a promise to contribute to both the perceived accuracy and objectivity in journalism. However, these very same qualities of immersive journalism may also undermine the perceived objectivity and accuracy of the imagery.

As Aitamurto discusses, in VR journalism/360° video journalism, the omnidirectional view is considered to provide a more accurate representation of events. This omnidirectional view is the 'God's eye view' or 'fly on the wall' view that we are familiar with from other factual formats. The idea is that the multidimensional aspects in immersive journalism can support the illusion of objectivity, as the viewer has access to more unrestricted field of views to the imagery. The illusion of objectivity may also come from the seeming lack of editing of the spherical view (for example, lack of 'continuity cuts' or other editing transitions within a scene). The omnidirectional field of view is meant to provide more freedom to the viewer to choose where to focus on. Aitamurto argues that this freedom means that the journalist loses control over the denotative and connotative aspects of the storyline, aspects that in more traditional visual journalism are more closely in journalists' control. This, she tells us, means that the viewer's freedom to choose the field of view can lead to a less accurate picture of the story. Precisely because of the expanded freedom to focus on or ignore details that may or may not contribute to eliciting the intended meaning of the scene, the viewer is much more of a collaborator/co-creator in this kind of format.

Holger Pötzsch continues with a similar line of thinking in Chapter 7, 'Promises, pitfalls and potentials of immersive journalism', where he presents his highly critical perspectives on immersive journalism. As several other authors have argued previously, Pötzsch thinks that the concept of immersive journalism has given rise to new (and perhaps too high) expectations regarding audience engagement with journalistic products (Pérez-Seijo, 2017; Jones, 2017). Cutting-edge VR technology combined with 3D-modelling and simulation techniques will immerse audiences in events and open new venues to a much-needed younger 'reader'ship (Pérez-Seijo, 2017). However, Pötzsch sets as his task to debunk some of these myths and offer a critique of a series of implicit assumptions built into mainstream discourses about immersive journalism. As an alternative, he presents a new way of conceptualising potential benefits of this emergent journalistic practice.

Pötzsch's position is that immersive journalism is not so much about depicting events as they happened, but about contextualising, explaining and interpreting these events in a rational and reflected fashion. For him, it is not a given that immersion and interactivity can contribute to highlighting the history or context of a simulated incident or to laying out various possible and often competing understandings of what happened. Immersive journalism, Pötzsch tells us, does not offer 'unfiltered audio-visual access to an event as it supposedly occurred' – it is always also a negotiation and interpretation of reality that can give rise to different versions of truth that need to be balanced and understood in relation to one another.

In a similar way that Steinfeld argues in her chapter, Pötzsch thinks that a narrativisation of real events in text or film can explain contradictions and thereby invite non-violent approaches to conflict resolution (Falke, 2017). Producing immersion as if there was no such obvious 'narrativisation' runs the danger of inviting a hedonistic, voyeuristic and cannibalistic form of reception that can paralyse audiences rather than facilitate critical and reflective long-term engagement (Sontag, 2003). For Pötzsch, the solution is to turn to the theory of the stage of Augusto Boal (1979; also Boal and Jackson, 2002), which can indicate how genuinely positive potentials of the emerging new technology of immersive journalism can be realised. In his texts on forum theatre and spect-actors, Boal describes a theatre where audiences are empowered to enter the stage and intervene in the play at any moment. Rather than passive spectators they become spect-actors and co-constitutive of the overall direction and message of a play. In contrast to, for instance, Brecht, Boal assumes the main point of a theatre play not to be the overall message of an orchestrated production on stage, but the discussions and debates about the play that take place among audiences, actors and director while it is staged (Pötzsch, 2017a). Boal perceives of these dialogues and shared struggles over meaning as the main aspects of political conscientisation processes and democratic deliberation. Boal's thinking opens new potentials for politically conscientious game play and development focused on engaging players in interventions and discussions about games and their politics during play (Pötzsch, 2019).

Pötzsch tells us that we could conceive of VR-based immersive journalism as an opportunity to not only engage with an authentically represented incident in simulated 3D settings, but also as an opportunity to problematise its technological frames and engage in ethical spectatorship (Kozol, 2014). In simulated 3D environments, one can vicariously witness an ultimately contingent past event in direct conjunction with others. The Levinasian face of the other this technology would make us 'response-able' to would then not be that of a simulated victim or perpetrator, but that of another witness exposed to the same artificial re-enactment yet still perceiving it from a differently situated personal vantage point (Butler, 2004, 2009). In times of increased mediatised tribalisation, filter bubbles and personal information customisation, such an exposure to the different perspective of a fellow other might serve a genuinely beneficial purpose for democracies. Pötzsch argues that the technologies behind immersive journalism could, if freely distributed and accessible, become conducive to shared immersive experiences that can be collectively engaged with and thereby appropriated.

An important assumption implicit in discourses of VR-based immersive journalism is about the capacity of virtual 3D environments to accurately represent news events in a supposedly more realistic and engaging manner thereby increasing potentials for empathy and therefore engagement. The questions that become pressing in this context concern the following: (a) what exactly is realistic about a representation, (b) why an increasingly accurate depiction of an incident's surface features should lead to enhanced empathy and (c) why increased empathy should lead to improved understanding and thereby to political conscientisation and mobilisation. In response to these questions, Pötzsch's chapter shows that realism in representations (both VR and otherwise) is highly selective (Pötzsch, 2017b) and that it is not necessarily a photorealistic depiction of the event itself that leads to long-term engagement (Pötzsch, 2012). On the contrary, an immersive, yet still simplistic, surface realism in depictions of violence and conflict might lead to a spectacularisation of news (Kellner, 2002). Immersive journalism might be open to voyeurism or politically debilitating shock effects (Sontag, 2003), can lead to a double injury of the depicted victims whose sufferings are enlisted on behalf of varying political projects (Dauphinée, 2007), or can be reconciled with a rationalisation of the depicted violence (Falke, 2017). On a more sombre note, Pötzsch argues that rather than opening audiences for the ethical obligations, an increased verisimilitude of 3D VR environments can invite to unpolitical pseudo-experiences of watchable surface features and consumable suffering.

In Chapter 8, 'Journalism, technology and truth in the age of digital', Robert Hassan invites us to look beyond the limited realm of immersive journalism. He asks us to consider that the original journalistic technology, the written word, continued to be central in the framing and in the narration of a reliable accounting of events even as journalists began adopting new technologies such as photography and film. However, something more radical seems to be happening with digital technology, which, as he argues, has transformed the craft of journalism in ways that are far from clear to most journalists and their public. For Hassan, immersive journalism represents one such area of practice where it is the technology itself that is claimed to lead in the search not simply for truths or facts to be consumed, but to bring the individual closer to the event such that it renders an ontological experience making truth and fact apparent. Hassan discusses the idea that augmented or virtual reality claims unmediated witnessing, lack of framing and lack of narrative artifice. The underlying assumption is that knowledge of the world can become virtually first-hand through immersion in the increasingly powerful representation of reality through computation.

Hassan strongly criticises this technology-led transformation of the ethical economy of public journalism through a critical comparison of the technologies involved. He takes us on a journey through the analogue technologies of the original craft tools of writing and the culture of print that it created, also covering the literary journalism of George Orwell and Christopher Hitchens as examples of the genre. He then considers the political commitment to truth, the Socratic method and the fundamental importance of writing over visual communication. He thereafter discusses the instrumental technology of virtual reality as the simulation of human activity as data to be manipulated and organised in a digital economy operating from an invisible and impenetrable cloud.

Hassan's argument is that despite the 'can-do ideology' from a hegemonic culture of solutionism that is behind immersive journalism, the technology cannot deliver on the experiential promises of virtuality. Even if it could, he tells us, immersive journalism is still ill-equipped to deliver on the first principles of journalism in respect of truth. Hassan's chapter centres around arguing that immersive journalism, by giving the criteria of truth to the judgement of the individual in the context of a semi-magical technology, is in effect a neoliberal abnegation of journalism and its modernist commitment to the public sphere. It simply means a 1980s-vintage adherence to free-market ideology by governments in the West has compromised their commitment to a functioning public sphere. The 'abnegation', he argues, is that of governments and states who have allowed or encouraged the public sphere to become a privatised social media sphere. The chapter ends by pointing out that there are signs of that changing, though, but nothing definitive yet, by way of substantive curtailing of the power of the platforms.

What this part of the book tells us is that utopian views about the potential applications of virtual reality technologies to journalism have dominated the rhetoric around immersive journalism. However, as virtual representations of news become increasingly vivid, journalists must also consider the heightened manipulative potential of these technologies. Where should the rights of audiences lie in terms of controlling their experience of immersive media? How should journalists be prepared to protect viewers when they enter a news event through a very vivid virtual reality? In sum, in what ways can the creation of synthetic versions of news events disrupt current notions of journalism?

References

Baía Reis, A., and Coelho, A. F. V. C. C. (2018). Virtual reality and journalism: A gateway to conceptualizing immersive journalism. *Digital Journalism*, 6(8), pp. 1090–1100.
Boal, A. (1979). *Theatre of the Oppressed*. London: Pluto Press.
Boal, A., and Jackson, A. (2002). *Games for Actors and Non-actors* (2nd ed.). London: Routledge.
Bohil, C., Alicea, B., and Biocca, F. (2011). Virtual reality in neuroscience research and therapy. *Nature Reviews. Neuroscience*, 12(12), 752–762.
Butler, J. (2004). *Precarious Life: The Powers of Mourning and Violence*. London: Verso.
Butler, J. (2009). *Frames of War: When Is Life Grievable?* London: Verso.
Conover, T. (1984). *Rolling Nowhere: Riding the Rails with America's Hoboes*. New York: Vintage Departures.
Conover, T. (2000). *Newjack: Guarding Sing Sing*. New York: Vintage Books.
Cummings, J., and Bailenson, J. (2016). How immersive is enough? A meta-analysis of the effect of immersive technology on user presence. *Media Psychology*, 19(2), 272–309.

Da Costa, L. G., and Brasil, A. (2017). Realidade virtual: Inovação técnica e narrativa no jornalismo imersivo [Virtual reality: Technical and narrative innovation in immersive journalism]. *Contemporanea-Revista de Comunicação e Cultura*, 15(1), pp. 141–161.

Dauphinée, E. (2007). The politics of the body in pain: Reading the ethics of imagery. *Security Dialogue*, 38(2), pp. 139–155. www.jstor.org/stable/26299649

De la Peña, N., Weil, P., Llobera, J., Giannopoulos, E., Pomés, A., Spanlang, B., and Slater, M. (2010). Immersive journalism: Immersive virtual reality for the first-person experience of news. *Presence: Teleoperators and Virtual Environments*, 19(4), pp. 291–301.

Deuze, M. (2004). Journalism studies beyond media: On ideology and identity. *Ecquid Novi: African Journalism Studies*, 25(2), pp. 275–293.

Dominguez Martinez, E. (2013). *Periodismo inmersivo: Fundamentos para una forma periodística basada en la interfaz y la acción*. [Immersive journalism: foundations of a journalistic format based on interface and action] (PhD), Universitat Ramon Llull.

Falke, C. (2017). Reading terror: Imagining violent acts through the rational and narrative sublime. In: H. Meretoja and C. Davis (eds.), *Storytelling and Ethics: Literature, Visual Arts and the Power of Narrative*. London: Routledge, pp. 253–266.

Gellhorn, M. (1994). *The View from the Ground*. New York: Atlantic Monthly Press.

Herman, E. S., and Chomsky, N. (2010 [1988]). *Manufacturing Consent: The Political Economy of the Mass Media*. New York: Random House.

Jones, S. (2017). Disrupting the narrative: Immersive journalism in virtual reality. *Journal of Media Practice*, 18(2–3), pp. 171–185. DOI:10.1080/14682753.2017.1374677

Keeble, R. L. (2020). *Journalism beyond Orwell*. Abingdon, Oxon: Routledge.

Kellner, D. (2002). *Media Spectacle*. London: Routledge.

Kozol, W. (2014). *Distant Wars Visible: The Ambivalence of Witnessing*. Minneapolis: University of Minnesota Press.

LeBlanc, A. N. (2003). *Random Family: Love, Drugs, Trouble and Coming of Age in the Bronx*. New York: Scribner.

Metzinger, T. (2018). Why is virtual reality interesting for philosophers? *Frontiers in Robotics and AI*, 5, pp. 101.

Murray, J. (1997). *Hamlet on the Holodeck : The Future of Narrative in Cyberspace*. New York: Free Press.

Pérez-Seijo, S. (2017). Immersive journalism: From audience to first-person experience of news. In: F. C. Freire, X. R. Araujo, V. A. M. Fernandez, and X. L. Garcia (eds), *Media and Metamedia Management*. Hamburg: Springer, pp. 113–119.

Pötzsch, H. (2012). Imag(in)ing painful pasts: Mimetic and poetic style in war films. In: A. Grønstad and H. Gustafsson (eds.), *Ethics and Images of Pain*. London: Routledge, pp. 251–278.

Pötzsch, H. (2017a). Playing games with Shklovsky, Brecht and Boal: Ostranenie, V-Effect and spect-actors as analytical tools for game studies. *Game Studies*, 17(2). http://gamestudies.org/1702/articles/potzsch

Pötzsch, H. (2017b). Selective realism: Filtering experiences of war in the first- and third-person shooter. *Games & Culture*, 12(2), pp. 156–178.

Pötzsch, H. (2019). Positioning players as political subjects: Forms of estrangement and the presentation of war in 'This War of Mine' and 'Spec Ops: The Line'. In: P. Hammond and H. Pötzsch (eds.), *War Game: Memory, Militarism and the Subject of Play*. New York: Bloomsbury, pp. 241–258.

Roeh, I. (1989). Journalism as storytelling, coverage as narrative. *American Behavioural Scientist*, 33(2), pp. 162–168.

Schudson, M. (2001). The objectivity norm in American journalism. *Journalism*, 2(2), pp. 149–170, DOI:10.1177/146488490100200201

Slater, M., and Wilbur, S. (1997). A framework for immersive virtual environments (FIVE): Speculations on the role of presence in virtual environments. *Presence: Teleoperators & Virtual Environments*, 6, pp. 603–616. DOI:10.1162/pres.1997.6.6.603

Sontag, S. (2003). *Regarding the Pain of Others*. London: Penguin Classics.

Steinfeld, N. (2020). To be there when it happened: Immersive journalism, empathy and opinion on sexual harassment. *Journalism Practice*, 14(2), pp. 240–258.

Triberti, S., and Riva, G. (2015). Being present in action: A theoretical model about the "interlocking" between intentions and environmental affordances. *Front Psychol* 6, pp. 2052. DOI:10.3389/fpsyg.2015.02052.

Walters, P. (2015). Cracking a closed culture as an immersion journalist. *Teaching Journalism & Mass Communication*, 5(1), pp. 1–14.

Waterworth, J. A., Waterworth, E. L., Mantovani F., and Riva, G. (2010). On feeling (the) present: An evolutionary account of the sense of presence in physical and electronically-mediated environments. *Journal of Consciousness Studies*, 17(1–2), pp. 167–188.

Zelizer, B. (2005). Definitions of journalism. In: G. Overholser and K. H. Jamieson (eds.), *Institutions of American Democracy: The Press*. New York: Oxford University Press, pp. 66–80.

PART I
Practicing and teaching immersive journalism

1
A PROSPECTIVE ANALYSIS OF IMMERSIVE JOURNALISM FROM THE PERSPECTIVE OF EXPERTS[1,2]

Susana Herrera Damas and Mª José Benítez de Gracia

In 2011, researcher Nonny De la Peña and Professor Robert Hernández were participating in a conference at the University of Southern California that was focused on the economic precariousness and adversity faced by some groups. De la Peña then suggested an idea to her colleague: 'Look at this person. Imagine what it would be like to be standing there, hungry, waiting in those food lines' (Hernández, 2018). A year later, De la Peña managed to materialise this idea in the project 'Hunger in Los Angeles', which recreated the diabetic crisis suffered by a person while waiting for their turn at a food bank. The researcher and her group, Immersive Journalism,[3] had developed a complex piece of equipment designed at the university's ICT Mixed Reality Lab, which made it possible to recreate this situation in a CGI environment, so that the viewer could visualise and walk through the scene from a first-person perspective, approaching and moving around the person who had collapsed to the ground.

Although De la Peña had already been working on this type of representation since 2007, mainly to address social issues centred on the defence of human rights, it was precisely the attempt to transfer and present this project to the Sundance Independent Film Festival that gave definitive impetus to this new journalistic modality, which she and her team had called immersive journalism just a year earlier (De la Peña et al., 2010: 291).

It was during a conference in which De la Peña was giving an account of the difficulty of moving the equipment when a student named Palmer Luckey offered to help her with a project he had in mind: The Oculus Rift virtual reality goggles system. De la Peña considered the young man's offer and he went on to work in her laboratory. Three years later, his recently founded company, Oculus Inc., would be bought by Facebook for USD $2 billion, (some €1.9 billion).

Meanwhile, on the other side of the United States, in New York, Ignacio Ferrando, a Spanish specialist in panoramic and spherical photography, was

DOI: 10.4324/9781003217008-3

observing with Joergen Geerds the structure that Sony Ericsson had commissioned from the latter to create a spherical video with one of the company's telephones. Having seen this, Ferrando had the idea of also creating a structure for GoPro action cameras to record spherical video in the same way, but with higher quality. Thus began the project of what would be the first rig used to record 360° video, a more accessible and cheaper piece of equipment than those that existed at the time.

From the coming together of these two systems, virtual reality glasses and recording equipment, comes a new format that allows narration from real images with 360° video. Although this recording technique was not new, the use of this equipment achieved a very significant reduction in the cost of these recordings, facilitating their rapid adoption and extension to a wide range of fields.[4]

This ability to represent scenarios in such an innovative way did not go unnoticed by the media involved in the search for new formulas that would guarantee their survival in a 'fragmented and viral media scenario' (Martínez Rodríguez and Torrado, 2017: 148). Gradually, some of the most prestigious media outlets joined this way of reporting events and, from April 2015, several began to adopt it, especially during the period between 2015 and 2018. The first to do so was *The New York Times*, in April 2015, with the report 'Walking New York'. It was followed by Discovery, *USA Today*, Associated Press, *The Washington Post*, ABC News, Frontline, CNET, *The Wall Street Journal* and Vice News as well as European media such as Euronews, the BBC, RTVE or RT and production companies specialising in this format such as RYOT, Vrse or Jaunt.

This was the birth of a form of journalism that is characterised by the representation of events on a spherical stage generated from real images and which the viewer accesses from a first-person perspective that he or she controls at will, giving the sensation of being present in the place where the events have taken place.

Immersive journalism with spherical video provides a series of advantages that add value and distinguish it from other narrative formulas. In fact, before this journalistic modality even had a name, some authors had already anticipated its advantages. Among them (Benítez and Herrera, 2020):

1. The immersion of the spectator in the event. By putting on the viewfinder, the spectator is isolated from the real physical environment, so that they only see and hear what is reproduced through the viewfinder.
2. The representation of a spherical stage through 360° video with a three-dimensional appearance and a hyper-realistic level of depth.
3. The control of the point of view by the spectator. By moving their head, the viewer modifies the field of vision in a way that is like the human gaze.
4. The use of spatial audio. This technology is essential to ensure that the viewer perceives the sound as coming from the direction in which it is produced.
5. The more active role that the spectator demands within the event, whether as an observer, as a character or even as the protagonist of the action that is being represented.

6. The illusion of presence. The spectator can perceive that they are in the place where the events are taking place and react to them as if they were there, something which, as can be understood, provides important advantages over conventional narrative.

In Spain, we witnessed a rapid adoption of this format by some media at the beginning of 2016 and a progressive popularisation in 2017 because it was then when several local and regional media began to produce them experimentally (Benítez and Herrera, 2018). However, this production slowed down almost entirely in both large media and digital natives in 2018 (Pérez-Seijo, 2021). Since then, there has been a progressive decline that has become more abrupt during the global crisis caused by Covid-19, which, logically, has not helped either. Although several projects have aimed to cover this anomalous situation in an immersive way, this type of production has gradually slowed down, which raises doubts about the sustainability of this form of journalism today, one that faces many challenges but which, at the same time, offers undeniable potential.[5]

Methods

In this context, the question arises as to what to expect from immersive journalism from now on. This is therefore the general objective of this research, which focuses on examining the prospects for immersive journalism with 360° video from the perspective of experts. More explicitly, the specific objectives we are pursuing are:

SO1: To examine the strengths and weaknesses of immersive journalism.
SO2: To examine what the best applications for immersive journalism and some of its best practices are.
SO3: To explore what the main challenges are and how to overcome them.
SO4: To explore what the experts see as the future of immersive journalism, also in relation to the evolution that the metaverse may undergo.

To address these objectives, we employed a qualitative and exploratory methodology by conducting a focus group. This technique consists of asking a series of questions to one or more groups of participants with the aim of gathering their responses while generating and analysing the interaction between participants (Barbour, 2007: 27). The underlying idea is that interviewees talk about different issues in a relaxed and informal atmosphere and exchange information with each other and with the interviewer (Hernández Sampieri, Fernández Collado and Batipsta, 2014: 418). The constant interrogative and comparative method required avoids impressionistic bias on the part of the researcher (Barbour, 2007).

In this case, we conducted two focus groups:

1. One to ascertain the views of academic experts who have studied immersive journalism in depth.

2. Another to explore these issues from the perspective of professionals who have had to face the different technical challenges related, above all, to its production and distribution.

To set up both groups, we contacted a total of 24 experts in this format through an email invitation. Finally, the group of academics was made up of eight people and the group of professionals consisted of seven. The interviewees came from Spain (7), the United States (3), Portugal (1), Norway (1), Colombia (1) and Brazil (2). In Tables 1.1 and 1.2, we present a brief biographical profile of each of them.

The two sessions, held online via Blackboard Collaborate on Friday 10th of December 2021, were guided by a list of eight questions plus a final, open-ended, question to give interviewees the opportunity to add any additional points of interest:

List of questions asked in each of the discussion groups:

1. What strengths or advantages do you consider immersive journalism to have over other forms of journalism?
2. And what do you consider to be its main weaknesses or disadvantages?
3. From your perspective, what specific issues do you think immersive journalism should be reserved for?
4. What advice would you give as best practices for those who want to undertake an immersive journalism project?
5. What are the most important challenges immersive journalism faces?
6. From your point of view, how can these challenges be overcome?
7. What do you see as the future of immersive journalism?
8. What do you think about the metaverse in relation to immersive journalism?
9. Can you add any additional points, comments or personal assessments about immersive journalism?

Before proceeding to the debate and in line with the extended focus group modality, we posed the total of nine questions, leaving a minute and a half of reflection after each one so that participants could think about their answers and thus make the discussion more productive.

After the debate, we transcribed the interviews, modifying some grammatical aspects to correct errors in agreement that are typical of spoken language and colloquial register. From there, we identified the nodes or keywords in each of them, highlighting the different paragraphs or adding annotations to easily recognise and identify the aspects that had been dealt with.

Once the information had been processed, we outlined the findings in the different results that we now present. For clarity of exposition, we grouped them according to the specific objectives we had set out at the beginning.

A prospective analysis of immersive journalism 21

TABLE 1.1 List of participants in the academics' focus group

Surname	Name	Biographical profile	URL
Baía-Reis	António	Researcher and Assistant Professor at the Centre for Media and Communication of the University of Passau in Germany. He has a BA in International Relations, an MA in Communication Sciences and a PhD in Digital Media with a focus on immersive media.	www.antoniobaiareis.com
Blein	Jorge Esteban	Narrative Consultant in Virtual Reality for several agencies and professor of immersive storytelling. PhD Cum Laude in cinematography, he has written and directed multiple VR 360° video – 3D fiction pieces.	
Domínguez Martín	Eva	Holds a degree in Journalism from the Autonomous University of Barcelona and a Master's in Interactive Telecommunications from New York University. In 2013, she defended her first doctoral thesis on immersive journalism. Currently, she combines teaching with consultancy and the creation of digital narratives.	www.evadominguez.com
Barbosa	Suzana	Professor at the Department of Communication and the Postgraduate Programme in Contemporary Communication and Culture at the Federal University of Bahia (UFBA). Researcher and one of the directors of the research group on online journalism (GJOL).	
Sánchez Laws	Ana Luisa	She is Professor of Interdisciplinary Methodologies and Methods at UiT The Arctic University of Norway. She had developed theoretical and practical work for this topic within the area of immersive journalism, with the book *Conceptualizing Immersive Journalism* and in a series of research articles.	https://en.uit.no/ansatte/person?p_document_id=716283
Pérez-Seijo	Sara	PhD in Communication and a researcher in the Novos Medios Group at the University of Santiago de Compostela. Her research focuses on the study of immersive narratives, innovation in public service media and engagement formulas in cybermedia.	
Sidorenko	Pavel	Holds a PhD in Communication and a Master's in Social Communication, he researches new narratives and technologies in journalism, advertising, marketing and corporate communication. He is the author of numerous publications on new narratives and new technologies in communication.	https://1oft360.wordpress.com
Lima	Lucielle	He has been a PhD student at the Federal University of Bahia in Brazil since 2018, working on immersive journalism under the supervision of Dr. Suzana Oliveira Barbosa.	

TABLE 1.2 List of participants in the professionals' focus group

Surname	Name	Biographical profile	URL
Coloma	Javier	A graduate in journalism from the CEU Cardenal Herrera University and co-founder of Zakato, a production company specialising in 360° video and immersive narratives, where he has developed and directed a great many 360° video projects. He currently teaches at the Miguel Hernández University of Elche.	https://emblematicgroup.com
De la Peña	Nonny	She is an American journalist, documentary filmmaker and entrepreneur. She is the founder and CEO of Emblematic Group, a digital media company focused on immersive virtual, mixed and augmented reality. She was selected by *Wired* magazine as #MakeTechHuman Agent of Change and has been called the 'Godmother of Virtual Reality' by Forbes, Engadget and the *Guardian*.	www.abaco-digital.es/web/es/
Ferrando	Ignacio	A specialist in 360° photography and video, virtual reality and augmented reality. Founder of one of the first production companies specialising in virtual reality and immersive experiences. He has participated in hundreds of projects around the world for clients such as NatGeo, Ikea, UNICEF and the United Nations.	http://blog.webjournalist.org
Hernández	Robert	He is a professor of professional practice at USC Annenberg. His primary focus is exploring the intersection of technology and journalism. His most recent work includes augmented reality and virtual reality. He and his students produce VR experiences under their brand: JOVRNALISM.	https://webdocc.net
Prat	Clàudia	She is a journalist specialising in 360° video and innovation. She has worked at AP since 2016. She is the 360° video editor of *House to House: The Battle For Mosul* and has contributed to around 40 360° video stories working for media organisations such as *The New York Times*, Univision and Fusion Media Group.	www.gmrv.es/~lraya/
Raya	Laura	PhD Cum Laude in Computer Engineering and Virtual Reality Project Manager at U-tad and a university professor since 2008. She has published more than 40 books and worked on more than 16 research projects since 2006. She is a member of the European projects The Blue Brain and The Human Brain Project.	www.danielrojasroa.com
Rojas Roa	Daniel	Photographer and graduate in Systems and Computer Engineering with an emphasis on electronic media and computer graphics from the Universidad de los Andes in Bogotá. He is co-founder of 3GO°Video, where he works in creation, production, direction and editing of virtual reality content.	

Results

The strengths of immersive journalism

One of the main advantages of immersive journalism is the ability to transport the viewer to places that are not easily accessible, or are even remote (Blein), which brings them 'to different emotional and physical human geographies' (Baía-Reis) by placing them

> in the centre of a space, of a reality or an event so that, having the sensation of really being there, this sensation of presence allows them or better understand a certain reality, to obtain a more complete image, to put themselves in the shoes of another person or to better understand a certain event.
>
> *Pérez-Seijo, 2021*

For Clàudia Prat, immersive journalism allows the viewer to be 'tele-transported' as no other medium has done before. The recently presented Space Explorers exhibition, The Infinite,[6] exemplifies in a very clear way some of these advantages that she considers revolutionary:

> The incredible thing about immersive journalism is that it allows us access to spaces and places where the audience can't be. Taken to the ultimate level, it's this project of being able to be in the space. And I think immersive journalism, one of the things about it, not just the space but wherever you put your camera, communicates details that might seem mundane but that add so much value to the story. For example, to go back to this space project, you are inside the Space Station and you can see all the stickers, all the details that for years the astronauts have had in their home living outside the planet Earth. If I write a good story, I could describe that space, but in immersive journalism, the magic is that you are there and you explore it from your body or, at least, with 360° video, from your head you can see and read the space with your body. That is what is revolutionary about immersive journalism and that is surely what has led those of us who are here to experiment in this medium, isn't it? It is unique, no other medium can do it: we have not been able to teleport in this way before.
>
> *Prat, 2021*

In a similar sense, Robert Hernández adds that the concept of presence can refer not only to a place, but also to a person, such as a migrant whom the viewer has never met and only sees from a distance in the news. And he adds that this is a highly relevant advantage.

In addition to the capacity for presence, Domínguez highlights other aspects, such as a higher sensory level and less cognitive effort, which makes it easier to generate experiences and allows for action. And this connects with the demands of younger audiences:

> For me, immersive journalism has two qualities: one is the ability to immerse (oneself) in a different space and the other is the ability to act. These are the two great characteristics that being immersed in any space allow and these technologies underline this. So, what are the strengths and advantages? That there is less cognitive effort with these formats because they are more sensory. The three-dimensionality, the sensory spatiality requires less cognitive effort … And, if you combine all that with interactivity, then that ability to have an experience, right? It's not just seeing or listening and feeling but also acting. And what is the advantage of this? Centennials are looking for experiences.
>
> Domínguez, 2021

Laura Raya also highlights the 'great leap' and the 'enormous advantage' that means that the viewer is no longer just someone to whom the news is told but becomes a 'user' who can interact with the information, even if that interaction simply consists of 360° movement. In similar terms, for Ignacio Ferrando, interactivity is one of the greatest advantages of these technologies:

> Yes, it is clear that the main advantage of 360° video, 360° photo, of immersive things, is interactivity, that is clear. It's not the same to be sitting in a place watching TV or watching the news as it is to put on a pair of glasses and turn it around or even turn it around on a cell phone. That's the absolute main advantage and that allows for immersion in a story.
>
> Ferrando, 2021

Therefore, that 'ability to generate the perceptual sensation of presence' (Raya) generates a greater 'emotional reach' (Blein), a greater 'empathetic connection' (Baía-Reis) which, in turn, offers 'a great potential for interaction, a more effective involvement' (Lima) and a 'different perspective from the one we normally have' (Baía-Reis). Empathy is also something that Daniel Rojas highlights:

> I think that the strength of immersive journalism compared to other tools and media is that it generates empathy, which allows you to understand more about the other person's situation and it also generates a context. It places you in another reality and that allows you to understand and live that experience. You no longer have to imagine it as when it is published in a newspaper, on the radio or on television, but now you are living it and that will allow you to understand the explanation of what is happening.
>
> Rojas, 2021

In turn, that greater emotional reach allows the audience to 'connect with the content in another way' (Sidorenko) and the viewer to feel present within the event and be able to empathise with the people and the story:

> Whether it's 360° video or computer-generated content, virtual reality allows you to feel present and this breaks all the schemes because, really, it's you in the news. You don't hear it from someone else: you interpret it' (which not only allows you) 'to have a better allocation of information, but it is true that you empathize more with the different people and with the content that can be followed from there.
>
> *Raya, 2021*

Sidorenko highlights the opportunity that all this represents today for journalism, in a context in which we are so 'powerfully infoxicated', we 'consume in a very nomadic and rapid way in social networks' and the disinformation 'industry' poses incredible challenges:

> For these reasons, immersive journalism could end up doing what slow journalism is trying to do, which is to motivate the person to stop and see, to understand something and to comprehend what is happening and obviously, what this allows is to bring them closer.
>
> *Sidorenko, 2021*

In a similar vein, Professor Barbosa points out the potential of these technologies in allowing journalism to reconnect with its audience:

> We know that journalism is going through many crises at the moment. One of them has to do with the issue of credibility, or the fact that the audience is somewhat distant and we also have the whole fake news movement. So, this offers an opportunity to recover the value of experiencing journalism.
>
> *Barbosa, 2021*

In addition to the above, Jorge Esteban Blein adds the advantage of the wow effect that this kind of technology continues to have:

> I thought it would've disappeared in these five years, but no way! It's still very much alive. It's the wow effect of VR itself and journalism has to continue using it extensively because the vast majority of people still haven't tried virtual reality glasses. So that effect is still there. At some point, the excitement will wear off, just like when people got used to the cinema over a century ago … That fairground feeling. I think in the case of VR, it's still there for most people and well, the feeling of being present and sharing the embodiment that VR generates is something that I think is fundamental for emotional journalistic content.
>
> *Blein, 2021*

Consequently, all these advantages make it possible to offer

> a first draft of the story that's much richer if you consider that it can capture all the aspects of a bodily presence that a person experiences in the events, with limitations and possible distortions, of course, but it's like a new layer that's added to this snapshot of events.
>
> Sánchez Laws, 2021

Weaknesses of immersive journalism

Among the shortcomings of immersive journalism, some of the experts agree that it has one very basic flaw, which is the need to have devices that not everyone possesses. Moreover, this situation affects both smartphones and virtual reality glasses.

> One of the weaknesses of immersive journalism and in this case, I'll focus only on immersive journalism that uses virtual reality, is that it needs an accessory, which is the glasses. If the journalist or media wants the user to have a real, 100% sensory experience, or the most immersive experience in terms of sensation, then it would be a drawback.
>
> Pérez-Seijo, 2021.

> The glasses are a problem. For example, how do you expect the public to experience our content if they don't have the glasses?
>
> Barbosa, 2021

António Baía-Reis adds the highly specific physical risk of cyber-sickness or dizziness in those cases in which the pieces are not well produced, while Ana Luisa Sánchez Laws points to the risk of 'sensory hyper-saturation':

> The emphasis on sensory experience can create a lack of space for interpretation and reflection – that critical level of distancing that Brechtian theatre speaks of –. At the same time, sensory hyper-saturation can be a mechanism used as an exclusive market logic that minimizes the civic function of journalism. Along these lines, I would add María Ressa's criticisms of the current information ecosystem, the role of journalists and the digital autocracy in which actors such as Facebook/Meta and other social media operate and which are currently investing in virtual reality.
>
> Sánchez Laws, 2021

Coloma adds that the productions are very expensive:

> Disadvantages? The high cost of everything. Putting together any small story costs a lot of money. Those of you doing research know that every time you

need to start a new project at the university you have to ask for huge budgets. I still think it's a tool that will be used for very specific things.

Coloma, 2021

Along the same lines, Barbosa mentions the lack of funding faced by many large journalistic companies, while Baía-Reis and Sidorenko point to monetisation as another serious weakness.

We also find other shortcomings related to ethical implications due to the power of immersive narratives, which can leave the viewer in a situation of great emotional vulnerability (Sánchez Laws, 2020; Benítez, Pérez-Seijo and Herrera, 2021). In this sense, for De la Peña 'it's a responsibility of any of us to think that this media has the kind of power and the potential that it does and perhaps re-visit what the best practices are':

> How do we apply what are the best practices that we have learnt in journalism previously to this explosion that is going to happen? How do we talk about the fact that, in a situation, maybe a bomb goes off? Are we going to let people step over the bodies? I think this is a moment in which we need to start defining what may work, what may not work and you have to imagine that future now, because we have not seen it yet'
>
> *De la Peña, 2021*

Blein also considers these implications, perhaps not at this very moment, but as an imminent risk that could occur in the future:

> We know that there have always been ethical issues in journalism. To what extent can showing an image, or not showing it, hurt a viewer's feelings? Here the issue is not that it can hurt them. The point is, it can upset them psychologically in a very profound way if we put them in the middle of a tragic situation, or in the middle of a place that can be … There's also a strong factor of morbid fascination. So, if journalism is able to manage the extent to which it can put the spectator in a place that's not good for their health and emotional well-being then … We've already seen graphic images in recent years that seem to indicate there's almost no limit, right? Children's corpses … So, if we continue down that road … In short, VR and AR might have consequences that are devastating for the user. Totally counterproductive, right? I think that's going to be the main weakness. It's not going to happen immediately, because obviously, immersive journalism is not yet mainstream enough for journalists to adopt this kind of approach. But it will happen. And I think it needs to be heavily regulated, starting now. I think that in general, VR is so powerful that we have to be very careful with how it's used because of the emotional and psychological damage that might be caused by its improper use. It won't happen

tomorrow, but it will come to that in the future. It's definitely going to happen at some point.

Blein, 2021

In more general terms, several of the experts agree in pointing out the scarcity of narrative and technological knowledge when it comes to producing this type of journalism, which is still an 'emerging and experimental' practice (Baía-Reis). Similarly, as Robert Hernández argues, 'The disadvantage is that it's a new culture, a culture not only for the user, but for the newsroom as well'. At the same time, Eva Domínguez points out that not all productions have achieved a sufficient level of quality:

> It's true that there's been a lot of production, but we also have to ask ourselves how much of that production had the level of quality and attraction for the audience that made it worth the effort to watch it in 360° video. In that sense, I think we have to put ourselves in the citizens' shoes, don't you think? I believe we still haven't done that. There have been some great productions that have been very well done, but many others that are kind of like, 'Well, why am I going to waste my time watching this? Time is short for everyone. So, what are the disadvantages? The fact that it's a new narrative that we really don't know enough about … There are many people who are producing and experimenting, but this is changing the way narratives are being produced. We're talking about three-dimensionality. We're talking about spatiality. These are spatial narratives and that … we don't know how to do yet. And I say this by using what I've learned – whether it's a little or a lot – in seven years working for a start-up, doing augmented reality and spatial narratives. We're still creating the language. So those are the disadvantages and drawbacks. There is a lack of narrative and technological knowledge and the media are not technologically prepared because they're not familiar with these platforms. In this context, there are many negatives for journalism in incorporating these formats.

Domínguez, 2021

In this regard, some of the experts point out that the media have made several mistakes. On the one hand, there has been a certain amount of confusion and lack of understanding in relation to this format, which requires 'building a storytelling' and not just 'grabbing the camera and putting videos on YouTube' (Sidorenko). In turn, as the media have been 'somewhat motivated by their eagerness to be the first to try out the technology … as a differentiating value and to have a competitive edge over other media', they have begun to produce this type of content intensely with 'an almost daily rhythm', perhaps replicating 'the logic of conventional audiovisual media', when in reality, 'the conventional model truly clashes with the unique features of the spatial narrative', which requires a lot of time in production, postproduction, narrative design and in consumption as well (Pérez-Seijo). The third mistake has been the attempt to direct this type of narrative at all types of audiences:

At least from my perspective, the problem with this immersive digital journalism is that it's interesting for a niche audience. And what the media have done is promote and sell this way of producing content as a format that might be of interest to the general public, which is not the case. Due to their own characteristics, these formats are more focused on certain audiences, such as those that are younger, due to their greater familiarity with video games or other types of content.

Pérez-Seijo, 2021

In this regard, Baía-Reis points out that the situation of technological frenzy faced by newsrooms does not leave enough time for the media, production companies or academics to assimilate all these innovations in a more structured way:

I think it's experimental. There are no standards. The emergence of new, associated technologies is becoming more and more frenetic and crazy. We're just trying to understand 360°, yet we already have full blown, volumetric virtual reality. Just as we were starting to understand volumetrics, now integrated immersive ecosystems with artificial intelligence are on the way. We just don't have enough intellectual or academic capability for all of this. It doesn't mean we shouldn't think about it. It just means we should think about it with the idea of slow (journalism) in mind.

Baía-Reis, 2021

Applications of immersive journalism

When asked about the best applications for which immersive journalism should be reserved, given the impossibility of telling everything in this way, most experts agree on the importance of providing an experience and fostering a sense of presence. However, this statement has various nuances.

Pérez-Seijo stresses the value of experiences that allow the spectator to 'better understand what is happening', reducing the distance between them and reality. She emphasises stories with a social background, or of human interest. This a point on which she agrees with Ferrando, who has had the opportunity to gain considerable experience specialising in these types of 'documentary or social projects, where get you into the story much more than if you are watching a documentary on TV'. For Pérez-Seijo, content that requires 'showing historical enclaves so the spectator can perceive the sensation of spatiality and really understand the scale, height and distance involved' is also important.

Robert Hernández agrees with the possibility of reliving historical events, to which he adds others, including sporting contests, protest demonstrations and war. In particular, he stresses the importance of point of view in offering the audience a relevant event to which they normally have no access, or when it is appropriate to 'show the other person's point of view' (Hernández).

Sidorenko also recognises the appropriateness of showing social issues that 'require greater involvement or understanding by the audience, such as social conflict, armed conflict and humanitarian or climate crises'. He also highlights its importance 'for the coverage of spectacular events, where the impressiveness of the moment can be captured'.

For Ana Luisa Sánchez Laws, immersive journalism is not only conducive to reporting topics related to current affairs by showing an event. It can also be used to verify or re-examine evidence of something that has already happened. However, she insists on the need to avoid sensational content. For Laura Raya, 'Generating immersive content is a complex, costly process'. As the cost-benefit ratio 'does not pay off' in many cases, it seems advisable to focus production on applications in which (i) the viewer truly feels present in the environment represented; (ii) the viewer can adopt a detached point of view and (iii) the re-created content requires interaction.

For Ferrando, the concept of presence is also essential, because in his experience, 'What gives the best results is the type of documentary in which you allow the viewer to go inside the story and live or feel the story as well'. He also adds the advantage that live broadcasts will offer when the technology allows it.

Rojas highlights the ability to reach impossible places, as well as risky or dangerous situations. He also remarks that immersive journalism requires time, dedication and production, which is why he points to documentaries as the most suitable genre when providing this type of content with greater depth.

Clàudia Prat disagrees with the idea of reducing immersive production to one type of content. Instead, she recommends continued exploration, because 'the more we experiment and test this technology, the better':

> There is another type of immersive journalism that we may not have tried to do, such as spatial data journalism or immersive audio journalism. I think there are many paths we can take and this is not the time to hold back or set limits.
>
> *Prat, 2021*

Best practices for producing immersive journalism

Regarding best practices that should be considered when starting a project of this type, Clàudia Prat recommends 'starting with simple ideas and giving yourself time to experiment and make mistakes'. For Daniel Rojas, such experimentation is also fundamental: 'Experiment, test and make mistakes. See how it works and learn how to see the way it works'. In short, this is a process of knowledge acquisition for which, according to Blein, 'It's necessary for journalists to educate themselves in these new media'. They must start by watching a lot of videos, because traditional audio-visual culture is no longer useful:

> Don't start by making a 360° video, a virtual reality, or a CGI experience until you've seen a lot of immersive 360° videos. It's not enough to watch them on YouTube. That's not immersive ... We have to be trained in this new medium. We have to be humble in the sense that we don't know anything, not even those of us who think we know something. We know nothing. We have no idea.
>
> *Blein, 2021*

Most experts agree with Blein on the differences between this new technology and traditional audio-visual narratives and that the new format has to be envisioned by 'always remembering that it's a spatial narrative' (Pérez-Seijo, 2021). The productions that are created by trying to replicate conventional audio-visual logic simply do not work:

> Not all stories are valid for this type of format. The user must always be at the centre of the experience and more specifically, must always guide the narrative and lead in building the story.
>
> *Pérez-Seijo, 2021*

In this regard, the script is essential, as it is highly relevant in building narratives of this type. For Coloma, there are two types of immersive journalism: That which is based on a script and that which is not. For productions in which the objective is to show live news, such as a volcano, hurricane, football match or concert, it would be enough to position the camera. However, when the aim is to give visibility to situations that are unfolding, it is necessary to have a script:

> A good script is 99% of a short film or report … A good script is important when carrying out immersive journalism in order to allow the user to enjoy a report, documentary, safari, or a story told about the people who live in the Sahara … However, there is a difference between in-person immersive journalism that sometimes involves showing occurrences that are inherently brutal and scripted immersive journalism that shows the events happening in the world that we should denounce, because in journalism, I think the most important thing is to denounce.
>
> *Coloma, 2021*

In writing this type of script, Ferrando considers it fundamental to 'forget the frame' and consider the point of view instead:

> Always thinking about the point of view is the key. This means you have to remember that the user's point of view is always going to be where you are positioned with the camera. You have to think more about that place; think more about a point of view rather than framing.
>
> *Ferrando, 2021*

He also adds the crucial need to plan the narrative structure beforehand, so as not to cause dizziness. Raya agrees with this aspect as well and affirms that if the content is not well designed, the result can be dizziness and, consequently, rejection:

> We produce content in 360° video or CGI, either stereoscopic or non-stereoscopic, with such a casualness that people later say that the immersive

technology makes you dizzy. But it's not true. Actually, it's the design that makes you dizzy. The technology doesn't necessarily make you dizzy.

Raya, 2021

For his part, Sidorenko recommends 'not saturating the content with extraneous material during the post-production process'. Following on from Prat, he also believes it is important 'to be clear about the distribution channel, which is something that should be considered from the beginning of the project and not be left to the last minute':[7]

> Right now, we don't have a good way to distribute this content, so I would think about whom I'm addressing and how I'm going to get the project to them and that can be anything from putting a 360° video on a website, although maybe not many people would see it, to thinking about more original ideas. For example, imagine we organise an event. We'll have the possibility of showing this content and this very unique kind of story that we've done in this special format.
>
> *Prat, 2021*

Along with this advice, the need to pay attention to ethical issues was also mentioned, due to the impact that these narratives can have:

> The sensation of being present means that the user can respond physically and psychologically to the experience in the same way as they would in real life, including the ability to create memories in that world, just like what happens in dreams.
>
> *Raya, 2021*

For this very reason, she warns of the 'psychological impact' that this very realistic experience can have on the viewer and that the effect will be different depending on each viewer's previous experience. Several experts also agree with this idea.

For De la Peña, 'the way that we tell the truth without trauma is going to be the most important thing to consider in immersive journalism'. In this sense, Hernández argues that this situation implies that 'the journalist will present the truth in an ethical and responsible way, without being voyeuristic or just looking for clicks', but also that the viewer is willing to 'watch the drama, even if it's negative news or includes different points of view'.

For Sánchez Laws, the ethical component is also crucial and must be present throughout the project development process:

> Working together as a team, all the members of the production staff need to have a deep understanding of the ethical issues of the project, whether they come from journalism or not. It's important to identify examples where

technologists fully incorporate ethical guidelines and good journalistic writing practices.

Sánchez Laws, 2021

Challenges facing immersive journalism

Among the challenges that immersive journalism must confront, several stand out that could affect different phases of production. To begin with, Hernández points to the lack of knowledge about this technology on the part of some individuals in charge of newsrooms:

> The biggest, most serious challenge for me is with those in charge of newsrooms; those who have been managers since before Internet, during Internet, during social networks and in the cellphone era, who don't move aside and adapt to the real world. The young people who are entering the field now get frustrated and go elsewhere.'
>
> *Hernández, 2021*

In a similar vein, De la Peña points to the challenge of applying everything that has been learned so far in immersive journalism to the explosion of this type of content that will be generated by imminent technological innovations: Similarly, Sánchez Laws asks herself how the civic role of journalism can be integrated into these technologies and adds the following challenges:

> The metaverse as a purely commercial space: clickbait, market logic and the manipulative potential of technology are all challenges that will be present in the immediate future.
>
> *Sánchez Laws, 2021*

Along with this situation, another challenge is understanding the audience, their preferences and their consumption patterns based on reception studies that include quantitative and qualitative questions: Numbers and context, metrics, platforms, mobility, access models and consumption profiles; 'What is this audience really willing to consume' (Lima). In a similar vein, Dominguez asks the following question:

> Where are the audiences? That's the question we need to ask. The audiences, especially the generation we are going to target. That generation is the one that's going to consume this technology. They want experiences more than anything else. They're looking for experiences because they're sociable and they use social networks for that purpose. But it's through this immersive technology that's arriving just now.
>
> *Domínguez, 2021*

Other experts point to the challenge of making technology accessible. For example, Raya mentions the importance of allowing information to be transmitted through different channels, 'because if not, it might be the coolest thing, but only about four people will see it and that's not the ideal situation' (Raya):

> I think that's the main challenge – how to get there and how the spectator sees it–. And right now, it's very limited. The truth is that the headsets that exist now, which are a lot better than before, are still heavy. They're a hassle … Nobody's going to watch a football game for an hour wearing one of those. It's ridiculous. The productions we make normally don't last more than 10 minutes and that's exactly the reason why: because nobody can stand any more.
>
> *Ferrando, 2021*

Clàudia Prat also addresses the challenge posed by the publication of this type of content on platforms such as Oculus, Facebook and even YouTube and she brings up the following question: 'Who are we benefiting by publishing all these projects on platforms, when we don't know what those platforms are going to do with our data, or the fact that they use algorithms in very non-transparent ways'. Faced with this reality, she poses the challenge of 'how to create immersive journalism that is open' (Prat).

To all these challenges, De la Peña adds one more, which is that of trying to tell the story without being too explicit, as there are different perceptions regarding what kinds of images are acceptable: 'I feel pretty strongly that you convey a story without having to be so graphic violent'. Likewise, for De la Peña, 'it is so important now to be more inclusive and critical, inclusive with voices and critical of information', a challenge that is also supported by Hernández:

> We have to be active as well as proactive so we can be inclusive about who is creating this content. It should not be only the rich … It has to be everyone, with all points of view, empowering all users to create content and tell their own story. That's extremely important, so that all people can be present in the future … We have to fight to include that point of view and put these new tools in the hands of all people so we can create a balanced world with the support of Facebook, Google, Apple and Amazon, but with the independence of having the power of your data, your presence and your work. The future that's coming will be interesting. By interesting, I mean that it could be both good and bad, but it's necessary to be active in reporting that future.
>
> *Hernández, 2021*

Baía-Reis points to a strong paradigm shift in comparison to the 1990s, when the (scarce) consumption of virtual reality was done in a very isolated way: With the arrival of certain platforms, 'we are gradually entering a space where we can be there, with a very systematic, intuitive performance, talking to people everywhere'. Along the same lines, Blein poses a challenge for immersive journalism to 'get on the bandwagon of sociability':

There's one thing I always say about immersive media, whether it's AR, VR, or extended reality. I think they'll either be sociable, or they won't. And for that reason, I think in applications and cellphones, what works the best are social networks. We have millions of applications on our cellphones that we hardly ever open, except for those that allow us to communicate with society, with other people. What I'm saying is that the same thing is going to happen with VR … It is essential for journalism to also think about how it can jump on the bandwagon of sociability and how stories or experiences can be enjoyed from a social point of view … Regarding this social aspect, it's absolutely necessary that in some way and I have no idea how, the journalistic profession should try to get its foot in the door and take advantage of positioning itself for when metaverses and extended realities become a phenomenon and most of all, a social phenomenon. We have to see how to get in there, even though I don't have the answer. I'm just posing the problem.'

Blein, 2021

Sidorenko also points out that:

immersive journalism is faced with the need to evolve by providing more spaces related to socialization dynamics: forums, meetups, etc. In social networks today, loyalty and community-building are paramount (Discord, TikTok, Twitch, Patreon, etc.) and the metaverse reaffirms this need.

Sidorenko, 2021

To a lesser extent, academics also face the theoretical and conceptual challenge involved in confronting a plethora of changes in grammar, codes and even paradigms, which is a question that 'must be investigated in greater depth in order to reduce theoretical problems and make progress in these studies' (Lima, 2021). In line with this idea, Sánchez Laws points out that for scientists 'the challenge is also to continue with research in this area despite the downturn in the market'.

How to overcome challenges

When asked how these challenges can be overcome, Domínguez criticises laying the blame on the audience for its lack of interest. Instead of trying to 'make them literate', she proposes another attitude: That of being very humble, simply because 'there is a lot of learning to be done':

I think we have to be extremely humble. I've worked in many other sectors and as a hypothetical situation, imagine you have a chain of shoe stores and you put a certain shoe in the store. If people don't like the shoe, you have to teach them to like it. So, is the customer the one who doesn't understand? Of course not. I think sometimes in journalism we have this idea. We've been carrying out our journalistic profession without knowing how the audience consumes our content and what does or doesn't interest them. We've been working in journalism for more than a century using our journalistic instincts, but now we have more metrics. But even though we're still a sector that carries out journalism for the audience, we don't take the audience into account. So, the problem is not with the audience. The problem is with the journalistic sector. And I'm involved in it, right? We're responsible for it. Any other sector is always trying to understand consumer behaviour, where trends are going and so on, but not in journalism. So, the problem is never the audience … I believe wholeheartedly in the saying that the customer is always right. But in order to really be better as content creators, as journalists of new formats, we have to ask ourselves if we are the ones doing things wrong, not the audience, because we immediately blame the audience. We all agree that there has been a lot of 360° video that we haven't even watched ourselves.

Domínguez, 2021

Within this new context, it seems appropriate to assume that from this point forward, journalists should always be in beta mode:

We're there, we're all experimenting, we're all learning, building this alphabet. But it's an alphabet that's constantly changing because language is changing, because technology is changing. So, we shouldn't pretend to know things because what's coming is always going to be like this. Because it's evolution. Technological evolution. Digital evolution, etcetera. We're evolving, so we'll never know everything. We're always in beta mode and we're always going to be in beta mode. And we have to feel comfortable with it.

Domínguez, 2021

In the immediate future, it is advisable to take advantage of the current spaces as well, starting 'with the little that can be done now within the productive logic of the media. Do they have Instagram? On Instagram, there's a fantastic Augmented Reality platform called Spark AR.[8] 'We should start there, so we can start developing' (Domínguez). She continues, 'At the same time, it would be a good idea for the media to make sure they're present in the new spaces'.

In order to do so and given the fact that they have structures that hinder 'people from being up-to-date', Domínguez advises partnering with start-ups and other professionals who have the necessary capabilities, thereby searching for a way 'to infuse yourself with innovation and with knowledge that other people have, because it's impossible to do highly innovative things if you don't have people with engineering-type backgrounds, just to give one example' (Domínguez). Along the same lines, Baía-Reis believes that 'journalistic media must get closer to people who are early adopters. Even though these people don't know what's going to happen in 10 years' time, they're already involved in such technology. They're already experimenting with it' (Baía-Reis).

For his part, Coloma adds university education to the list as another very specific way of overcoming the diverse challenges faced by immersive journalism:

> We should invent something that could be used in classrooms so that students could work with devices that are not too complicated, but that would allow them to change the way of doing things, starting in the classroom. And from there, these new generations would enter the workforce with knowledge of what immersive journalism is all about. Because I get the feeling from what's happening, … that if we don't start developing in a different way, we're going to have to wait 10 to 15 years until everything is easier to use.
>
> *Coloma, 2021*

'In turn', he adds, 'the media should join forces with universities' (Coloma, 2021). Moreover, regarding teaching, Ferrando highlights the need to systematically organise knowledge in the form of guides and manuals:

> Also, on the issue of education and I do see this as important, with regard to universities and most of all with the issue of technicians. I've been involved in this since it began and there are no books, no documentation and no theory. We just learned it by doing. The 360° video cameras have been created by a few of us lunatics who have been making cameras, together with the people I collaborate with and with brands that ask for feedback all day long … But we can safely say there are no books on this subject, whereas photography has many books … It's true that there are forums and all of those things. All of us who started with these forums and other sources have used them to share information and we have all evolved, but at an academic level, I suppose you can't just say to your students, 'Join a forum or a Facebook group, about I don't know what' … You have to give them something more academic.'
>
> *Ferrando, 2021*

The future of immersive journalism

When asked to forecast the future of immersive journalism, the experts agree that we are still at a very early stage. In any case, the technological development that is expected in the coming years is a reason for optimism.

Nonny de la Peña states categorically that 'immersive journalism today has more possibilities than ever', specifically due to the evolution of smartphone cameras:

> I think the opportunities for immersive journalism now are bigger than ever. Everyone is buying smartphones; the smartphones are starting to come with a 'live art camera'. Everyone would be capturing the world with dimension and that means that the immersive experience will become normal. So, this opportunity that we have right now is astonishing to start to establish what it means to build the 'tail spatial stories', especially in journalism.
>
> *De la Peña, 2021*

Eva Domínguez is also convinced that despite the drawbacks, immersive journalism 'has a much better future than its present' and strongly reassures that 'the best is yet to come':

> I believe the future of immersive journalism is going to be increasingly more approachable. It's getting closer as time passes; it's an evolution of digital journalism; it's three-dimensional; I'm totally convinced. So, it's probably going to be in 10, maybe 15 years before it will be more immersive.
>
> *Domínguez, 2021*

Blein also has no doubt that 'the future is going to be bright for immersive journalism'. However, the road is long and patience is required, because in the end 'virtual, augmented and mixed reality will eventually merge':

> We have to learn step by step, investing and making mistakes and acquiring a background that will allow us, in 10 or 15 years, to be grounded in these new means of interaction that are going to change everyone's life.
>
> *Blein, 2021*

Clàudia Prat shares an optimistic vision of the future of immersive journalism that involves two possible directions. On the one hand, there is the media's commitment to the documentary genre. On the other hand, there is the creation of immersive experiences in public spaces such as museums, 'where it is easy to put on virtual glasses and have a shared experience with other people watching a project' (Prat).

In the immediate future, Sánchez Laws suggests an uncertain scenario with multiple directions possible, in which we will need to ask ourselves how to 'integrate the civic role of journalism into this technology':

> The information system is crippled. We have a dominance of clickbait and high consumption of instant information and to me, what that means in terms of what might happen in the metaverse is sensory saturation ... Zuckerberg's metaverse is a model of society, which to me, personally, is terrifying. It's a limitation of what human experience can be, which is limited to consumption ... I think we have to get back on the right track of finding that difficult balance between the economic and civic aspects of journalistic activity. It is also extremely important in the context of immersive journalism, precisely because of the capability of this medium and all the sensory information in which we can be immersed.
>
> *Sánchez Laws, 2021*

For Sidorenko, there is no specific future on the horizon and he states that 'immersive journalism today is at the bottom of a valley in which it's difficult to see the next hill', since the current reality is that 'the media today are not interested in moving forward with this type of format because of the scarce attention they receive from audiences'.

However, even though the development of immersive technologies and greater consumption by the public will be decisive for the consolidation of immersive journalism, a learning curve will be required which, as the experts agree, will continue to develop and become consolidated over the next 10 to 15 years. For Hernández, this requires 'a learning period for this new technology', as he points out that the cellular phone was not well-received in its early stages and the low quality of its photographic lens led to rejection. Twenty years after the appearance of the first cellular phones with cameras, the current scenario is very different. In fact, it is so different that as Rojas points out, 'Mobile technology has begun to generate spatial information through integrated 3D cameras'.

For Pérez-Seijo, immersive journalism will have a stable future 'when all of these mixed realities are finally integrated, which will make this way of practicing or envisioning journalism much more portable and widespread'. In the meantime, she sees immersive journalism as something complementary, 'not as daily journalism, but as a slower process that requires more production time'.

Coloma also envisions the convergence of technologies into simple devices that will facilitate immersion when immersive technologies are compressed into some kind of contact lenses or small glasses with 3D vision that are easy to use: 'When this immersion becomes extremely simple and easy-to-use, I believe at that point, immersive journalism will start to work' (Coloma).

De la Peña and Ferrando agree: 'The future is going to be different; we are going to create it all together'. Both journalists and producers must adapt to the new technologies and never put a halt to research (Ferrando). At the same time, the content, as well as the quality of the content, must not be neglected. For Hernández, it is necessary to practice and learn from a responsible point of view:

> We have a responsibility to create those opportunities and what we are doing now in the present are the first versions of that journalism. We have to practice, learn and teach each other the good and the bad, especially the things we've done wrong. We have learned to improve the quality of these experiences.
> *Hernández, 2021*

Immersive journalism considering the (imminent) arrival of the metaverse

The evolution of social networks and the diverse extended realities could converge in metaverses where immersive journalism would have its own space. When asked about this issue, the experts agree that despite media expectations following the announcement of Meta, or Facebook's metaverse, at the present time, 'There is basically nothing'; 'There is really nothing, even though it seems like there's something every day' (Domínguez); 'It's an economic question of pure marketing'

(Baía-Reis); 'Something that distracts' (Hernández); 'We still don't know what it's going to be' (Rojas); 'Probably, the coming metaverses will not be what we imagine' (Raya).

As if that were not enough, Raya stresses the possibility that in the coming years metaverses could play a 'very important role in the economy and social dynamics, because they specifically involve reproducing all the social dynamics that we can have in real life'. The metaverse will present a serious challenge for journalism. According to Raya, 'The more users there are in that metaverse and the more actions and social dynamics they want to be present there, then obviously, they will want to be informed within that metaverse'. Baía-Reis adds that 'the media must bear in mind that journalistic practices are going to take place in these metaverses and that the technology for telling their stories are already being transferred to other realities parallel to our real reality'.

Domínguez agrees that it would be advisable for the media to be present and test these new spaces, which are not exclusive to a single platform:

> Nowadays, everyone wants to prevail in the metaverse and they want their metaverse to triumph over others. So, Zuckerberg introduces Meta, when there's really nothing there, even though it seems like there's something new every day. Everyone is out there, rushing around trying to impose their metaverse. We'll see what happens, but there is going to be a huge number of platforms. In fact, some metaverses are already working. Fortnite is a metaverse with people playing, but it's a metaverse where a lot of things are being done. There are a lot of metaverses already. I would experiment to see what's being done there, what kinds of things people are doing, how blockchains work and how they are going to evolve. All these technologies are going to be joined together. I think we have to be very attentive to this situation and well, try to do what all of us are doing, which is testing this language, don't you think?
>
> *Domínguez, 2021*

In keeping with this notion, Hernández believes the metaverse is important and will emerge, but not in the way Meta or Facebook would like:

> They want to control it. The real metaverse is coming; a world where we can all interact. It doesn't matter what brand of glasses you use or where the content is embedded. That's decades away. The first true version of metaverse is going to be real life with augmented reality.
>
> *Hernández, 2021*

Regarding control of our own data, De la Peña mentions the capability for interconnection between different platforms or metaverses:

> Not only we should be able to own our data to go in all these places, but we should be in all cross places. We shouldn't be limited to have to go to each

place with new software to enter those spaces. We need to demand interoperability and that will be the only way to control who we are, to control ourselves and that may be a way to help us make sure the voices who tell stories are told in a way that lets people control their own virtual data.

De la Peña, 2021

Prat also stresses the importance of protecting data and states that 'the ideal situation would be an open and decentralised metaverse that protects users' data, with interconnected communities or platforms where we can engage with the content in a much more interactive, almost bodily way'. Moreover, we still can try to define it without a large corporation doing the task for us:

> I think we have to start creating a critical mass of people who will decide what kind of web 3.0 we want, what kind of metaverse we want and how we want to navigate the web with the tools and gadgets available, which might be our phone, a bracelet, or virtual glasses. We will also need to decide how we want to interact with the internet, what we want to see happen with our data and try to learn from the mistakes that have been made in web 2.0, social networks, disinformation and the bias of algorithms, let us learn from it and create a metaverse, or an Internet that will really serve us as citizens of different worlds in the future.

Prat, 2021

In a similar vein, Sánchez Laws suggests the desirability of establishing greater alliances between journalists and academia for a 'critical investigation of how to reshape the information system regarding the new challenges and opportunities presented by virtual reality'.

However, as Raya observes, the metaverse 'requires previous training for the people who are going to create journalism within it, so that it makes sense both inside and outside the metaverse and it can truly be consumed'. Baía-Reis highlights the challenge posed by the metaverse for the educational training of future journalists, given the need for new professional profiles.

Conclusion

The results reveal few differences between producers and academics on the various issues involved. Specifically, we found a strong consensus in the areas of strengths and weaknesses. Among the strengths, the interviewees agreed on the importance of immersive journalism in transporting the viewer to remote places that are difficult to access, bringing them closer to new realities and placing them in the centre of the situations, as if they were there. Moreover, the experts also highlighted the capability it offers for acting and for interactivity, which represents a great leap forward in terms of how information has been accessed to date, offering a different perspective, greater emotional reach, increased empathetic connections and more effective involvement with the content. In the current, multi-factor crisis afflicting journalism today, all these advantages are of particular interest.

On the other side of the coin, however, professionals and academics agree that there are several weaknesses, such as the need for devices that not everyone has, as well as more specific physical and economic risks resulting from the continued high cost of the equipment.

The fact that the return on investment is not assured means that monetisation remains an unresolved problem, as it paralyses necessary experimentation by the media. The experts refer to other weaknesses as well, such as those related to ethical issues, which are exacerbated by the power of this technology. Furthermore, both narrative and technological knowledge are lacking when it comes to producing this type of journalism, which has resulted in the media having made several mistakes, one of which has been producing too much of this content without considering the complexity of this type of spatial narrative, but also by massively directing it towards all kinds of audiences, when it seems more appropriate to produce specific items with a very defined purpose aimed at a 'niche' audience.

Regarding the best applications for immersive journalism, most experts highlight the importance of providing the viewer with an experience and fostering a sense of being present.

In practice, this can be achieved in many ways, such as through the representation of human-interest stories, or social backgrounds when covering humanitarian crises, sporting events, protest demonstrations, wars, spectacular events and even historical sites. The potential for live broadcasts in cases where the technology allows has been mentioned as well, in addition to the benefits of continuing to carry out experiments and tests of this technology as much as possible.

In terms of best practice, the experts refer to several issues, almost all of which relate to the start of production. First, they point to the need to be very humble, bearing in mind the change of paradigm about conventional audio-visual projects. They also make several other key recommendations, such as the following: Obtain the necessary intensive training in this new visual culture; start with simple ideas; be very willing to experiment and learn; work thoroughly on the script, especially when it involves making situations visible for the purpose of denouncement; forget the framing of conventional audio-visual culture and think instead about the point of view that the spectator is going to have; plan a narrative structure that avoids dizziness; and finally, define the distribution channel beforehand. In post-production, it is advisable not to saturate the content with extraneous elements. In essence, it is important to learn how to 'tell the truth without generating trauma', which requires considering all ethical implications, given the power of these technologies in terms of 'psychological impact'.

Among the challenges, several have been highlighted that affect different phases of production: The lack of a culture of innovation on the part of some newsroom managers; the challenge of applying all that has been learned so far to the next upsurge of this type of content; finding ways to integrate the civic role of journalism into all these technologies; and the crucial need to understand the interests of the audience, as well as what they are truly willing to consume. They also point to the difficult task of making technology accessible, preferably on platforms that are open and decentralised. Two of the experts add the challenge of immersive journalism being able to 'jump on the bandwagon of sociability' and two others refer to the advisability of telling immersive narratives in an inclusive way.

As the challenges are numerous, the strategies to face them should also be diverse. To begin with, the experts agree on the importance of being very humble, as there is still 'a lot of learning to be done'. In the immediate future, it seems advisable to take advantage of the current spaces that allow for the productive logic of the media, while at the same time being present in the new spaces, including the metaverses that are already in operation. Other proposals include partnering with start-ups and professionals who have the necessary capabilities, reinforcing the university-based training and gradually organising the new knowledge into guides and manuals.

As for the future of immersive journalism, the experts agree that even though we are in the very early stages and there are doubts about its immediate future, the technological development expected in the coming years is a reason for optimism. Specifically, part of this future might involve the media's commitment to the documentary genre, as well as to the creation of immersive experiences in public spaces like museums.

The evolution of social networks and diverse, extended realities might converge into metaverses where journalism would have its own space. Despite the media hype following the announcement of Meta and the fact that 'there is still nothing yet', the metaverse could possibly become highly relevant regarding social dynamics and the economy, which in turn would pose a new challenge for journalism. In this context, once again it is necessary to be attentive to what might happen while still testing this new language to help define the metaverse before a large corporation takes the initiative to do so.

Discussion questions

- Have you experienced immersive journalism in a VR headset and do you agree with the experts in that it is very different from 360° videos watched on YouTube? Discuss your experiences with your peers.
- In addition to the specific characteristics of immersive journalism discussed by the experts, what other aspects do you consider to be unique to this practice?
- What do you think should be the future uses of immersive journalism?

Notes

1 This chapter is an extended and reworked version of a previously published journal article entitled 'Immersive Journalism: Advantages, Disadvantages and Challenges from the Perspective of Experts', *Journalism and Media* 3(2), 330–347, published in May 2022, DOI:10.3390/journalmedia3020024.

2 The work has been supported by the Madrid Government (Comunidad de Madrid-Spain) under the Multiannual Agreement with Universidad Carlos III de Madrid in the line of Excellence of University Professors (EPUC3MXX) and in the context of the V PRICIT (Regional Programme of Research and Technological Innovation).
3 Nowadays called The Emblematic.
4 Among them, the tourism, real estate, museum and educational sectors. It is also being used therapeutically in psychology clinics to correct certain anxiety disorders such as social phobia, vertigo, fear of flying, agoraphobia, etc. In the field of education, in 2016 Google launched the 'Expeditions' initiative, which offers more than 1,000 tours of different places in the world for students to discover and explore with the help of virtual reality glasses.
5 To promote good use of this modality, in the book, *Cómo Producir Reportajes Inmersivos Con Video en 360°* [*How to Produce 360° Video Immersive Features*] (Benítez and Herrera, 2020), we propose a total of 20 good practices that affect different moments of the production process, how to guide attention, how to generate the sensation of presence and good practices from an ethical point of view.
6 The Infinite is a Space Explorers exhibition, produced by PHI and Felix and Paul Studios in association with TIME Studios https://theinfiniteexperience.world
7 In this sense, the exhibition 'Infinite', by Space Explorer, offers an immersive experience based on the NASA missions. Spanning 1,160 square metres, viewers can experience the sensation of living and working in Earth's orbit. The exhibition, which opened in Houston, will travel to Canada and other US cities. In 2023, it is scheduled to travel to other countries as well.
8 https://sparkar.facebook.com/ar-studio/

References

Barbour, R. (2007). *Doing focus groups*. New York: Sage Publications.

Benítez, M.J. and Herrera, S. (2018). 'Los primeros pasos del reportaje inmersivo a través de vídeos en 360°'. [First steps in immersive journalism using 360° video] *Historia y Comunicación Social*, 23(2), 547–566. DOI:10.5209/HICS.62784

Benítez, M.J. and Herrera, S. (2020). *Cómo producir reportajes inmersivos con vídeo en 360°* [*How to produce immersive journalism using 360° video*], Barcelona: UOC.

Benítez, M.J., Pérez-Seijo, S., and Herrera, S. (2021). Ethics in 360-Degree Immersive Journalism. In *News Media Innovation Reconsidered: Ethics and Values in a Creative Reconstruction of Journalism*. Edited by M. Luengo and S. Herrera-Damas. Hoboken: John Wiley & Sons.

De la Peña, N. (2011). Physical world news in virtual spaces: Representation and embodiment in immersive nonfiction. *Media Fields Journal: Critical Explorations in Media and Space*, 3, 1–12. http://mediafieldsjournal.org/physical-world-news-in-virtual/2011/7/22/physical-world-news-in-virtual-spaces-representation-and-emb.html

De la Peña, N., Weil, P., Llobera, J., Spanlang, B., Friedman, D., Sánchez-Vives, M.V., and Slater, M. (2010). Immersive journalism. Immersive virtual reality for the first-person experience of news. *Presence*, 19(4), 291–301. DOI:10.1162/PRES_a_00005

Hernandez, R. (2018). Interview by María José Benítez. Online in-depth interview. May 25.

Hernández Sampieri, R., Fernández Collado, C., and Baptista, P. (2014). *Metodología de la investigación* [*Research methodology*] (5th ed.). Ciudad de México: McGraw Hill.

Martínez Rodríguez, L. and Torrado, S. (2017). Reflexiones en torno al periodismo y la narrativa transmedia. In *Territorios Transmedia y Narrativas Audiovisuales*. Edited by S. Torrado, G. Ródenas, and J. G. Ferreras. Barcelona: UOC, 145–164.

Pérez-Seijo, S. (2021). Uso del vídeo 360° por los medios nativos digitales. Análisis exploratorio de los primeros pasos en el ecosistema español [Uses of 360° video in native digital media. Exploratory analysis of first steps in the Spanish ecosystem]. *El Profesional de la Información*, 30(3). DOI:10.3145/epi.2021.may.04

Sánchez Laws, A.L. (2020). *Conceptualising immersive journalism*. New York: Routledge.

2
SCREENPLAY WRITING FOR IMMERSIVE JOURNALISM

Nili Steinfeld

Introduction: Journalism as storytelling

One of the main goals of immersive journalism projects is to allow participants to have a first-person experience in a virtually recreated scenario representing a news story (De la Peña et al., 2010). In the projects led by De la Peña, for instance, audio recorded during an event was used in an animated simulation of the event. But not all news stories can be recorded in real-time. For cases aiming at allowing participants to enter a representation of a news story which cannot be recorded, can a script written based on testimonies, simulating both the visual and audio of a representative event, still be considered journalism?

One of journalism's basic goals is to create an affective relationship between the public and the news (Baía Reis and Coelho, 2018). This is not new and has not been invented with immersive journalism. In fact, storytelling forms of journalism, aimed at increasing audience immersion and engagement with the story, gained prominence during the 20th century, long before virtual reality (VR) was introduced to journalism. An example is Martha Gellhorn's reporting, especially as a war correspondent. Gellhorn's writing, as reflected in her book 'The view from the ground' (Gellhorn, 1994) featuring the author's descriptions of political and social issues, crisis and conflicts over the course of six decades, is read and structured like a story. Dell'Orto (2004) describes Gellhorn's reporting as 'Literary Journalism', a social and cultural construct that creates, not just represents, reality. Another classic example of literary journalism is the writing of George Orwell, designed to 'make political writing into an art' (Orwell et al., 1968, as cited in Keeble, 2020). Orwell has promoted his political ideology through the issues he covered in his writing, as well as through developing a unique and close relationship with his readers. He has maintained this relationship by responding to letters sent to him or to the *Tribune*'s desk in his writings and encouraged readers to respond to his columns (Keeble and

Wheeler, 2007). Can screenplay writing for immersive journalism be perceived as a development of literary journalism?

Journalism scholarship provides varying, complex, sometimes contradictory definitions to journalism and of journalists. However, it is quite clear even with the more conservative approaches that journalistic coverage is practically never a mere reporting of events. Good journalism is expected to make complex events and issues into simple and understandable stories (Zelizer, 2005). Therefore, editing and interpretation is a necessity. Although some perceptions of journalism still aspire for it to be a strict mirroring of events, without filtering or editing, completely objective and clear of bias, many contemporary reporters as well as scholars consider this approach nonviable (Zelizer, 2005). Some scholars note that storytelling has always been a common, even central, journalistic practice. In that spirit, Roeh (1989) argues that journalism is and always has been a form of storytelling and that coverage always follows a narrative. There is no such thing as objective, fact-only reporting of news. Anything other than that is already storytelling.

One main reason contributing to the literary nature of journalism is the existence of the audience. Audience engagement has become a crucial condition for successful media outlets (Ekström, 2000; Nelson, 2021). Revenue models recently adopted by digital media outlets, which are dependent on audience support and loyalty, lead news publishers to focus much more on audience engagement as they seek to better understand what encourages audience loyalty (Krebs and Lischka, 2019; Nelson, 2021). Audience engagement can be in the form of online practices such as commenting, sharing or rating news items (Krebs and Lischka, 2019). But the audience plays a crucial role even while reading the story, with the practice of sensemaking of the journalistic story. Zampa and Perrin (2018) move beyond the common perception of journalism as storytelling and contend that journalism is more than merely storytelling, as often described. Journalists create fragments of stories, story parts, which are understood, complemented and completed by their audience. These 'story-parts' and the journalistic practices in general are also largely dictated by limitations, such as limited time, as stories keep evolving and need to be written and published in a short period of time and limited space (Zampa and Perrin, 2018). These limitations effect a central part of the storytelling journalistic practice, i.e., the editing of the stories. Indeed, editing is an integral part of storytelling journalism. Much of the storytelling aspects of the news story are created during and by editing: The drama, the suspense, the narrative structure (Ekström, 2000).

Ekström (2000) proposes a model of three modes of communication to evaluate journalism, focusing on TV journalism: Information, Storytelling and Attraction. Each mode of communication corresponds to different bases for audience engagement, or involvement: Information corresponds to audience thirst for knowledge. Attention – with desire to gaze, to see something extraordinary. Storytelling corresponds to lust for adventure, propensity to empathise and experience suspense and drama. Given the characteristics of immersive journalism, often designed to promote empathy, to promote user engagement with distant events and cultures and to provide users first-person experience of journalistic stories by entering a virtual representation of the appearances and sounds of the actual event (De-la Peña et al., 2010; Sánchez Laws, 2020; Wang et al., 2018), it is obvious that immersive journalism is an especially successful form of storytelling journalism.

The unique narrative characteristics of immersive journalism

Immersive journalism is a form of storytelling journalism, but it adds some unique features to more traditional forms of journalism: First, it introduces a new dimension into the field of journalism which has not been relevant before: UX – User Experience, borrowed from the fields of software, user behaviour and computer games (Paíno Ambrosio and Rodríguez Fidalgo, 2019a). Second, the readers/viewers of the story become users in immersive means of storytelling: They are more than consumers of content. They are either witnesses, or protagonists/victims. But they are never merely readers, viewers, or consumers of the media (Paíno Ambrosio and Rodríguez Fidalgo, 2019b; Rodríguez, 2018). Considering the importance of editing as part of the story creation, made by the journalist and editor in classic forms of journalism, in the case of immersive journalism we meet additional, media-specific forms of editing. At the very basic level, Pérez-Seijo and López-García (2019) note that removing the camera tripod in 360° video news items, or eliminating the journalist from the scene, is a form of editing that needs to be considered. Is this an acceptable form of manipulation of reality?

Furthermore, Paíno Ambrosio and Rodríguez Fidalgo (2019b) contend that the user of the immersive experience also takes part in the editing process during the experience, when she decides where to look, what scenes or areas to focus on or how to respond. In immersive experiences of actual events, the user may be placed in a recreated scene as the protagonist, the victim or one of the original participants in the event. The user becomes a participant in an event she was not originally part of. De Bruin et al. (2022) make an interesting remark on embodiment and note that virtual body representation in the immersive experience can increase the sense of realness of the virtual environment. This integration of the user into the story requires integrating fiction into the news content. In practice, this entails manipulating the story in a significant way (Paíno Ambrosio and Rodríguez Fidalgo, 2019b).

Paíno Ambrosio and Rodríguez Fidalgo (2019a) conclude that due to its unique practice and characteristics, immersive journalism reformulates the basics of the 5 W's of journalistic stories: The 'Where' is the place where the story happened, but in immersive journalism it coincides with the 3D environment recreated by the creators and experienced by the user. The 'When' is when the story happened, but in immersive journalism it is also now, every time the user puts on the device and relives the story. 'To-whom' also becomes the spectator, the user of the experience, who is reliving the news story – as either a witness, the protagonist, the victim or others in the scene.

The story is not told in a past tense, something that happened and ended in the past. It is dynamic, ongoing and evolving with users actively unfolding the story as they participate in the experience. Users are a part of the story. In fact, they are at the centre of the story (Bösch et al., 2018). Maschio (2017) concludes by using the term 'storyliving' (rather than 'storytelling') to describe the distinctive experience of VR that conveys the sense that users are living the story, not merely listening/reading, or being told the story. An interesting observation to complement the image of users' storyliving the news story is that, unlike other forms of news consumption, users experiencing immersive journalism through head-mounted displays cannot be engaged with any other activities and multi-task, as they often do while watching television, listening to the radio, or reading a newspaper. The story gets their complete attention (Jones, 2017).

An important observation should be noted here. Despite its great potential in introducing advanced engaging narrative elements to traditional journalistic practice, most immersive journalistic projects today still fail to fully exploit the medium's capabilities. In an examination of immersive journalism projects by de Bruin et al. (2022) it was found that 92.1% of the works placed the users as observers and rarely did users have a main role in the story. In only 3.2% of the projects, users had a virtual representation of themselves (i.e., embodiment). Moreover, most productions only use few interactive features, with the most common (featured in 98.9% of the productions) was the option to change viewpoint. The second most common form of interactivity is controlling the pace of the experience and it was only featured in 5.8% of the productions. These results suggest that immersive journalism in its current form is still far from fully exploiting the capabilities made possible by this innovative technology.

The role of journalism

Following this line, which considers storytelling a basic form of journalism, perhaps the appropriate question may not be which practice is journalism, but rather, what is the role of journalism and how is it served by means of screenplay in immersive journalism. Witschge and Harbers (2018) contend that journalism scholarship has been occupied with normative expectations of journalism, particularly with its role in the maintenance of democracy and democratic systems, that it prevented new understandings of journalism's role for society from developing. Deuze proposes a view of journalism as an (occupational) ideology consisting of five core values: Public service, obligation to objectivity, autonomy, immediacy and ethics (Deuze, 2004).

Relating to immersive forms of journalism, Jones (2017) notes that they seek to make the journalist a part of the story. To involve the journalist in the story, defying traditional news values according to which 'good news' are factual, objective and lack emotional involvement.

The aim of immersive journalism, or non-fiction VR, according to McRoberts (2018), is not necessarily to inform or bring the audience 'closer to the truth'.

Rather, non-fiction VR offers users different ways of looking at the world and potentially induce more empathic perspectives on issues.

But journalism has other roles and relevancies for society. Stories, narratives and myths are compelling, attractive, easier to follow and engaging. News reporting as storytelling is often exploited by governments, when incidents are reported to the press framed as (often incredible, extraordinary) stories. The press adopts and accepts the narrative, takes part in the creation of myths and serves the government's agenda, often contrary to its perceived role as a watchdog (Bird and Dardenne, 2009). And if the press indeed serves state and power interests and functions as a 'propaganda machine' (Herman and Chomsky, 2010 [1988]), the compelling power of storytelling makes it an especially successful practice to that end as well. In the case of immersive storytelling, this power might increase dramatically.

Immersive storytelling practices

Immersive journalism practices vary in format, structure, interactivity and narrative elements. To set the ground for a discussion around screenplay writing as a storytelling practice, let us start by briefly describing several examples of immersive journalistic projects, describing their narrative characteristics.

'The fight for Fallujah'[1] is a *New York Times* 11-minute 360° video experience following the traditional format of documentary films. The director, writer and narrator of the video, Ben C. Solomon, also appears in the movie as he accompanies Iraqi troops fighting to retake the city of Fallujah from the hands of ISIS soldiers. The narration by Solomon provides context to the scenes in the video, background information on the war in Iraq and its current state during the shooting of the video. The user here is a spectator, accompanying the events alongside Solomon. The video presents real-life battles, missile firing, patrols through the ghost town, abandoned ISIS camps and prisoner cells. One especially dramatic scene places the user (by the placement of the camera) into a prison cell, which is an actual cage, while Solomon closes the cage bars. This piece is an example of immersive storytelling that follows common non-immersive documentary practices: The reporter appears in the video, but the narration is added as a voice-over posterior recording providing description and interpretation for what the user is witnessing. The soldiers that appear in the video are real Iraqi soldiers and the refugees are real refugees. Solomon interviews a refugee and the user hears simultaneous voice-over translation of her answers. The story does not illustrate, recreate or otherwise mediate the reality it describes. Because of the natural setting of the recording, in the battlefield, refugee camp or soldiers' rest areas – the surroundings are crowded with visual information, objects and people and the user's role as editor of her own experience (Paíno Ambrosio and Rodríguez Fidalgo, 2019b) is quite apparent. The piece can be viewed several times by the same user and each time a different image (different parts of the story) will be revealed, according to the choice of gaze and focus during the experience. There is no embodiment in this experience, and the user does not play any role in the story.

A step forward in terms of narrative elements, or storytelling techniques, can be seen in the project 'After solitary',[2] a collaboration between Emblematic Group and PBS's investigative series Frontline. This 360° video experience tells the story of 39-year-old Kenny Moore, a released inmate who spent over five years in solitary confinement. The video presents Kenny, but places Kenny's image on a photogrammetric scan of solitary confinement cell that serves as a recreated scene for Kenny's story. It is not Kenny's cell but an illustration. Kenny is not physically present in the cell, but his image is visually edited into the cell which serves as a background. The video places Kenny in different positions – sometimes standing, sometimes seated as though on his cell bed. In another scene, the image displays the cells doors and Kenny's video is edited to look as though he is talking from inside the cell, looking outside at the user. In another scene, a video tape of a cell extraction of a distressed inmate, not Kenny, is presented on the same background, while Kenny's voice continues to narrate his story. 'After solitary' presents an example of immersive video that combines protagonist narration and visual appearance on a recreated scene, with narrative elements (e.g., family pictures appearing and disappearing on the cell wall when Kenny describes his decision to focus on getting back to his family) that support the story and serve to enhance the sense of drama and relatedness to the main character. In this project too, the user is a spectator and is not a part of the story, nor is the user embodied in a virtual character.

Other projects by Emblematic group create animated recreation of scenes and events, often with original audio recorded on the field. A renowned example is *Hunger in L.A.*,[3] the group's first and flagship project, a recreation of an actual event that occurred at a food bank outside the First Unitarian Church in Los Angeles. The audio is an actual, real audio recording. The animated experience is an illustration of the incident, in which a diabetic man waiting in line collapsed when his blood sugar level dropped too low and was evacuated by ambulance. The figures in the animation represent the participants in the incident. The user experiences the humiliation of standing in line, hearing insults by passengers on the street, the sense of helplessness at the face of a men seizing due to malnutrition and others standing idle by until help arrives. In this experience, although the user is not embedded in an avatar, the sense of embodiment is strengthened by the ability to walk around the scene, which animated 3D environments enable and 3D video does not. The user has greater agency and ability to control her point of view, or approach elements of the story that she wants to focus on and explore. This type of production moves a step further from factual reporting and introduces VR-specific storytelling elements to the content. It increases the user's role as editor and co-creator of the content, as well as user agency and involvement in the story. Although there is no avatar embodiment in the experience, the user becomes part of the story, a person standing on the same line as the others. She can choose to investigate further the incident, the status of the man needing help, or look around and focus on other characters or parts of the scene.

'We Wait'[4] is a BBC short animated illustration of the refugee crisis in Europe as it is experienced from the perspective of a Syrian family trying to cross the border from Turkey to Greece by sea. The user is entered into a boat with the family in a frightening and dangerous sail through the sea at night. The user is placed into the scene as one of the passengers, by thus it is inferred that the user is a refugee herself, making the journey into Europe. There are several narrators in the film: A woman tells her story and describes the journey, her fears, how they encountered another boat of refugees that sank during the journey but they could not help and save the passengers; a man recalls how the Turkish coastguard found their boat in the previous attempt and made everyone go back. The experience is an animation illustration of a fictitious family's journey, based on BBC News interviews with migrants. This example introduces screenplay writing for immersive journalism as a form of storytelling technique. The story is based on real events, collected by the BBC in interviews with refugees, which inspired the creation of the story. But the family in the experience is not a real family and its story is an illustration of real refugee stories. The event that the user participates in did not happen, but it is an example of many other similar events that did.

In a recent paper (Steinfeld, 2020), I describe a study for which I have created an immersive 360° video entitled 'Workplace Sexual Harassment'. The screenplay for the video was written by the research team and was based on testimonies of employees reporting workplace sexual harassment, which were drawn from a publicly accessible Israeli Facebook page dedicated to the publication of testimonies of sexual harassment and sexual assault victims. The scenes follow office interactions between a female employee and her male manager. In each scene, the manager makes remarks referencing the employee's appearance and attractiveness, asks about her relationship status and finally attempts to convince her to sit closer to him during a meeting. The script ends with the employee storming out of the room. The video is filmed from the point of view of the employee. This way, the employee's face is never shown, but her hands and legs are shown from beneath the camera. This is another example of immersive content featuring a fictitious story based on real events and testimonies. The experience is very real for the users in the sense that it presents video materials and is shot from the point-of-view of the victim so that participants embody the victim (when they look down they see the employee's hands and legs as their own). Participants in the study were introduced to the story in one of three formats: As a written script; as a 2D video; or as a 3D immersive experience using head-mounted display. Participants were informed beforehand that they would be witnessing a fictitious story based on real testimonies. And indeed, a follow-up study found that the participants, male and female, regardless of the format of watching the video (2D or 3D), have agreed that the video realistically simulates a familiar phenomenon (Steinfeld and Lowenstein, 2022). Moreover, participants of the VR experience specifically noted that they felt like they were physically present in the office and that they have fully embodied the victim's character, and expressed a total identification with the victim during the experience ('I felt that I was her'; ibid.).

The examples above demonstrate a range of immersive journalism experiences spanning a variety of storytelling techniques. The first example, 'The fight for Fallujah', features the least amount of narrative elements: It follows documentary guidelines almost entirely, presents reality and from-the-field footage and makes a clear distinction between reporting and commentary (reporter's narration). The last two examples: 'We Wait' and 'Workplace Sexual Harassment' represent, perhaps, the other end of immersive journalism, as they integrate significantly more immersive narrative elements. In fact, they are stories rather than reports. They are fictitious, but they are still journalistic in the sense that they illustrate a real phenomenon, based on research and collection of testimonies and real stories. They recreate a scene, an example, so that users can experience from a first-person perspective the phenomenon they engage with. Recreating a fictitious facts-based illustration enables the experience to be significantly more 'immersive', in the sense that it can integrate more narrative elements – primarily, the user can be placed into the scene as a character and not just a passive observer (de Bruin et al., 2022), to 'storylive' the story (Maschio, 2017). In 'Workplace Sexual Harassment', the embodiment of a victim of sexual harassment contributes to user engagement and attachment to the story and to the victim. It has also led to change in stereotypical views on the phenomenon of sexual harassment. The experience makes use of the advanced story elements possible by 3D 360° video technology and has proven that by exploiting the technology's affordances it can have a significant effect on opinions.

But this understanding raises some serious ethical concerns. At what point does immersive storytelling manipulation become too much?

Ethical and societal dilemmas

Immersive experiences have demonstrated impressive abilities to produce empathetic responses (e.g., Archer and Finger, 2018; Breves, 2020; Gonzalez-Liencres et al., 2020; Kandaurova and Lee, 2019). In a TED talk he gave, Chris Milk, director of 360° video VR documentaries, has described VR technology's potential of being the 'ultimate empathy machine' (TED, 2015). And empathy, as a wealth of previous research has demonstrated, can lead to change in opinion (see Newman et al., 2015; Sirin et al., 2017). According to Bloom (2017), empathy can on the one hand encourage prosocial behaviour, but on the other hand can motivate cruelty and aggression. Empathy can lead to immoral decisions, for example when it creates a bias towards a person, at the expense of others.

Indeed, previous research has found that immersive VR experiences increase intention to donate money or volunteer for social causes (Kandaurova and Lee, 2019), and sense of telepresence in a VR experience increases brand recommendation intention (Shen et al., 2020), stronger liking of a touristic destination and higher levels of visitation intention (Tussyadiah et al., 2018) and reduction of intergroup stereotypes (Banakou et al., 2016). Embodied experiences affect emotions, opinions and behaviours related to the virtual content and these influence general attitudes and behaviours over time and after the virtual experience has ended (Ahn, 2021). One of VR's main features that has great persuasive power is the ability to computer-generate mimicry of characters and adjust them to the user – in appearance, body position or gestures (Miller, 2007). And indeed, a study by Hasler and colleagues (2014) found that mimicry in a simulated intergroup contact in VR led to increased empathy and sympathy towards the out-group member and perception of the interaction as more harmonious.

If VR is an empathy machine, were should we draw the line between story and manipulation? Between narrative journalism and propaganda that manipulates user emotions in an unethical way?

Sánchez Laws and Utne (2019) address another important ethical consideration in immersive journalism, related to the persuasive power of first-person perspective of an event: 'When journalists decide to invite audiences to witness a news event "as if they were there" through immersive journalism, they acquire new responsibilities toward audiences' (ibid.).

Users in immersive experiences are placed in the scene as if they are witnessing the event as it unfolds. There is a blurring of the mediation, due to the sense of presence and embodiment, that contributes to users' adoption of the narrative, because they 'see it in their own eyes' and are 'present right there in the scene'. Under these circumstances, story manipulation in the form of re-enactment or staging of a scene might be accepted as authentic by the users. Sánchez Laws and Utne (2019) mention the case of *The Displaced* by *The New York Times*, a documentary project following the stories of three refugee families. One scene in the immersive document produced within this project was a re-enactment, a staged scene featuring a child riding his bicycle. Sullivan (2015) responds to concerns raised regarding the ethics of staging scenes in this piece. She describes how some degree of editing and staging has always been necessary in still photography and videography, for example, setting up a portrait of a news subject for a photograph, or staging a school principal walking down a hallway. She mentions the need to 'hide' the reporter in a 360° video because there is no 'behind the camera' in this type of media. These manipulations are not meant to 'trick the viewer', but when the staging becomes too artificial, it does not belong in a news story (Sullivan, 2015).

Another key aspect to consider is that immersive experiences elicit higher arousal and presence, but users demonstrated lower focused attention, recognition and cued recall of information in immersive conditions (Barreda-Ángeles et al., 2021) and information recall is negatively associated with sense of telepresence (Shen et al., 2020). A possible explanation is that the psychological state of telepresence requires an extensive number of cognitive resources allocated to the experience, at the price of less cognitive capacity for memorising.

Combining impaired cognitive processing, which limits users' ability to process complex situations and events, with the powerful effect of empathy and its role in persuasion and behavioural change, immersive storytelling has an alarming potential to become a very powerful propaganda tool.

Immersive journalism and its potential for propaganda

Governments and political leaders turn to the media to convey their messages to the public. They feed the media with their version of reality, often partial, one-sided or biased, with the hope to win over public opinion and gain legitimacy and support for their actions (Nohrstedt et al., 2000). In the case of conflicts, competing versions of the conflict, its origins and the image of one side as being the 'good side', whereas the other side is the 'bad side', are contested. Media outlets may adopt one of the contested narratives for a variety of reasons: The complex nature of conflicts and of reality in general, the need to simplify the reporting, the desire to make news stories accessible and increase audience engagement with the stories. However, when doing this, they become part of the propaganda. Hobbs (2012) claims that propaganda is so common today that it triumphs traditional journalism that values fairness, accuracy and balance. The internet and, consequentially, the battle over audience attention and engagement have led to a blurring in journalistic content between journalism, art and advocacy, meant to attract attention. This blurring results in rising propaganda in journalistic content (Hobbs, 2012).

Bard (2017) summarises definitions of propaganda and notes that propaganda is employed through a manipulation of the recipient's individual and societal beliefs. It uses a combination of facts and lies, while disguising opposing facts and points of view.

Emotional appeal is a common technique of propaganda, as emotions are powerful mobilising mechanisms and can trigger automatic, instinctive responses that bypass reason (Jowett and O'Donnell, 2018; Shabo, 2008).

Immersive journalism in the form of narrative VR experiences has great potential to become a 'propaganda machine' – a combination of intense and highly engaging experience, which places the user in the event, operating emotions and producing empathy, more than any other medium. It is a storytelling, 'storyliving' platform inviting users to experience events from a first-person perspective, although they were not there when the event happened. Previous evidence that presence in an immersive experience, which is a main affordance of the medium and a goal of immersive experiences, comes at the expense of cognitive processing and memorisation. This leads to simplification of complex stories and possibly to limited critical consumption of the content by users. It may make it easier to content producers to create a highly biased, partial, one-sided content that is very convincing due to the sense of presence and first-person experience.

For immersive journalism content to be fully immersive, to exploit the potential of VR to its fullest, a relatively high level of editing, planning and downright manipulation is necessary. At the very basic level, an elimination of the tripod, of the reporter and of any 'backstage' material is required. But to be able to let users relive the story, relate to it, engage with it in a fully immersive experience, to let users become protagonists, victims, characters in the scene, or control the pace, the story, their positions, the story must be rewritten. A screenplay, recreating, illustrating or demonstrating the story, is required to make a journalistic story into a fully immersive VR experience.

Summary: Screenplay for immersive journalism

VR is by definition a 'fake medium'. Immersive experiences are all about creating fake content because they place users in fake environments, create a fake sense of presence and users embody a fake virtual body. The more fake the experience is, the more it enables users to fully immerse into it. For this reason, immersive journalistic projects that wish to exploit the potential and affordances of VR will be required to make significant manipulation in the story, possibly rewriting it completely, to enable the active participation and immersion of users in the story. This is also why ethical guidelines and journalistic standards need to be carefully guiding the production of such content.

There is an obvious blurring between art and journalistic practice within immersive storytelling journalism. This blurring raises ethical and societal dilemmas that result from the persuasive power of immersive experiences and their increased potential to evoke empathy, alongside the integration of fact and fiction, objectivity and bias, which characterise these productions. Immersive journalism is exciting exactly because it affords such blurring. Narrative, literary forms of journalism were not invented with VR and are certainly not novel. However, due to the sense of presence and first-person experience in VR, the persuasive power of stories increases. That calls for a reconsidering of the negotiated role of journalism – an ideology consisting of the obligation for objectivity and impartial interpretation of the world (Deuze, 2004), a tool to create affective relationship between the public and the news (Baía Reis and Coelho, 2018), or a propaganda machine serving the elite (Herman and Chomsky, 2010 [1988]).

Immersive journalists committed to producing quality news content that is engaging, attractive, thought-provoking as well as balanced and reliable should approach their projects with the full understanding of the level of manipulation that is required in processing the story into an experience, their obligation to avoid bias, avoid over-simplifying the story and fairly represent diverse points of view. They need to consider how to make it very clear to users which parts of the story are fictitious, which parts are realistic recreations and which parts are real and fully authentic. Aspiring for non-manipulation guidelines or adopting traditional journalism ethics will result in poor productions in terms of immersive features. Instead, I propose developing guidelines that address the medium-specific affordances, potential and challenges through full-disclosure, fair and balanced representation of what is ultimately a fact-based story.

Discussion questions

- Do you agree with the author's arguments about journalism as a form of storytelling? If yes/no, why?
- In addition to the concerns mentioned by the author, can you think of other ethical concerns in screenplay writing for immersive journalism?
- Have you attempted to write screenplays for your own journalistic productions? Discuss your experiences with your peers

Notes

1 www.nytimes.com/interactive/2016/08/14/magazine/fight-for-falluja-vr.html
2 https://emblematicgroup.com/experiences/solitary-confinement/

3 https://emblematicgroup.com/experiences/hunger-in-la/
4 www.bbc.co.uk/taster/pilots/we-wait

References

Ahn, S. J. (2021). Designing for persuasion through embodied experiences in virtual reality. In: T. de la Hera, J. Jansz, J. Raessens, and B. Schouten (eds.), *Persuasive Gaming in Context*. Amsterdam: Amsterdam University Press, pp. 163–180.

Archer, D. and Finger, K. (2018). *Walking in another's virtual shoes: Do 360-degree video news stories generate empathy in viewers?* New York: Tow Center for Digital Journalism, Columbia University.

Baía Reis, A. and Coelho, A. F. V. C. C. (2018). Virtual reality and journalism: A gateway to conceptualizing immersive journalism. *Digital Journalism*, 6(8), pp. 1090–1100. DOI:10.1080/21670811.2018.1502046

Banakou, D., Hanumanthu, P. D., and Slater, M. (2016). Virtual embodiment of white people in a black virtual body leads to a sustained reduction in their implicit racial bias. *Frontiers in Human Neuroscience*, 10, p. 601. DOI:10.3389/fnhum.2016.00601

Bard, M. T. (2017). Propaganda, persuasion, or journalism? Fox News' prime-time coverage of health-care reform in 2009 and 2014. *Electronic News*, 11(2), pp. 100–118. DOI:10.1177/1931243117710278

Barreda-Ángeles, M., Aleix-Guillaume, S., and Pereda-Baños, A. (2021). Virtual reality storytelling as a double-edged sword: Immersive presentation of nonfiction 360-video is associated with impaired cognitive information processing. *Communication Monographs*, 88(2), pp. 154–173. DOI:10.1080/03637751.2020.1803496

Bird, S. E. and Dardenne, R. W. (2009). Rethinking news and myth as storytelling. In: K. Wahl-Jorgensen and T. Hanitzsch (eds.), *The Handbook of Journalism Studies*. New York: Routledge, pp. 205–217.

Bloom, P. (2017). Empathy and its discontents. *Trends in Cognitive Sciences*, 21(1), pp. 24–31. DOI:10.1016/j.tics.2016.11.004

Bösch, M., Gensch, S., and Rath-Wiggins, L. (2018). Immersive journalism: How virtual reality impacts investigative storytelling. In: O. Hahn and F. Stalph (eds.), *Digital Investigative Journalism*. Cham: Palgrave Macmillan, pp. 103–111. DOI:10.1007/978-3-319-97283-1

Breves, P. (2020). Bringing people closer: The prosocial effects of immersive media on users' attitudes and behavior. Nonprofit and Voluntary Sector *Quarterly*, 49(5), pp. 1015–1034. DOI: 10.1177/0899764020903101

de Bruin, K., de Haan, Y., Kruikemeier, S., Lecheler, S., and Goutier, N. (2022). A first-person promise? A content-analysis of immersive journalistic productions. *Journalism*, 23(2), pp. 479–498. DOI:10.1177/1464884920922006

De la Peña, N., Weil, P., Llobera, J., Giannopoulos, E., Pomés, A., Spanlang, B., and Slater, M. (2010). Immersive *journalism*: Immersive virtual reality for the first-person experience of news. Presence: Teleoperators and *Virtual Environments*, 19(4), pp. 291–301. DOI: 10.1162/PRES_a_00005

Dell'Orto, G. (2004). 'Memory and imagination are the great deterrents': Martha Gellhorn at war as correspondent and literary author. *Journal of American Culture*, 27(3), pp. 303. DOI:10.1111/j.1537-4726.2004.00138.x

Deuze, M. (2004). Journalism studies beyond media: On ideology and identity. *Ecquid Novi: African Journalism Studies*, 25(2), pp. 275–293. DOI:10.3368/ajs.25.2.275

Ekström, M. (2000). Information, storytelling and attractions: TV journalism in three modes of communication. *Media, Culture & Society*, 22(4), pp. 465–492. DOI:10.1177/016344300022004006

Gellhorn, M. (1994). *The View from the Ground*. New York: Atlantic Monthly Press.

Gonzalez-Liencres, C., Zapata, L. E., Iruretagoyena, G., Seinfeld, S., Perez-Mendez, L., Arroyo-Palacios, J., Borland, D., Slater, M., and Sanchez-Vives, M.V. (2020). Being the victim of intimate partner violence in virtual reality: First- versus third-person perspective. *Frontiers in Psychology*, 11, p. 820. DOI: 10.3389/fpsyg.2020.00

Hasler, B. S., Hirschberger, G., Shani-Sherman, T., and Friedman, D. A. (2014). Virtual peacemakers: Mimicry increases empathy in simulated contact with virtual outgroup members. *Cyberpsychology, Behavior, and Social Networking*, 17(12), pp. 766–771. DOI:10.1089/cyber.2014.0213

Herman, E. S. and Chomsky, N. (2010 [1988]). *Manufacturing Consent: The Political Economy of the Mass Media*. New York: Random House.

Hobbs, R. (2012). The blurring of art, journalism, and advocacy: Confronting 21st century propaganda in a world of online journalism. *I/S: A Journal of Law and Policy for the Information Society*, 8(3), pp. 625–637.

Jones, S. (2017). Disrupting the narrative: Immersive journalism in virtual reality. *Journal of Media Practice*, 18(2–3), pp. 171–185. DOI: 10.1080/14682753.2017.1374677

Jowett, G. S. and O'Donnell, V. (2018). *Propaganda & Persuasion*. Thousand Oaks, CA: Sage Publications.

Kandaurova, M. and Lee, S. H. M. (2019). The effects of virtual reality (VR) on charitable giving: The role of empathy, guilt, responsibility, and social exclusion. *Journal of Business Research*, 100, pp. 571–580. DOI:10.1016/j.jbusres.2018.10.027

Keeble, R. L. (2020). *Journalism beyond Orwell*. Abingdon, Oxon: Routledge.

Keeble, R. L. and Wheeler, S. (2007). *The Journalistic Imagination: Literary Journalists from Defoe to Capote and Carter*. London: Routledge.

Krebs, I. and Lischka, J. A. (2019). Is audience engagement worth the buzz? The value of audience engagement, comment reading, and content for online news brands. *Journalism*, 20(6), pp. 714–732. DOI:10.1177/1464884916689277

Maschio, T. (2017). Storyliving: An ethnographic study of how audiences experience VR and what that means for journalists. *Google News Lab*. https://newslab.withgoogle.com/assets/docs/storyliving-a-study-of-vr-in-journalism.pdf

McRoberts, J. (2018). Are we there yet? Media content and sense of presence in non-fiction virtual reality. *Studies in Documentary Film*, 12(2), pp. 101–118. DOI: 10.1080/17503280.2017.1344924

Miller, G. (2007). The art of virtual persuasion. *Science*, 317(5843), pp. 1343–1343. DOI:10.1126/science.317.5843.1343

Nelson, J. L. (2021). The next media regime: The pursuit of 'audience engagement' in journalism. *Journalism*, 22(9), pp. 2350–2367. DOI:10.1177/1464884919862375

Newman, B. J., Hartman, T. K., Lown, P. L., and Feldman, S. (2015). Easing the heavy hand: Humanitarian concern, empathy, and opinion on immigration. *British Journal of Political Science*, 45(3), pp. 583–607. DOI:10.1017/S0007123413000410

Nohrstedt, S. A., Kaitatzi-Whitlock, S., Ottosen, R., and Riegert, K. (2000). From the Persian Gulf to Kosovo—War journalism and propaganda. *European Journal of Communication*, 15(3), pp. 383–404.

Orwell, G., Orwell, S., and Angus, I. (1968). *The Collected Essays, Journalism, and Letters of George Orwell* (1st ed.). New York: Harcourt Brace & World.

Paíno Ambrosio, A. and Rodríguez Fidalgo, M. I. (2019a). Proposal for a new communicative model in immersive journalism. *Journalism*, 22(10), pp. 2600–2617. DOI:10.1177/1464884919869710

Paíno Ambrosio, A. and Rodríguez Fidalgo, M. I. (2019b). A proposal for the classification of immersive journalism genres based on the use of virtual reality and 360-degree video. *Revista Latina de Comunicación Social*, 74, pp. 1132–1153. DOI:10.4185/RLCS-2019-1375en

Pérez-Seijo, S. and López-García, X. (2019). Five Ethical Challenges of Immersive Journalism: A Proposal of Good Practices' Indicators. In: Rocha, Á., Ferrás, C., Paredes, M. (eds) Information Technology and Systems. ICITS 2019. *Advances in Intelligent Systems and Computing* (918). Cham: Springer. DOI:10.1007/978-3-030-11890-7_89

Rodríguez, N. L. (2018). Immersive journalism design within a transmedia space. In: R. Gambarato and G. Alzamora (eds.), *Exploring Transmedia Journalism in the Digital Age*. Hershey, PA: IGI Global, pp. 67–82. DOI:10.4018/978-1-5225-3781-6.ch005

Roeh, I. (1989). Journalism as storytelling, coverage as narrative. *American Behavioral Scientist*, 33(2), pp. 162–168. DOI:10.1177/0002764289033002007

Sánchez Laws, A. L. (2020). Can immersive journalism enhance empathy? *Digital Journalism*, 8(2), pp. 213–228. DOI:10.1080/21670811.2017.1389286

Sánchez Laws, A. L., and Utne, T. (2019). Ethics guidelines for immersive journalism. *Frontiers in Robotics and AI*, 6, p. 28. DOI:10.3389/frobt.2019.00028

Shabo, M. (2008). *Techniques of Propaganda and Persuasion*. Clayton, DE: Prestwick House Inc.

Shen, J., Wang, Y., Chen, C., Nelson, M. R., and Yao, M. Z. (2020). Using virtual reality to promote the university brand: When do telepresence and system immersion matter? *Journal of Marketing Communications*, 26(4), pp. 362–393. DOI:10.1080/13527266.2019.1671480

Sirin, C. V., Valentino, N. A., and Villalobos, J. D. (2017). The social causes and political consequences of group empathy. *Political Psychology*, 38(3), pp. 427–448. www.jstor.org/stable/45094364

Steinfeld, N. (2020). To be there when it happened: immersive journalism, empathy, and opinion on sexual harassment. *Journalism Practice*, 14(2), pp. 240–258. DOI:10.1080/17512786.2019.1704842

Steinfeld, N. and Lowenstein, H. (2022, forthcoming). It's personal: An analysis of reactions to disclosure of sexual violence victimization in Israel, by online textual testimonies and by virtual reality immersive illustration. In: A. Baker and U. M. Rodrigues (eds.), *Journalism and Reporting on Sexual Violence in the Hashtag Era: #metoo #SayHerName #BlackLivesMatter*. London: Routledge.

Sullivan, M. (2015, 14 November). The tricky terrain of virtual reality. *The New York Times*. www.nytimes.com/2015/11/15/public-editor/new-york-times-virtual-reality-margaret-sullivan-public-editor.html

TED. (2015). Chris Milk: How virtual reality can create the ultimate empathy machine. www.youtube.com/watch?v=iXHil1TPxvA

Tussyadiah, I. P., Wang, D., Jung, T. H., and tom Dieck, M. C. (2018). Virtual reality, presence, and attitude change: Empirical evidence from tourism. *Tourism Management*, 66, pp. 140–154. DOI:10.1016/j.tourman.2017.12.003

Wang, G., Gu, W., and Suh, A. (2018). The effects of 360-degree VR videos on audience engagement: Evidence from *The New York Times*. In: F. Fui-Hoon Nah and B. Sophia Xiao (eds.), *HCI in Business, Government, and Organizations*. Las Vegas, NV: Springer, pp. 217–235.

Witschge, T. and Harbers, F. (2018). Journalism as practice. In: T. Vos (ed.), *Journalism*. Berlin and Boston: De Gruyter Mouton, pp. 105–123. DOI:10.1515/9781501500084-006

Zampa, M. and Perrin, D. (2018). Fragmentary narrative reasoning. On the enthymematic structure of journalistic storytelling. *Studies in Communication Sciences*, 18(1), pp. 173–189. DOI:10.24434/j.scoms.2018.01.012

Zelizer, B. (2005). Definitions of journalism. In: G. Overholser and K. H. Jamieson (eds.), *Institutions of American Democracy: The Press*. New York: Oxford University Press, pp. 66–80.

3
TEACHING IMMERSIVE JOURNALISM PRODUCTION

Tormod Utne

Media production is still characterised by the tradition of broadcasting, that is, sending out processed information from one-to-many perspectives with a strong and controlled narrator voice and a dramaturgy, where the producer is strongly present at the steering wheel. Yet the future of journalism is highly complex, perhaps even confusing, and producers are no longer solely at the helm. This has deep consequences for the teaching of journalism. As Bartnett (2004) argues, uncertainty is the rule, and not even the most developed knowledge or the best competencies and skills are enough to ensure a good professional life. Classical journalism education, as discussed by Kirchhoff (2022), is challenged by digital transformation. Educating journalism students to deal with an increasingly complex technological environment and training them to adopt emerging technologies in innovative ways becomes a key goal of journalism education.

How can we, the teachers, educators and trainers of the next generation of immersive journalists, help students build the competences and confidence they need for creating content for emerging media? And beyond that, how can training students in new digital media provide them with the stamina needed to survive in such a fast-moving news production environment?

Innovative technologies demand innovative pedagogies. One area where the need for innovative pedagogies in journalism training becomes clear is the area of spherical media production, which includes immersive journalism. Innovative spherical storytelling has developed as part of media production in the last ten years (De la Peña et al., 2010; Sánchez Laws, 2019; Sánchez Laws, 2020) opening for new theories, methods, and dilemmas, including ethical implications (Sánchez Laws and Utne, 2019).

In this regard, a key difference between more 'traditional' journalism education and education on spherical media concerns challenging traditional views of user involvement as passive, decentred third-person consumption. Placing users

DOI: 10.4324/9781003217008-5

at the centre is essential when teaching spherical storytelling methods. Practical advice on how to encourage this change of perspective is the focus of this chapter. The chapter summarises our pedagogical experiences from teaching in the field of spherical media and immersive journalism from 2016 onwards at Volda University College (VUC), one of the main institutions for professional journalism education in Norway.

Current state of immersive journalism/immersive media education

Immersive technologies have been used in various domains to help solve real problems within an ever-increasing range of fields. These emerging technologies have had heavy impact within fields such as medical training (Satava, 1993), tourism (Blumenthal and Jensen, 2019; Waern and Løvlie, 2022) and therapy (Osimo et al., 2015). Educational institutions have begun to implement offers for training with virtual reality. For example, in medicine it has been used for laparoscopic surgery training and nursing education (Samadbeik et al., 2018; Pottle, 2019).

Media research and education has more traditionally focused on uses of virtual reality for entertainment (Nyre and Vindenes, 2021) and for computer gaming (Calleja, 2010). However, new educational offers have begun to also include news reporting and documentary with spherical media.[1] At the time of writing, immersive journalism is being taught at the Stanford Journalism Program (COMM 280: Immersive (VR/AR) Journalism in the Public Sphere), City University of New York (Jour76007: Virtual Reality), the University of South Australia (COMM 3081: Virtual Reality Storytelling (immersive journalism)), Ryerson University in Toronto (JRN 841: Advanced Multimedia Journalism) and at the USC Annenberg School for Journalism and Communication, and has been the subject of graduate projects at the University of California Berkeley's Graduate School of Journalism, Oslo Metropolitan University and Universidad Ramón Llul.[2] It was also the subject of Massive Online Open Course (MOOC) by the Knight Foundation at the University of Texas in 2017. In the United Kingdom, the University of East London currently has a degree in Immersive Media, UWE Bristol offers an MA-level degree in Virtual and Extended Realities and the University of Salford's BA (Hons) in Journalism (Multimedia) involves an immersive storytelling component.[3]

Creating immersive journalism education in Volda

VUC offers one of Norway's most reputed profession-oriented journalism programmes, and 360° video technology has been incorporated into teaching at VUC since 2016. The motivation to start teaching with this technology was the rising interest in 360° video content in Silicon Valley in 2015, when the college established contacts with the Geo Media unit at Google, as well as research cooperation with professionals in national magazines and regional media funded by the Norwegian Research Council.[4]

The very first student projects containing 360° photos and videos were produced during the Spring of 2016, when the international course 'Web Documentary' was established. This course contained a module focusing on the use of 360° video, VR and AR and pivoted around teaching multimedia, nonlinear storytelling. The Web Documentary course at Volda is both for bachelor and master's students. The course provides practical and theoretical knowledge about fact-based or fact-claiming narratives on the web. It provides vocational and hands-on experience in the production of an interdisciplinary project and provides critical analytical perspectives to understand narrative strategies for web-based media. As an evolving media genre, production of web documentaries involves elements of film, animation, journalism, web design and Public Relations (PR) strategies.

Teaching immersive journalism is organised as an interdisciplinary lab-based activity. Groups are composed across programmes as journalism, design, media production and PR. Our practicum tradition additionally implies close collaboration with professionals. The need for more complex workflows is obviously present when producing advanced digital stories. The emphasis on interdisciplinary co-work and the complementary skills exchange among course participants is thus important for media educators. Students are given a lab-based space through which to explore non-linear narratives, and through which documentarists can expand the outreach of their projects. Their lab work involves understanding how to use multiple media channels and platforms, and understanding the uses of cutting-edge technologies (e.g. virtual and augmented reality in mobiles, location-based services) to materialise their fact-based stories.[5]

At Volda, we have structured the course around the following tasks and principles:

- As a first obligatory requirement, the teams must develop and pitch an idea for a web documentary for fellow students, teachers and industry partners.
- From the start, the students are instructed about creative processes in transdisciplinary groups, in a community of practice, learning by doing, socially and cognitively (Wenger, 1998).
- It is essential that the understanding of immersion is integrated early in the course schedule. Immersive productions are discussed at the beginning of the course. Requirements for user involvement and interaction are defined based on the use of 360° video material, VR and other emerging technologies in the professional examples highlighted.
- Students and examiners agree on expectations about the degree of interaction and non-linearity in the immersive journalism pieces to be produced, and there is an openness about the marking criteria from the very start. Clarity about expectations is crucial when discussing premises during the first lectures.
- The course is rich on workshops in filming 360° material, how to merge media elements into the spatial production.

Constructing the theoretical base for non-linear narrative forms and immersive journalism and forming the students' curriculum is vital. This brings its own challenges, as the literature on immersive journalism (especially pedagogy-oriented literature) is scarce. Instructors must allocate time to find, show and discuss examples of immersive multimedia documentaries.

Several resources are available online, but one of the challenges concerns keeping updated with the changes in technology. In Volda, we have been able to invite students to participate in industry conferences on immersive technologies (NxtMedia[6] conference in Trondheim, Norway), and have also been active participants in international conferences such as the renowned biannual I-Docs Symposium in Bristol.[7]

Our teaching philosophy

From the very beginning, our attention was drawn to the new collaboration possibilities that immersive media opened. In our case, the Web Documentary course was pivotal in creating a highly transdisciplinary collaborative environment where media industry, researchers and students would meet as equal partners. Wenger's (1998) idea that an organisation is a constellation of 'communities of practice' is highly recognisable in our approach. We embrace his argument that education in its deepest sense concerns the creation of new professional identities and modes of belonging, and only secondarily does it concern skills and information. Informal competence and 'social learning' are acquired by co-working with professional partners from editorial floors, technology companies and public bodies. Practicum traditions represented by Kolb (1984) and Kayes et al. (2005) are also close to the DNA of the teaching at Volda, what we informally call 'The Volda model' of practitioner-oriented media education.

Thus, to support our teaching philosophy, Google employees have been brought to our course to teach 360° video shooting workshops. We have also run seminars involving media and tech partners such as the Norwegian technology magazine Teknisk Ukeblad, the location-based storytelling app Hidden, the Norwegian daily newspaper VG, the regional newspaper Sunnmørsposten, amongst many others. The idea, however, is to not only learn *from* the professionals but learn *with* them (Schön, 1992). As an example, students co-created 360° materials with the Teknisk Ukeblad expert Eirik Helland Urke, who later published the collaborative results in the magazine (Helland Urke, 2018).

Introducing UX to journalism education

Inviting the users and giving them an opportunity to control the progress of the media experience can feel both unfamiliar and frightening. Some students are afraid of this shift – key principles of user engagement must be understood to create a good immersive User Experience (UX) for the end user.

Challenging traditional linear ways of thinking is central when entering an environment of non-linear, multimedia and immersive documentary production, yet we journalism educators tend to stick to traditional methods and storytelling perspectives. However, producers of immersive media obviously need to shift to a UX perspective. They need to adopt a different perspective on how to plan and technically produce content. They also need to rethink classical work methods – from idea development to UX. In spherical media, consumers are direct participants, and this affects the construction of narratives at many levels.

By placing the audience at the centre of their news productions and documentaries, media students as producers are forced to acquire new ways of thinking when it comes to planning, filming, coding, storyboarding and composing their narratives. In our course, we create groups of students from different disciplines in the Media department. This means that students majoring in journalism get to collaborate with students in media design, animation and film. The design students bring with them their knowledge on UX design principles. For their part, the journalism students bring with them their strong investigative skills and ethical knowledge. This creates a rich peer-based learning environment, where many aspects of what is involved when designing for a user can be brought forward. For example, the user can be conceived as a specific 'persona' (e.g. a middle-aged farmer living in Volda), and the students can then discuss ethical aspects, accessibility, usability and interaction design aspects, narrative and language aspects and other factors involved when creating a story for this specific person and the broader audience this 'persona' represents. Students can also discuss specific scenarios where the story can be viewed (for instance, considerations when using VR headsets contra AR experiences in the mobile, indoors or outdoors).

Encouraging transdisciplinary innovation within and beyond the classroom

Innovation is best created in collaboration with others. We are thus operating in a landscape described by Darsø (2011), where innovation competence is the ability to effectively navigate the interaction with others in complex contexts. Building from this premise, in recent years, we have changed our approach to transdisciplinary[8] team formation. At the very start of our course, we ask students to fill in a survey identifying skills, background and interests. The goal is to prevent the formation of homogeneous groups and to ensure complementary skills that can bring new energy from the intersection of disciplines.

Surveys among our students reveal that a broad majority have no experience with working with immersive media prior to entering the course. As shown in Figure 3.1, less than 10% of the students in the 2021 course had engaged in 360° video, VR or AR production prior to taking the Web Documentary course.[9]

Given the students' diverse backgrounds and experiences with the technology, we have moved away from voluntary group establishment in the courses, to a more deliberate, organised formation of transdisciplinary teams. This task is not easy, as it demands students to go out of their comfort zone – they are no longer only talking to their discipline peers but must engage with very different views about

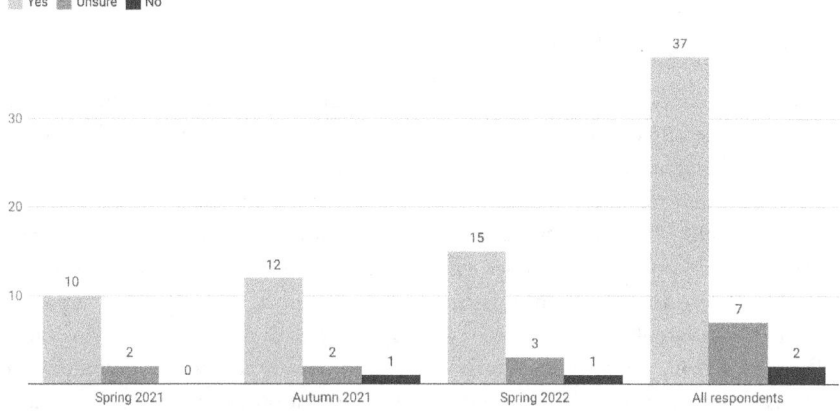

FIGURE 3.1 Pre-course survey questions
Source: https://datawrapper.dwcdn.net/XPMbE/1/

what is important when producing a factual story. Having only newspaper journalism students in a group leads to classic long-read article production. When only TV students are in a group, they quickly choose to make classic TV documentary productions. However, when purposefully putting together transdisciplinary teams, it is easier to foster an environment where teams are ready to test boundaries and break habits, to move forward in a more innovative direction.

The importance of the quality of relationships for innovation processes is not to be overlooked. Cultivating relationships and getting to know the talent, resources and skills available in the team are important to build a strong foundation for cross-disciplinary creative energy. Therefore, in the first phase of our course, we get students to present themselves and to be open and welcoming to each other. Students are encouraged to learn and understand each other's specialisation. Our aim is to prepare a ground for positive dynamic opportunities. Our hope is that innovation will emerge when several disciplines meet in practical problem-solving. In addition, a part of becoming a reflective practitioner is understanding related disciplines. As modern media professionals, students should know how to interact with designers and front-end developers, even though they will not become professionals within those disciplines.

The author of this chapter was Head of Innovation Units in media companies for many years before entering academia. For the author, social innovation/people-centred innovation is important. Innovation is not only the product or the process prior to creating the interactive media experience. It is also about the creation of a new, human infrastructure. The human relational infrastructure lives on after our courses and degrees are over. It forms a breeding ground for further collaboration with known or new partners, for instance in an editorial floor or within start-up companies. This is where the real value of innovation pedagogy is found.

Reflection-in-action

Creating a balance between the course's tasks and the student's freedom to be playful and use out-of-the-box creativity in narratives and immersive techniques is often a challenge in teaching immersive journalism.

Basic for such teaching is the approach to the epistemology of practice described by Schön (1992). The senior practitioners usually know more than they can express. Learning from knowing-in-practice gives students an enhanced form of reflection. This 'reflection-in-action' culture is incorporated into the transdisciplinary profile of immersive journalism teaching in Volda, especially with respect to involving close collaboration with professionals. Professionals are not only sources of inspiration for students – they also provide a real-life-oriented educational element to the course. Such 'real-life' elements involve using the same technology as professional media organisations do. Student projects are developed together with professionals and published for a larger audience.[10] Students are also respondents in research activities, thus learning about the academic research component. They contribute with valuable formative evaluation and testing of upcoming technology for professional partners. Working in real-world conditions is motivating for students, yet it also gives a completely different perspective on the usefulness of theory and methods that accompanies the course, since students recognise insights from theory in actual productions.

Examples

From 360° video to 3D reconstruction

Among the first stories produced by our students was a multimedia documentary about the relation between mountaineers and the Sunnmøre Alps. In this web documentary, audiences could follow speed flyer Marius Beck Dahle, who had recently recovered from a serious back injury. We follow him with a GoPro rig of six cameras on his helmet, flying down the steep mountains of north-western Norway in his speed flying parachute. The project was developed in collaboration with a media lab at a regional newspaper and was published for a broad regional audience (Kallevig et al., 2016).

The classical immersive idea for this project was to place the audience in a setting they would not otherwise experience – most of us would never consider flying down in a parachute at a very close distance to alpine pinnacles. Still, audiences could want to get an idea of how it could feel. Our students hoped that immersive journalism, as a storytelling documenting technique, might help understand better why Marius returned to speed flying even after suffering an injury. Perhaps a media experience that engaged more bodily motion would better communicate Marius' feeling of being like a bird in the mountains.

Projects like this present students with many learning challenges. Students experience the basic principles of creating immersive media content, yet without there being much previous guidance on the topic. When we started teaching this topic, the technologies for producing 360° video were very cumbersome. Thus, in addition to solving technical obstacles like 360° video stitching, editing and publishing immersive content, students effectively learned about motion stability, anti-nausea precautions and principles of placing 360° camera points.

After experimenting with 360° video and merging multimedia elements within 360° material, a further technical challenge was taken by students, who set off to create a 3D-based virtual world entitled 'The Viking Project'. The Viking project concept was to use a pile of stones (an unknown Viking grave in Volda) and trigger the cell phone of a passing pedestrian to lead her into an immersive experience of living in a Viking village in virtual reality (Sánchez Laws, 2017). A workshop aiming at creating media content out of physical objects taught students concepts related to placing the audience in an immersive environment and bringing ancient objects into life. Through this project, students discovered that the possibilities in VR and AR for reconstructing historical environments were huge and worked well for creating innovative dynamics with audiences, as well as exciting collaboration between researchers and students, since students collaborated with museum curators and journalists to create this 3D immersive environment.

AR workshop

During a two-day intensive AR workshop[11] in Volda, in collaboration with the University of Bergen, students explored the possible uses of Microsoft's Hololens and other advanced interfaces for VR and AR. Assignments connected to the workshops were constructed to encourage students to think outside the box, to disrupt traditional storytelling standards, and to embrace the innovation pedagogy principles embedded in the course (Darsø, 2011). Students were 'gently forced' to adopt innovative approaches by including an obligatory work requirement for formative evaluation of emerging technologies.[12] The spring 2022 students tested, evaluated and suggested improvements in the apps of *Hidden* and *Voice of Norway* by using the Nielsen's usability heuristics rating scale.[13]

Learning to deal with technical limitations

A unit of master's students were developing a gamified AR experience for Viti-Sunnmøre Museum. The concept of the project was that by scanning physical objects at the museum area, the ghost Lucille would be awakened and guide the user through a mixed reality historical tour through the outdoor museum area.[14] Students met certain limitations in the software supported by one of our tech partners, the company *Hidden*. *Hidden*'s locative technology worked optimally in many settings, but not all. The collaborative work with the company led students to do master productions on how to solve the technical issues. The students became truly problem-solving creative partners who proposed how to better bring immersion into gamified AR experiences. For professional partners, the way students pushed the boundaries of their technology was of great value.

The AR museum project is an example of learning as a process that takes place in a participation framework, not in an individual mind. The creation happens in communities of practice, where participation is at first legitimately, and expectedly, peripheral, yet gradually increases in engagement and complexity (Lave and Wenger, 1991).

This AR workshop also led to the birth of an augmented reality prototype finished in Spring 2022, , called 'Volda Virtual Buddy'. The Virtual Buddy was designed to help students from abroad to get to know the college campus in Volda. An augmented reality guide appears in front of students triggered by their location, guiding them around their new campus facilities.

Measuring learning outcomes

Measuring the learning outcomes of our immersive teaching indicates two interesting findings (see Figure 3.2). When asking students after delivering their exam productions and method reports what their most important learning outcomes from working with immersive media elements were, two outcomes stood out:

- Students found that learning about the *technical issues of immersive media* was very beneficial. Exploring and solving technical obstacles of the storytelling is challenging but rewarding when one succeeds. Building down the fear of technology is a great part of coaching students, and relatively small breakthroughs can lead to focus-shifting, from clinging to traditional methods, to be willing to

Most important learning outcome

56 students were asked: "If you made use of immersive elements in your documentary, what is your most important learning outcome by working with such user engagement?"

	Spring 2022	Autumn 2021	Spring 2021	All respondents
The technical use of immersive elements	11	2	3	16
The narrative challenge, how to implement it in the storytelling	6	6	4	16
Planning and organizing in new ways	1	1	1	3
My awareness of the user experience has been changed	0	2	2	4
Other	0	1	1	2

Table: Tormod Utne • Created with Datawrapper

FIGURE 3.2 End of course survey results (Survey no. 1)

explore new possibilities, aiming always for the ideal technology for the story to be told. A huge positive implication here is that students are becoming less afraid to fail. They learn to adopt a perspective of problem-solving and innovative creativity.
- *Narrative 'code cracking'* stands out as the second valuable learning outcome. Students learn to 'crack the code' of how to implement immersive elements in the storytelling and narratives in their documentaries, and in the surveys, they highlight this learning outcome as truly important. As one candidate pointed out, 'connecting it (the immersive element) to the whole storytelling/narrative was (positively) challenging and interesting with regard to finding new ways of integrating the user actively in the narrative'.[15] Classroom discussions connected to the level of linearity in web documentaries and when to let the user loose into exploring immersive elements were fruitful and interesting. Teaching immersive media production leads candidates to develop awareness and skills interactive storytelling techniques, which means that they will enter the professional world of media production better prepared to use new forms of audience engagement.

Changes in acceptance of new technologies

Emerging technologies mature, and so does their acceptance amongst practitioners, scholars and the public. After teaching immersive web documentary for some years, we see a shift among our students. We see that our future documentary makers have increased acceptance of immersive technologies, and they think that these technologies can enrich their storytelling (see Figure 3.3). 'The technical integration was not difficult at all. But it really enriched the story, since the user can participate in the story and experience it by him/herself', one student commented.[16]

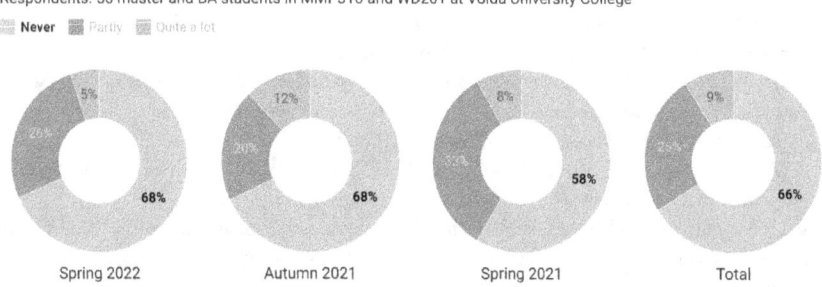

FIGURE 3.3 End of course survey results (Survey no. 2)

Developing the course in the future: Addressing the emotional impact of immersion

One last note concerns the emotional aspects of using immersive technologies for fact-based storytelling. Students themselves see the potential of interactive web documentaries for telling strong personal stories. For example, students can imagine that telling the story about a transgender person by entering the bathroom of a boy recently becoming a female and listening to her reflections as she puts her make up on, being able to consume bits for stories connected to physical objects inside her apartment, might help understand and get to know that person much more effectively and intimately than by using traditional storytelling techniques. When media students do projects like these types of portraits, the course works as innovative pedagogical method. This connects to the idea that VR enhances empathy, as discussed by Bujic et al. (2020). We have not run specific questions in our survey on this point, but we as teachers see the potential of expanding the course to cover these and other emotional aspects of immersion.

Discussion questions

- How do you think interdisciplinary student teams should be managed for the successful production of immersive journalism products? Have you had positive/negative experiences in these kinds of teams? Discuss with your peers.
- What are your views about collaboration between students and industry partners? What potentials and pitfalls do you see in these types of collaboration?
- For instructors: What measures are you taking to involve students, researchers and professionals in the teaching of topics such as web documentary and immersive journalism? What other strategies could you implement?

Notes

1. Spherical media here refers to both 360° videos and 3D-based virtual reality experiences.
2. Stanford University: https://explorecourses.stanford.edu/search?view=catalog&filter-coursestatus-Active=on&page=0&catalog=&academicYear=&q=COMM+280%3A+Virtual+Reality+Journalism+in+the+Public+Sphere&collapse=; City University of New York: www.journalism.cuny.edu/courses/virtual-reality/; University of South Australia: https://study.unisa.edu.au/courses/165041; Ryerson University: www.ryerson.ca/calendar/2020-2021/courses/journalism/JRN/841/
3. UWE Bristol: https://courses.uwe.ac.uk/I7101/virtual-reality; University of Salford: www.salford.ac.uk/courses/undergraduate/journalism-multimedia
4. VRI project with Teknisk Ukeblad and Sunnmørsposten, financed by the Norwegian Research Council and Møre og Romsdal county municipality.
5. Course description: www.hivolda.no/emne/MMP310/9700
6. https://nxtmediaconference.no/
7. http://i-docs.org/about-interactive-documentary-idocs/i-docs-symposium/
8. With transdisciplinary, we mean involving both academics and industry in the teams to go beyond our traditional higher education disciplinary boundaries.

9 Surveys collecting data from a total of 56 master's and bachelor students in 2021 and 2022, coming from a variety of media education programmes. Among the students, approximately 70% are international media students, both Erasmus and worldwide.
10 An example is the 'Dei lokkande tindane' documentary, developed and published in the Norwegian daily Sunnmørsposten, 2018: https://interaktiv.smp.no/2018/shorthand/sunnmorsalpane/
11 AR workshop arranged in cooperation with TekLab and Professor Lars Nyre (University of Bergen). 17 February and 18 February, 2022, in the Future Lab at Volda University College: https://teklab.uib.no/event/ar-workshop-i-future-lab/
12 https://teklab.uib.no/artikler/kritisk-vurdering-av-ny-teknologi/
13 www.nngroup.com/articles/how-to-rate-the-severity-of-usability-problems/
14 https://teklab.uib.no/medieproduksjon/vaerla-lille-aarsille/
15 Course evaluation WD201/MMP310 spring 2022. Survey with 19 student respondents.
16 Course evaluation WD201/MMP310 autumn 2021. Survey with 25 student respondents.

References

Bartnett, R. (2004). Learning for an unknown future. *Higher Education Research & Development*, 23(3), pp. 247–260. DOI:10.1080/0729436042000235382

Blumenthal, V. and Jensen, Ø. (2019). Consumer immersion in the experiencescape of managed visitor attractions: The nature of the immersion process and the role of involvement. *Tourism Management Perspectives*, 30, pp.159–170. DOI:10.1016/j.tmp.2019.02.008

Bujic, M., Salminen, M., Macey, J., and Hamari, J. (2020). "Empathy machine": How virtual reality affects human rights attitudes. *Internet Research*, 30(5), pp. 1407–1425. DOI:10.1108/INTR-07-2019-0306

Calleja, G. (2010). Digital games and escapism. *Games and Culture*, 5(4), pp. 335–353. DOI:10.1177/1555412009360412

Darsø, L. (2011). *Innovationspædagogik: Kunsten at fremelske innovationskompetence*. [*Innovation pegagogy: The art of stimulating innovation competence*]. Frederiksberg: Samfundslitteratur.

De la Peña, N., Weil, P. Llobera, J., Giannopoulos, E., Pomés, A., Spanlang, B., Friedman, D., Sanchez-Vives, M., and Slater, M. (2010). Immersive journalism: Immersive virtual reality for the first-person experience of news. *Presence*, 19, pp. 291–301. DOI:10.1162/PRES_a_00005

Helland Urke, E. (2018). *VR og AR - en norsk introduksjon til virtual og augmented reality*. Oslo: Cappelen Damm Akademisk.

Kallevig, G.K, Vik, F., Wiborg Karlsen, Ø., and Nordeide Kuiper, K. (2016). Fjellfolket på Sunnmøre. Ålesund: Sunnmørsposten. [Online] www.smp.no/nyheter/2016/09/29/Fjellfolket-på-Sunnmøre-13562926.ece

Kayes, A.B., Kayes, D.C., and Kolb, D.A. (2005). Developing teams using the Kolb team learning experience. *Simulation & Gaming*, 36(3), pp. 355–363. DOI:10.1177/1046878105279013

Kirchhoff, S. (2022). Journalism education's response to the challenges of digital transformation: A dispositive analysis of journalism training and education programs, *Journalism Studies*, 23(1), pp. 108–130. DOI:10.1080/1461670X.2021.2004555

Kolb, D.A. (1984). *Experiential learning. Experience as the source of learning and development*. Englewood Cliffs, NJ: Prentice Hall.

Lave, J. and Wenger, E. (1991). *Situated learning: Legitimate peripheral participation*. Cambridge: Cambridge University Press.

Nyre, L. and Vindenes, J. (2021) *Immersive journalism as witnessing 1. I: Immersive journalism as storytelling ethics, production and design* (1st Ed.). Abingdon, Oxon: Routledge.

Osimo, S.A., Pizarro, R., Spanlang, B., and Slater, M. (2015). Conversations between self and self as Sigmund Freud – A virtual body ownership paradigm for self-counselling. *Scientific Reports*, 5, 13899. DOI:10.1038/srep13899

Pottle, J. (2019). Virtual reality and the transformation of medical education. *Future Healthcare Journal*, 6(3), pp. 181–185. DOI:10.7861/fhj.2019-0036.

Samadbeik, M., Yaaghobi, D., Bastani, P., Abhari, S., Rezaee, R., and Garavand, A. (2018). The applications of virtual reality technology in medical groups teaching. *Journal of Advances in Medical Education & Professionalism*, 6(3), pp. 123–129.

Sánchez Laws, A. L. (2017). Viking grave ENG. YouTube. 24th of January 2017. (Online video) www.youtube.com/watch?v=ZPNklCN0Pkc

Sánchez Laws, A.L. (2019). *Conceptualising immersive journalism*. Abingdon, Oxon: Routledge.

Sánchez Laws, A.L. (2020). Can immersive journalism enhance empathy? *Digital Journalism*, 8(2), pp. 213–228. DOI:10.1080/21670811.2017.1389286

Sánchez Laws, A.L. and Utne, T. (2019). Ethics guidelines for immersive journalism. *Frontiers in Robotics and AI*, (6)28. DOI:10.3389/frobt.2019.00028

Satava, R.M. (1993). Virtual reality surgical simulator. The first steps. *Surgical Endoscopy*, 7(3), pp. 203–205. DOI:10.1007/BF00594110

Schön, D.A. (1992). *The reflective practitioner: How professionals think in action*. London: Routledge.

Waern, A. and Løvlie, A. (eds) (2022). *Hybrid museum experiences. Theory and design*. Media Matters Series. Amsterdam: Amsterdam University Press.

Wenger, E. (1998). *Communities of practice: Learning, meaning, and identity*. Cambridge: Cambridge University Press.

PART II
Researching immersive journalism

4
EVOLUTION OF IMMERSIVE JOURNALISM RESEARCH

A scientometric analysis

Seok Kang

Digital revolutions have transformed the journalism industry. Technologies have enabled users to engage, feel and empathise with the news. Audiences are no longer consumers of stories but participants in the news. Immersive journalism represents the trend of experiential news in the digital news landscape. Immersive journalism is referred to as a type of journalism that creates another reality and offers virtual experience from multiple angles or perspectives (Pavlik, 2019). Immersive news stories elicit a sense of presence in a three-dimensional narrative environment because audiences not only use but also experience the narrative (Mabrook and Singer, 2019). Immersive journalism is also dubbed as virtual reality (VR) journalism, experiential journalism and three-dimensional (3D) news. The emergence of immersive journalism is regarded as a culmination of the long arc of the experiential news media evolution.

With the rapidly adapting news landscape to the digital technology-based industry, academic interests in digital journalism in general – immersive journalism in particular – have been on the rise. Immersive news is still in its inceptive stage. Colussi and Reis (2020) addressed some limitations immersive journalism faces: Users do not likely feel engaged psychologically at a high level. However, the creation of innovative initiatives for immersion, presence and transportation can be the agendas to accomplish successful immersive journalism (Nielsen and Sheets, 2021).

As a sizable number of studies on immersive journalism have been conducted for the last several decades (e.g. Cruz and Fernandes, 2011; Mabrook and Singer, 2019; van Damme, All, De Marez, and Van Leuven, 2019), the research literature has grown substantially. Immersive journalism studies have either focused on conceptualisation (e.g. Jones, 2017) or audience responses (e.g. Meyer, Atkins, and Peko, 2020). As such, the studies illustrate some patterns in agendas and implications. However, themes and key concepts drawn from the topics on immersive journalism

DOI: 10.4324/9781003217008-7

have yet to be reviewed for constructive suggestions for the scholarship. Significant room remains for relevant approaches to immersive journalism research. The identification of valuable academic approaches to the topic is crucial because immersive journalism is considered the future of digital journalism (Pavlik, 2019). Even though much research has been done on immersive journalism, no systematic or comprehensive review of discussing the topic for the primary purpose of detailing themes has been conducted. An organised summary of the studies on immersive journalism can provide a structural assessment of empirical studies that can offer efficient suggestions for the immersive journalism research programme.

Ausserhofer and colleagues (2020) argue that a systematic survey of existing literature on journalism (e.g. data journalism and computational journalism) enables to identify related literature, influential publications and recurring theoretical frameworks, research designs and future directions. To better map research patterns and suggestive agendas, this chapter implemented a scientometric analysis on immersive journalism research conducted over the past several decades from its origin to the current advancement. This involves a systematic review on how immersive journalism allows researchers to pursue research agendas such as audience engagement, experience and evaluation in multimodal news media platforms.

Based on scientometrics of bibliometric data assessment, the structural analysis in this systematic review aims at quantifying and measuring the research topics of immersive journalism. Specifically, this chapter (a) identifies the main concepts and foci of research on immersive journalism, (b) visualises the conceptual and thematic structure of research on immersive journalism, (c) presents key components that are revealed in immersive journalism research and (d) suggests potential agendas for future immersive journalism research.

Using the *VOSviewer* (van Eck and Waltman, 2010) tools that construct and visualise bibliometric networks, the author of this chapter (a) collected data from the Web of Science (WoS) database, (b) selected units of analysis, (c) obtained frequencies of each unit, (d) calculated co-occurrences, (e) applied clustering techniques, (f) positioned and visualised the units and (g) interpreted implications of the visual representations. The mapping of immersive journalism research reveals what topics have received the most attention and what areas are understudied. Further, the results suggest future research directions in the immersive journalism field.

Defining immersive journalism

Starting with a fictitious book in 1935 (Weinbaum, 1935) and broader popularity with online/offline games such as video games and multiplayer games, the use of immersive technology has expanded its functionality to varying sectors, including the news industry. The fundamental principle of immersive journalism is represented as connection, first-person, interaction, telepresence, participation and experience (De la Peña et al., 2010). The audience transports itself to the narrative and becomes part of the narrative. The psychological connection can generate empathy and engagement.

A main digital technology used for immersive journalism is VR. Some scholars define immersive journalism as vivid and interactive journalistic storytelling using VR eliciting experience within the constructed world (Mabrook and Singer, 2019; Steinfeld, 2020). The consumption of a news story in the virtual world can be immersive and participatory being in the moments. VR is a computer-simulated environment of images and scenes enabling users to experience telepresence with the aid of head-mounted display (HMD) gears (Bardi, 2019). Technology companies have invested in developing HMDs to provide users with a more immersive VR experience. Facebook Oculus Rift, HTC Vive, Samsung Gear and Sony PlayStation VR have accelerated the spread of VR and contributed to expanding its reach from the innovator to the early majority phases of technology diffusion.

Nearly 90 years of the VR development span (1935–2021) demonstrate that immersive technology holds both opportunities and challenges. As Rogers (2003) suggests, factors influencing the adoption of technology, users and the industry are at the crossroads of the threshold of massive diffusion. Immersive technology for news has relative advantage, compatibility, complexity, trialability and observability. However, are audiences satisfied with the relative advantage of immersive news over other storytelling narratives? Do audiences use immersive VR news often? Such studies on VR news have seldom been conducted. In the news industry, immersive journalism is available in multiple formats, including headset viewing, 360° videos without a headset and interactive visuals. The experience differs between formats, but users view the same story for the possibility of immersion and telepresence. News publishers are still experimenting with VR technology to best reach the audience with optimal effectiveness.

An immersive narrative offers a space where everyone in the context becomes an actor exercising a level of agency (Mabrook and Singer, 2019). The degree of experience can vary depending on the depth, length, relevancy and functions of the narrative (Lewis and Westlund, 2015). That is, technology is a practical factor that determines the experience and may influence the effect of narrative consumption. In fact, news consumption in the 2D (two-dimensional) environment requires a certain level of immersion to truly learn the story. Transportation to the narrative leads the user to being with the characters of the story. One possible difference between 2D news consumption and immersive news viewing could be the level of immersion. The level of immersion with a VR story could potentially be deeper, higher and more engaging than the 2D version of the same story.

VR journalism is 'story-living' going beyond 'storytelling' in which the user plays an active role in the narrative, in other words, 'spatial storytelling' (Kukkakorpi and Pantti, 2021). VR journalism transports users from digital spaces to a sense of place by manifesting real places (Usher, 2019). When audiences connect the story to the space in terms of feeling, understanding and engaging, the narrative can be regarded as successful, because news organisations aim to amplify audiences' space-time proximity through immersive reporting (Kukkakorpi and Pantti, 2021). Hence, immersive journalism enables spatial narratives in multiple points of interest, which allows the audience to gain information from the environment, learn the context and generate subjective interpretations (Tricart, 2018).

In sum, immersive journalism can be defined broadly as a news storytelling method that utilises interactive and multiple-angle perspectives to provide sensorial and experiential news. As the news industry transforms to a participatory news environment, a systematic review of immersive journalism research can gauge where the scholarship stands and envision the direction research should head to.

Immersive journalism research

Research studies related to immersive journalism delve into the effectiveness of technology, narrative and user environment in reception, processing and acceptance. Colussi and Reis (2020) compared 360° video news stories published in the news application of three countries' publishers: El País VR (Spain), Folha 360° (Brazil), Estadão RV (Brazil) and NYT VR (United States). They found that users' spatial immersion levels were significantly higher than the sensory levels in the consumption. The user experience was not notably immersive nor experiential except for NYT VR. The researchers suggested refined accessibility with innovative initiatives to offer a truly immersive experience. Kang, O'Brien, Villarreal, Lee and Mahood (2018) reported a similar finding in which users did not distinguish significant differences between VR news viewing with a headset and 360° news consumption. The study used testing variables consisting of presence, telepresence, credibility and immersion. These parameters may play key roles in accounting for the influence of immersive journalism on audience responses, evaluation, attitudes and intentions.

The complexity of the segmented audience is an apparent trait of news consumers in today's news media environment. To meet the diverse needs, preferences and technology affordances, the measurement of immersive journalism needs to embrace the traits from adoption factors to information processing (Mateo, Bautista, and Pintado, 2020). Mabrook and Singer (2019) claim that users of VR journalism play actor roles in the story. The actors judge the context of the story to engage. By extension, the users of immersive news narratives are likely to have a deeper belief in being social members of the narrative.

As the level of engagement is known to be higher for immersive news use than for traditional news consumption, researchers insist on the influence of VR journalism on opinion change in controversial social affairs. For example, immersive news viewing and emotional empathy contributed to a decrease in stereotypical views of workplace harassment (Steinfeld, 2020). Another example demonstrates that exposure to disaster news in the 360° video format led to a higher level of presence, enjoyment, involvement toward the topic and empathy with the sufferings. As far as the comparison between the viewing with a headset and 360° video exposure, users tend to prefer the latter, indicating that the headset experience does not yet surpass the convenient 360° video use (van Damme et al., 2019).

A physiological measure of immersive news viewing through heart rate variability and electrodermal activity indicated that immersive news consumption elicited higher arousal and presence and lower attention, recognition and cued recall of information (Barreda-Ángeles, Aleix-Guillaume, and Pereda-Baños, 2021). As the effect on focused attention and memory was not mediated by arousal and presence, some improvements are suggested for immersive news experience. Relatedly, VR users tended to explore the space around them while being exposed to the virtual narrative despite their perceptions about the risk of diverting attention (Hoffman, 2021; Newton and Soukup, 2016).

The literature review suggests that immersive journalism research discovers fragmented results in audience responses. Consequences of immersive news exposure we measured through self-reported evaluations and neurological reactions. Immersive journalism is expanding its scope of news presentation to video, games and data visualisation. Identifying research patterns on immersive journalism enables to discuss its potential in journalism studies and the news industry.

Bibliometric research from co-word analysis perspective

In this chapter, the purpose of the scientometrics analysis is to quantify a batch of published literature and verify patterns in the field (Gálvez, 2019). Two broad categories are adapted to bibliometric studies: Evaluative and structural (Soos, Kampis, and Gulyas, 2013). The evaluative bibliometric analysis is designed to measure the impact of research in terms of evaluation, whereas the structural analysis uses relational indicators based on the co-occurrences of units of analysis including keywords and citations.

This chapter adopted the structural bibliometric analysis that uses relational and multidimensional indicators for the topic immersive journalism. By finding co-occurrences of at least two terms in each text, the structure of the academic domain is identified, interrelated and summarised (Gálvez, 2019). Bibliometrics, also called scientometrics, webometrics and altmetrics, detect, analyse, quantify, organise, measure and articulate research topics to build systematic presentations of the empirical body of literature (Türkay, Baykasoglu, Altun, Durmusoglu, and Türksen, 2011). A systematic analysis of literature over a given timespan enables one to investigate the structure, pattern, focus and emphasis of the research. Particularly, bibliometrics pivot a complex batch of information to a visualised format of messages called schematics (Niederer, Fink, Noble, and Smith, 2009). This mapping process reconfigures a corpus of knowledge in the form of scienciograms and offers directions in future research.

This chapter used co-word analysis that classifies concepts into relational dimensions. Co-occurred words are identified in the conceptual and thematic structure of the explored discipline. Some terms are selected from the literature of interest. From the selected terms, co-word matrices are constructed and the related words build thematic networks. The generated data can be used for statistical analysis and visualisation (Gálvez, 2019). Eventually, the analysis represents a conceptual map of the topic.

Few bibliometric analyses on journalism studies are found in the literature. Some past research reviewed journalism ethics in bibliometric analysis and found that new ethical dilemmas arise as digital technologies appear to determine news practices in the field (Redondo, Sánchez-García, and Etura, 2017). The study further suggests that academic debate on digital ethics and adaptation of it to curricula are possible courses of action. Research on journalism regarding systematic analysis has been also conducted in meta-analysis studies. In a meta-analysis of articles on narrative journalism, the analysis found that most articles were essayistic and qualitative, whereas a dearth of research was done on systematic research on the impact and functions of the topic (van Krieken and Sanders, 2021). A meta-analysis on data journalism discovered influential studies in the field. Studies on precision journalism and computer-assisted reporting were cited most by researchers in data journalism (Ausserhofer et al., 2020). Walter and Tukachinsky (2020) systematically analysed studies on misinformation and concluded that source credibility and time lag were significantly related to the effect of untruthful news.

The review suggests that a bibliometric analysis on immersive journalism is worth conducting given scarce systematic reviews and its impact and value in the news industry. A mapping of journals, topics and their strengths in order would provide a structural picture of immersive journalism and suggest relevant research agenda for contribution. Research questions guiding the inquiries are,

> **RQ1:** What keywords are found in immersive journalism research over time?
> **RQ2:** How are keywords on immersive journalism research interconnected with each other?

Method

The co-word analysis performed in this chapter followed several stages suggested by past scientometric analysis research (Gálvez, 2019). This chapter selected units of analysis; obtained frequencies of each unit of analysis; calculated co-occurrences; applied clustering techniques; positioned and visualised the analysis units in two-dimensional maps; and interpreted the visual representations. In the entire data analysis process, *VOSviewer* was used for the co-word and visualisation of units of analysis.

Data collection

Data were collected using WoS's advanced search features. WoS lists the Science Citation Index Expanded (SCIE), Social Sciences Citation Index (SSCI) and Arts & Humanities Citation Index (A & HCI) databases for academic articles, book chapters, proceedings papers and editorial materials. The literature review suggested keywords referring to immersive journalism as follows: Immersive journalism, or VR journalism, or experiential journalism, or immersive news, or 3D news, or immersive video news, or 360° video news, or interactive news, or augmented reality news or experiential news. The database retrieved results from multiple layers of search, including categories and topics. As immersive journalism is termed in many ways, those additional topic terms bearing similar meanings were included by connecting with the conjunction 'or'.

The search strategy started with searching the WC field (WoS Categories) for the term 'WC = Communication'; the field TP (type of document) for the term 'TP = Article', the field TS (topic) for 'TS = (immersive journalism, VR journalism, experiential journalism, immersive news, 3D news, immersive video news, 360° video news, interactive news, augmented reality news, experiential news)'. To do this, the advanced search query builder was used. As each category and term were selected, they were added to the query. These documents were downloaded in plain text for further analysis.

Exclusion criteria were articles published in languages other than English, journals in other fields, book chapters, editorial materials, letters, reviews, books, proceeding papers and book reviews. The data included only academic articles with empirical research outcomes in the communication field. Therefore, this data set was regarded as the one that reflects on results through scientific analysis.

The data were collected throughout the month of September 2021 and the ending date of collection was 31 September. As a result, a total of 223 research articles that examined immersive journalism in the communication field were obtained. The publication years of the articles ranged from 1994 to 2021. From WoS, the collected data finalised from the sorting process were exported to other data formats. In the export setting, full records and cited references were selected. The exported text file was imported to *VOSviewer* for analysis.

Data processing for analysis

This chapter used all keywords obtained from the scientific production indexed in the WoS data as the units of analysis. From the 223 articles, two types of keywords were used: Author Keywords from the authors and KeyWords Plus (KP), generated by the frequency of the words in the citations. To analyse the keywords, this chapter followed through step-by-step data export and import instructions. First, the data were extracted from WoS using data export in a tab-delimited file. Second, in *VOSviewer*, the option 'create a map based on bibliographic data' to obtain keyword co-occurrence data was used. Third, the option 'read data from bibliographic database files' was chosen to collect the data from WoS. Fourth, the type of analysis was co-occurrence; the units of analysis were all keywords; and the counting method was full counting. As a result, there appeared a total of 382 keywords. The minimum number of occurrences of the keyword option chose '2' to garner as many meaningfully linked keywords as possible. When the minimum number was set to 2, 68 keywords met the threshold. Therefore, square matrices of 68 × 68 between pairs of keywords were built and used for mapping.

Keywords in science maps

VOSviewer implemented multiple steps for creating keyword network visualisations and mapping (Gálvez, 2019). *VOSviewer* yielded the number of co-occurrences and link strength. Based on the normalisation of the associations of keywords, the results generate the number of links from one keyword to other keywords. Therefore, link strength is an indication of the significance of each keyword.

Mapping in a 2D space presented nodes by strength. Strongly related nodes were positioned closely with each other, whereas weakly related nodes were small and positioned farther from each other. *VOSviewer* displayed the results based on clustering algorithms. Mapping results in different resolution parameters in clusters. Keyword groups were presented in label view, density view and publication time view bibliometric maps. The label view showed keywords by a circle with a label. The size of the circle indicates significance. Different brightness distinguishes groupings of keywords by cohesiveness. The keywords linked with large circles represent the connectedness of the research topics. The density view is an image in which each zone is composed of keywords with different brightness. The publication time view was represented with different brightness for each time span.

Results

In a preliminary analysis, the refined final data on WoS found the top 20 communication journals that published immersive journalism studies. The two journals that published the topic most were *Digital Journalism* ($n = 21$) and *Journalism Studies* ($n = 21$), followed by *New Media & Society* ($n = 19$), *Journalism* ($n = 18$), *Journalism Practice* ($n = 18$), *Communication Research* ($n = 12$), *Convergence* ($n = 10$), *Mass Communication and Society* ($n = 8$) and *Journal of Communication* ($n = 7$). Some of the journals in the 'Other' category include *Visual Communication Quarterly*, *Asian Journal of Communication*, *Human Communication Research* and *International Journal of Communication* (see Table 4.1).

RQ1 asked what keywords exist in immersive journalism research. The results of the top 20 keywords for immersive journalism studies showed that journalism ($n = 12$) was used most followed by media ($n = 11$), virtual reality ($n = 10$), news ($n = 8$), immersive journalism ($n = 7$), online ($n = 6$), credibility ($n = 5$) and engagement ($n = 5$; Table 4.2). The highest link strength was found in media ($n = 56$) followed by virtual reality ($n = 49$), journalism ($n = 48$), news ($n = 45$), online ($n = 40$) and credibility ($n = 31$). In an additional analysis, Figure 4.1 demonstrates the number of publications about immersive journalism over time. As of 30 September 2021, 23 publications were found. In 2020, a total of 38 immersive journalism studies were published, followed by 2019 ($n = 25$), 2018 ($n = 21$), 2017 ($n = 20$), 2016 ($n = 16$) and 2015 ($n = 14$).

RQ2 inquired about the interconnected structure of immersive journalism research in terms of keywords. The label view for the 68 keywords was clustered into six groups (Figure 4.2). Cluster 1 entailed 19 items: Attitude, credibility, incivility, information, internet, media, media sociology, moderation, newspapers, online, online comments, online news, participation, patterns, people, public sphere, quality, trust and user comments. Cluster 2 had 17 items: Attention, content analysis, data journalism, data visualisation, emotion, experience, eye tracking, immersive

TABLE 4.1 List of top 20 communication journals with published articles on immersive journalism

Journals	Number of articles (%)
1. Digital Journalism	21 (9.41)
2. Journalism Studies	21 (9.41)
3. New Media & Society	19 (8.52)
4. Journalism	18 (8.07)
5. Journalism Practice	18 (8.07)
6. Communication Research	12 (5.38)
7. Convergence: The International Journal of Research into New Media Technology	10 (4.48)
8. Mass Communication and Society	8 (3.58)
9. Journal of Communication	7 (3.13)
10. Journalism & Mass Communication Quarterly	7 (3.13)
11. Asia Pacific Media Educator	6 (2.69)
12. Discourse Communication	5 (2.24)
13. Chinese Journal of Communication	4 (1.79)
14. Media and Communication	4 (1.79)
15. Business and Professional Communication Quarterly	3 (1.34)
16. Communication and Society-Spain	3 (1.34)
17. European Journal of Communication	3 (1.34)
18. Media International Australia	3 (1.34)
19. Nordicom Review	3 (1.34)
20. Social Media and Society	3 (1.34)
Others	45 (20.17)
Total	223 (100%)

journalism, information processing, interactivity, involvement, knowledge, memory, model, presence, reality and responses. Cluster 3 had 16 items: Audiences, digital journalism, documentary, engagement, Facebook, future, immersion, journalism, multimedia, news, news audience, perceptions, power, rise, social media and Twitter. Cluster 4 included six items: Authorship, empathy, storytelling, user agency, video games and virtual reality. Cluster 5 had five items: Coverage, gamification, news games, self-censorship and virtual reality. Lastly, Cluster 6 included augmented reality, communication, fear, place and space.

The density view demonstrates the significance of keywords (Figure 4.3). The heavy-density areas included journalism, virtual reality, media, social media, immersive journalism and online. The moderate-density areas located keywords such as engagement, Facebook, experience, video games, newspapers, incivility, information, eye tracking, data visualisation, memory, presence, empathy, involvement, data journalism, fear and credibility. The light-density areas encompassed trust, online news and quality.

Figure 4.4 shows the keywords categorised by publication time. Bright circles and lines indicate recent publications whereas darker ones are early publications. The topics published in recent years include data journalism, immersion, multimedia,

TABLE 4.2 Top 20 keywords with the number of occurrences and link strength

Keyword	Occurrences	Total link strength
1. Journalism	12	48
2. Media	11	56
3. Virtual reality	10	49
4. News	8	45
5. Immersive journalism	7	40
6. Online	6	35
7. Credibility	5	31
8. Engagement	5	30
9. Social media	5	20
10. Emotion	4	25
11. Experience	4	25
12. Information	4	21
13. Augmented reality	4	18
14. Digital journalism	4	18
15. Empathy	4	14
16. Newspapers	3	26
17. User comments	3	25
18. Incivility	3	22
19. Interactivity	3	22
20. Attention	3	19

Note: Total link strength indicates the number of links from the keyword to other keywords.

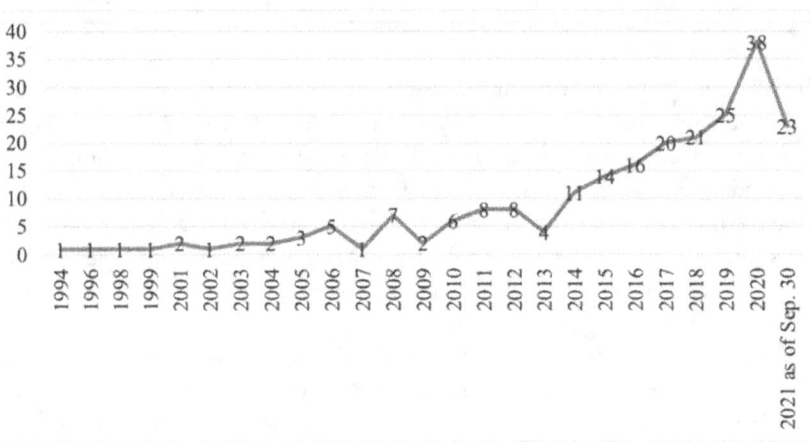

FIGURE 4.1 Number of publications on immersive journalism by year
Source: Own elaboration.

Evolution of immersive journalism research 85

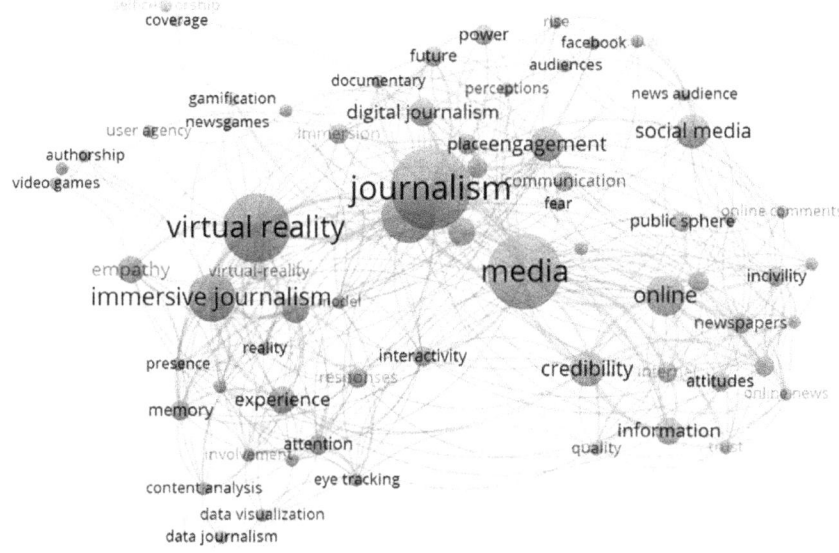

FIGURE 4.2 Labels of keywords with different groups
Source: Own elaboration.

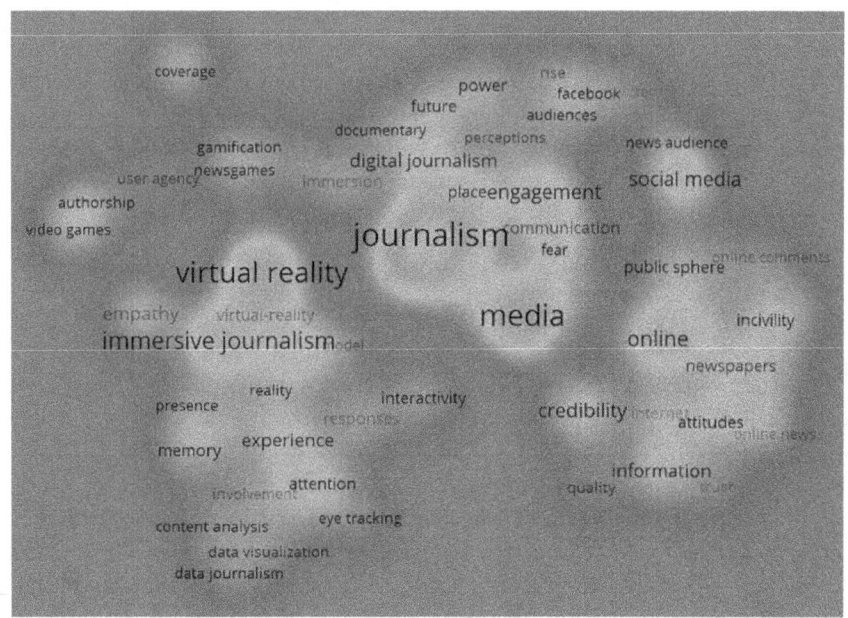

FIGURE 4.3 Density view with keyword connections
Source: Own elaboration.

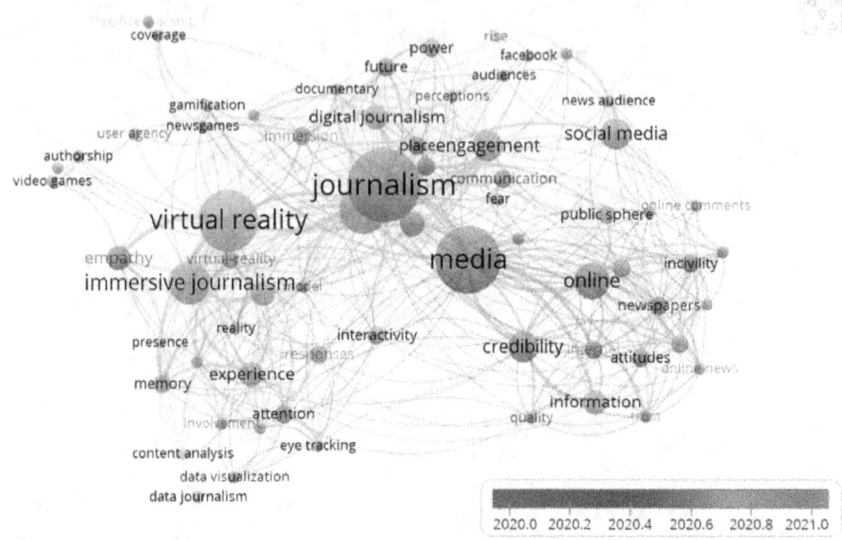

FIGURE 4.4 Publication time view with keyword connections
Source: Own elaboration.

experience, information processing, memory, user agency, documentary and online comments. The topics published in earlier years are journalism, digital journalism, immersive journalism, emotion, virtual reality, empathy, self-censorship, credibility, media, augmented reality, internet, information, attitude, trust, online, public sphere, incivility, engagement, place, space and future. The topics published in the earliest years were involvement, eye tracking, interactivity, quality, online news, user comments, social media, news audience, gamification, video games, storytelling, Twitter, Facebook, coverage and power.

Discussion

This chapter was designed to conduct a scientometric analysis of immersive journalism research in terms of themes, topic strengths and publication time in the journalism field. In the top 20 communication journals that published immersive journalism articles, journalism-specialised journals published the topic primarily (e.g. *Digital Journalism* and *Journalism Studies*). *New Media & Society* published immersive journalism studies as well as other new media topics.

The most studied keywords in immersive journalism were journalism and media. It is understandable that the segmented keywords ranked top on the list (e.g. journalism, media and news). On the other hand, keywords such as virtual reality, credibility, engagement, emotion, social media and experience in both co-occurrences and link strength imply that immersive journalism researchers are focused on news credibility and psychology, especially emotional aspects in their studies (e.g., Kukkakorpi and Pantti, 2021; Steinfeld, 2020). A possible area that may need attention in immersive journalism research can be the cognitive processing of experiential news content and behavioural intentions. The continued growth of the immersive journalism articles published in journals indicates an increase in the use of the stories in news reports. As emerging devices, including wearables, are drivers of the diffusion of VR and AR in the audience (Nagel, 2021), it is expected that immersive journalism research will continue to increase. Future studies can focus on behavioural outcomes of immersive news experiences.

The label view of keywords from the data shows groups that cluster with each other. The online newsgroup was related mainly to news credibility, public sphere, attitudes and information quality. The digital journalism group was related to the topics of social media, perceptions, immersion, engagement, Facebook and perceptions. The results imply that social media may be the main channel for audiences to consume experiential news. In those studies, the researchers tested perceptions and audience responses. Therefore, the journalism and media groups tend to measure immersive journalism effects and audiences' psychological reactions to the news consumption experience (e.g. Meyer et al., 2020; Shin and Biocca, 2018). Another cluster represented memory, experience, eye tracking, data visualisation and presence. The results address that immersive journalism researchers are interested in audiences' physiological reactions to the news. Therefore, competent research areas in immersive journalism have been emotional responses, neurological measures and content engagement (e.g. Barreda-Ángeles et al., 2021; Jeong, Kim, Yum, and Hwang, 2020). Notably, immersive journalism studies are linked with video games. Cinematic or documentary storytelling formats in immersive news are a convergence of experiential engagement with procedural rhetoric of digital games. Immersive journalism storytelling can be presented as a participatory game and audiences experience involvement (Dowling, 2020). Immersive journalism researchers may need to continue to investigate experiential news in engaging game formats and documentaries in future research.

In the density view results, some areas that need more attention as topics for future research in immersive journalism can be online comments, behaviours and social participation. The results show only a weak relationship between immersive news and real-life engagement and behavioural intention. Such behavioural level studies can offer new implications about the influence of immersive news on action by going beyond audiences' perceptive and attitudinal evaluations.

The publication time of immersive journalism studies shows recently rising topics in the field. Memory, presence, online comments, documentary, data journalism and experientiality are what immersive journalism researchers used as topics for recent publications. Despite the prevalent news consumption on social media, the studies on immersive journalism and social media were published in relatively early years. As increasing social media platforms offer a VR or AR (augmented reality) format for stories, continued research on immersive journalism and audiences' experience with VR/AR news on social media is necessary (Sheller, 2015). Data journalism through the lens of immersive news is promising. The effects of interactive, 3D and immersive data visualisation on audience responses and behaviours may open an additional area of research agendas in immersive journalism.

Overall, changes were observed in the evolution of immersive journalism research during the last three decades. Journalism researchers' growing interest over time, emphasis on topics and journals that published immersive journalism were presented in this analysis. The analysed data and results demonstrate that immersive journalism is a constantly growing area of research in the journalism field by expanding the scope of topics. Researchers have tested the influence of immersive journalism on emotional, sensorial and attitudinal responses.

Limitations and Suggestions

Although the analysis in this chapter offers some significant implications in identifying the scholarship of immersive journalism research, the methodological approach bears some limitations. Since this analysis was based only on one database (WoS), the search results might have overlooked other reliable resources for data. The integration of data sources from multiple databases can increase sample validity. Another limitation is the exclusion of studies in different languages. Studies published in languages other than English would likely represent varying aspects of immersive journalism, because the topic is a global phenomenon. There can be some blind spots that may add important implications to the current findings. Not only a scientometric analysis but also inferential statistics for frequencies and other indices can provide insights into the authenticity of the data and relevant interpretations of the immersive journalism research status.

Conclusion

This scientometric data analysis in combination with visualisation provided a structure of multidimensional and evolving trends in immersive journalism research. A refined study list from WoS allowed for the identification of thematic clusters of immersive journalism keywords. The results of publications over time suggest that immersive journalism is gradually playing an important role in journalism research. The upward trends of publications and the expanded scope of topics including engagement, power, empathy, documentary, games and credibility offer opportunities to further explore the topic in future studies. Journalism researchers may focus more on the role of immersive journalism in adoption, civic engagement, emotion, information processing, intention and behaviours than the current efforts. Immersive storytelling can be not only VR news viewing with a headset but also immersive news in the forms of games, AR, experiential documentaries and interactive data. The current chapter enabled to observe the study trends and provided possible future directions in immersive journalism research.

Discussion questions

- Which topics in immersive journalism research are you interested in? Discuss with your peers.

- After reading this analysis, what are your conclusions on what topics should be emphasised in future research on immersive journalism?
- How do the findings affect the research you were planning to conduct? Will you alter your topic? If yes/no, why?

References

Ausserhofer, J., Gutounig, R., Oppermann, M., Matiasek, S., and Goldgruber, E. (2020). The datafication of data journalism scholarship: Focal points, methods, and research propositions for the investigation of data-intensive newswork. *Journalism,* 21(7), pp. 950–973. DOI:10.1177/1464884917700667

Bardi, J. (2019). *What is virtual reality?* Marxent. www.marxentlabs.com/what-is-virtual-reality/

Barreda-Ángeles, M., Aleix-Guillaume, S., and Pereda-Baños, A. (2021). Virtual reality storytelling as a double-edged sword: Immersive presentation of nonfiction 360° video is associated with impaired cognitive information processing. *Communication Monographs,* 88(2), pp. 154–173. DOI:10.1080/03637751.2020.1803496

Colussi, J. and Reis, T.A. (2020). Periodismo inmersivo. Análisis de la narrativa en aplicaciones de realidad virtual [Immersive journalism. Analysis of narratives in virtual reality applications]. *Revista Latina de Comunicación Social,* 77, pp. 19–32. DOI:10.4185/RLCS-2020-1447

Cruz, R. and Fernandes, R. (2011). Journalism in virtual worlds. *Journal of Virtual Worlds Research,* 4(1), pp. 4–13. DOI:10.4101/jvwr.v4i1.2110

De la Peña, N., Weil, P., Llobera, J., Giannopoulos, E., Pomés, A., Spanlang, B., Friedman, D., Sanchez-Vives, M.V., and Slater, M. (2010). Immersive journalism: Immersive virtual reality for the first-person experience of news. *Presence: Teleoperators and Virtual Environments,* 19(4), pp. 291–301. DOI:10.1162/PRES_a_00005

Dowling, D.O. (2020). Documentary games for social change: Recasting violence in the latest generation of i-docs. *Catalan Journal of Communication & Cultural Studies,* 12(2), pp. 287–299. DOI:10.1386/cjcs_00033_1

Gálvez, C. (2019). Evolution of the field of social media research through science maps (2008–2017). *Communication & Society,* 32(2), pp. 61–76. DOI:10.15581/003.32.2.61-76

Hoffman, H.G. (2021). Interacting with virtual objects via embodied avatar hands reduces pain intensity and diverts attention. *Scientific Report,* 11, 10672. DOI:10.1038/s41598-021-89526-4

Jeong, S.-H., Kim, S., Yum, J.-Y., and Hwang, Y. (2020). Effects of virtual reality news on knowledge gain and news attitudes. *International Journal of Mobile Communications,* 18(3), pp. 300–313. DOI:10.1504/IJMC.2020.107098

Jones, S. (2017). Disrupting the narrative: Immersive journalism in virtual reality. *Journal of Media Practice,* 18(2/3), pp. 171–185. DOI:10.1080/14682753.2017.1374677

Kang, S., O'Brien, E., Villarreal A., Lee, W.S., and Mahood, C. (2018). Immersive journalism and telepresence: Does virtual reality news use affect news credibility? *Digital Journalism,* 7(2), pp. 294–313. DOI:10.1080/21670811.2018.1504624

Kukkakorpi, M. and Pantti, M. (2021). A sense of place: VR journalism and emotional engagement. *Journalism Practice,* 15(6), pp. 785–802. DOI:10.1080/17512786.2020.1799237

Lewis, S.C. and Westlund, O. (2015). Actors, actants, audiences, and activities in cross-media news work. *Digital Journalism,* 3(1), pp. 19–37.

Mabrook, R. and Singer, J.B. (2019). Virtual reality, 360° video, and journalism studies: Conceptual approaches to immersive technologies. *Journalism Studies,* 20(14), pp. 2096–2112. DOI:10.1080/1461670X.2019.1568203

Mateo, R.C., Bautista, P.S., and Pintado, P.G. (2020). Hacia un modelo de narrativa en periodismo inmersivo [Towards a narrative model in immersive journalism]. *Revista Latina de Comunicación Social,* 75, pp. 341–365. DOI:10.4185/RLCS-2020-1430

Meyer, H.K., Atkins, A., and Peko, S. (2020). Virtual community: Can community journalists use non-linear, VR storytelling to improve credibility, increase community connection? *Grassroots Editor,* 61(3/4), pp. 11–20.

Nagel, D. (2021, 5 October). *Augmented and virtual reality leading growth in emerging devices. The Journal.* https://thejournal.com/articles/2021/10/05/augmented-and-virtual-reality-leading-growth-in-emerging-devices.aspx

Newton, K. and Soukup, K. (2016, 6 April). *The storyteller's guide to the virtual reality audience. Medium.* https://medium.com/stanford-d-school/the-storyteller-s-guide-to-the-virtual-realityaudience-19e92da57497

Niederer, S.A., Fink, M., Noble, D., and Smith, N.P. (2009). A meta-analysis of cardiac electrophysiology computational models. *Experimental Physiology,* 94(5), pp. 486–495. DOI:10.1113/expphysiol.2008.044610

Nielsen, S.L. and Sheets, P. (2021). Virtual hype meets reality: Users' perception of immersive journalism. *Journalism,* 22(10), pp. 2637–2653. DOI:10.1177/1464884919869399

Pavlik, J.V. (2019). *Journalism in the age of virtual reality.* New York: Columbia University Press.

Redondo, M., Sánchez-García, P., and Etura, D. (2017). Research on ethics education for journalists in Spain. Bibliometric analysis and applied educational terms (2005–2015). *Revista Latina de Comunicación Social,* 72, pp. 235–252. DOI:10.4185/RLCS-2017-1163

Rogers, E. (2003). *Diffusion of innovations* (5th ed.). New York: Simon & Schuster.

Sheller, M. (2015). News Now. *Journalism Studies,* 16(1), pp. 12–26. DOI:10.1080/1461670X.2014.890324

Shin, D. and Biocca, F. (2018). Exploring immersive experience in journalism. *New Media & Society,* 20(8), pp. 2800–2823. DOI:10.1177/1461444817733133

Soos, S., Kampis, G., and Gulyas, L. (2013). Large-scale temporal analysis of computer and information science. *European Physical Journal Special Topics,* 222, pp. 1441–1465. DOI:10.1140/epjst/e2013-01936-6

Steinfeld, N. (2020). To be there when it happened: Immersive journalism, empathy, and opinion on sexual harassment. *Journalism Practice,* 14(2), pp. 240–258. DOI:10.1080/17512786.2019.1704842

Tricart, C. (2018). *Virtual reality filmmaking: Techniques & best practices for VR filmmakers.* New York: Routledge.

Türkay, D., Baykasoglu, A., Altun, K., Durmusoglu, A., and Türksen, I.B. (2011). Industrial applications of type-2 fuzzy sets and systems: A concise review. *Computers in Industry,* 62(2), pp. 125–137. DOI:10.1016/j.compind.2010.10.006

Usher, N. (2019). Putting 'place' in the center of journalism research: A way forward to understand challenges to trust and knowledge in news. *Journalism & Mass Communication Monographs,* 21(2), pp. 84–146.

van Damme, K., All, A., De Marez, L., and Van Leuven, S. (2019). 360° video journalism: Experimental study on the effect of immersion on news experience and distant suffering. *Journalism Studies,* 20(14), pp. 2053–2076. DOI:10.1080/1461670X.2018.1561208

van Eck, N.J. and Waltman, L. (2010). Software survey: VOSviewer, a computer program for bibliometric mapping. *Scientometrics,* 84(2), pp. 523–538.

van Krieken, K. and Sanders, J. (2021). What is narrative journalism? A systematic review and an empirical agenda. *Journalism,* 22(6), pp. 1393–1412. DOI:10.1177/1464884919862056

Walter, N. and Tukachinsky, R. (2020). A meta-analytic examination of the continued influence of misinformation in the face of correction: How powerful is it, why does it happen, and how to stop it? *Communication Research,* 47(2), pp. 155–177. DOI:10.1177/ 0093650219854600

Weinbaum, S.G. (1935). *Pygmalion's spectacles.* Whitefish, MT: Kessinger.

5
MAIN CONCEPTS IN IMMERSIVE JOURNALISM
Immersion and presence

António Baía Reis, Lukas Kick and Marina Oliveto

Since the introduction of the concept of immersive journalism by Nonny De la Peña et al. (2010), technological advancements have led to major changes and virtual reality technologies have made extensive progress. This has led to today's hype around the idea of the so-called metaverse. Discussions about different display formats and about the potential use of immersive media in journalistic contexts have also increased over the past years (Owen, Pitt, Aronson-Rath and Milward, 2015; Bösch, Gensch and Rath-Wiggins, 2018). However, despite the wide variety of research about immersive media technicalities (e.g. distinct formats, case studies, issues regarding production standards and emergent ethical concerns), we find that an in-depth debate about the core conceptual elements of immersive media – immersion and presence – is still missing.

Given that immersive journalism is inherently interdisciplinary, and its potentialities and challenges are rather nuanced and complex, it is not our intention to reduce immersive journalism to two major terms. Nevertheless, and given that immersion and presence are central for the understanding and further discussions about other effects of immersion (such as empathy and emotion), a focused examination of these two core elements is needed.

In this chapter, we investigate definitions of immersion and presence in the field of immersive journalism. With this, our goal is to unveil the current conceptual consensus. We also wish to underline the importance of making this consensus explicit as a guideline for further discussions and future research on immersive media.

The concepts of immersion and presence are not something exclusive to immersive media. In fact, they are not even new to media theories and practices at large. 'Transporting' the audience to a news story or media event or bringing them closer to the depicted stories is not something exclusively enabled by immersive media technologies such as 360° video or augmented reality applications. On the contrary, the aim of immersing audiences in news stories has been present in news contexts long before the digital era. Highly descriptive and emotionally engaging news coverage by Martha Gellhorn during World War II or CBS News anchor Walter Cronkite's show 'You are there!' posits the idea that being immersed, or present can be something that does not need to be triggered by digital technology, but by meaningful storytelling (Baía Reis and Castro Coelho, 2018: 1095–1096).

Against this historical background, it becomes even more apparent why immersion and presence must be dissected, outlined and discussed in the context of immersive journalism. This chapter's main goal is to investigate the growing body of work dealing with immersive journalism, beginning with the seminal studies by De la Peña et al. (2010) and onwards, to try to systematically obtain an all-encompassing view on how the two concepts, immersion and presence, have been defined throughout the last decade. We adopt a two-pronged approach. First, we provide a systematic overview of the various current approaches and ways of describing and defining immersion and presence in immersive media. Second, we use the results of this systematic mapping to contextualise distinct perspectives within their historical roots. In the discussion section, we condense our findings as a holistic definition of immersion and presence that can serve as a guideline for future research.

Methods

A qualitative content analysis was conducted to identify and map definitions of 'immersion' and 'presence' in existing literature. The research design was based upon the content analysis scheme of Philipp Mayring (2015). The analysis was applied to a data sample collected exclusively within Scopus database. Using a systematic review approach, we collected a sample of scientific texts on immersive journalism containing definitions of 'immersion' and 'presence'. To do this, search results were first filtered by the search term 'immersive journalism' and these first-pass results were further filtered by the search terms 'immersion' and 'presence'. Only texts published in English were included in the study's sample. We excluded results that were inaccessible or unavailable. A total sample of 135 scientific texts on immersive journalism with the keywords 'immersion' ($n = 69$) and 'presence' ($n = 66$) was collected.

This sample was analysed by using the model of content structuring by Philipp Mayring (2015: 103). This method involves qualitative content analysis of related characteristics of texts, which opens the possibility to identify different topic elements within texts. As a first step and drawing from existing literature, a deductive category system was created. This served as a reference for the actual coding process. Besides the pre-established deductive categories, Mayring's (2015: 103) method allowed us to add inductive categories to our category system as needed (Mayring, 2015: 97–99).

For the analysis of the terms 'immersion' and 'presence', a category system was used for each term separately. Based on our sample, the following categories were outlined: (1) 'technically-centred', (2) 'emotionally-centred', (3) 'bodily-centred,

(4) interactivity-centred, (5) 'psychologically-centred' and (6) 'not assignable'. The 'technically-centred' category encompassed definitions stressing *immersive technologies* as core aspects for the feeling of immersion and presence. The 'emotionally-centred' category included definitions that focused on the emotional aspects and feelings of participants. For the category 'bodily-centred', the feeling of a bodily experience within the virtual or immersive environments was central. The 'interactivity-centred' category included definitional approaches that centred around possible interactivity in the immersive contents. The 'psychologically-centred' category contained definitions where the feeling of immersion and presence were connected to psychological effects. 'Not assignable' served as a necessary exclusion category. Our analysis concentrated only on 'immersion' and 'presence'. The term descriptions of 'immersion' and 'presence' contained in our sample were coded according to the six categories listed above.

In addition to the qualitative analysis approach and in order to obtain a holistic understanding of the various features of definitions of 'immersion' and 'presence', we also included a quantitative approach. This also provided us with a first impression of trends in concept definitions contained in our sample. For this, we used MAXQDA 2020 as our main analysis tool. The qualitative collected data were evaluated quantitatively by capturing the numbers of results for coded categories, which allowed for a certain degree of comparability. The overall goal of this combined approach was to achieve an all-encompassing characterisation of the terms 'immersion' and 'presence' as they were used in the literature.

The concept of *immersion* – 'feeling as if you are there!'

After little more than a decade of the first experiments in immersive journalism, a wide variety of productions were carried out using virtual and augmented environments and technologies. This was part of a new narrative format that allowed telling news stories in unique ways and provided innovative means for audiences to experience those news stories, moving from the 'storytelling' to 'storyliving' paradigm (Pavlik, 2019). The work done throughout the last ten years led the way to other related formats and emergent ecosystems.[1] For our research and with the purpose of defining productions that are characterised as immersive media, we see the immersive media technological spectrum as comprising 360° photography, 360° or spherical video, virtual reality, augmented reality and mixed reality.

Within this spectrum and within each category, experiences can have higher or lower interactivity and/or complexity. For example, virtual reality experiences can allow to walk around a digital environment by means of hand controls and 360° videos usually only allow for a passive one-person perspective from a given stationary point of view.

Over the years, journalists have experimented with the whole spectrum of these emergent technological possibilities to explore new and innovative ways of telling news stories. Much has been said about the technological aspects, yet theoretical foundations using concepts such as immersion and presence are lacking in the popular debates on immersive journalism. More problematically, they also seem to be somewhat left out from the scientific literature. Different authors provide only brief definitions of the concept of immersion as preambles for their empirical investigations. To address this gap, drawing from our data collection, we outline a comparison between the different conceptualizations and interpretations offered by researchers over the last decade.

Our data reveal a clear consensus: Immersion has been consistently defined as an essential part of the sensorial and perceptual construction of being in a place or reality that is not the same as the one in which you physically find yourself. Our data also shows that historically, the experience of an imaginary image space is part of an ancestral desire to 'enter' images or even create illusionistic visual spaces (Grau, 2003: 25). The creation of content that takes place in the physical world but is intentionally projected in a virtual world by means of digital technologies and tools is part of multiple attempts to generate realistic representations of news content that take news experiences into new levels. Immersion is not a new concept: It emerged in the late 1980s when the advancement of digital entertainment technologies began to create games using virtual reality technologies (Heim, 1993). The driver for focusing on a concept such as immersion is the need to 'transport' the user inside emerging virtual worlds. Biocca (1997) speaks about how virtual reality technology enables the user to gradually bring the human body into these digital environments. This progressive virtual embodiment – or 'avatar anthropomorphism' if one embodies an avatar in a computer-generated environment – is part of the 'constant immersion in advance of sensorimotor channels in computational interfaces through a closer and more pervasive coupling of the body with sensors and interface displays' (Biocca, 1997). Since Biocca's (1997) definition, a technologically driven conceptualization of immersion has been guiding the theoretical discussion of immersive media research at large. Nonny De La Peña (2010) and colleagues, pioneers in the field of immersive journalism, used Biocca's (1997) theoretisation as starting point to the process of establishing the seminal definition of immersive journalism:

> The fundamental idea of immersive journalism is to allow the participant to enter a virtually recreated scenario representing the news story. The participant will be typically represented in the form of a digital avatar—an animated 3D digital representation of the participant and see the world from the first-person perspective of that avatar.
>
> De La Peña (2010: 292)

In an immersive system such as a CAVE (i.e. an automatic virtual environment; Cruz-Neira et al., 1992), the person was invited to see his or her own real body and the avatar only through shadows and reflections in virtual objects in the environment, though other online people could also see the avatar directly (De la Peña et al., 2010: 292).

Within studies of cyberjournalism, immersion has been characterised as a psychological state, a state in which the spectator is deeply involved with the narrative

(Bailenson, 2018). Thus, the degree of involvement within the narrative is directly linked to psychological dynamics. In addition, this form of interaction and involvement requires that the viewer's attention is fully directed towards the immersive display, which makes each viewer able to react to the content in varying levels of depth (Bailenson, 2018). Consequently, system attributes are essential to enable immersion in digital environments; thus, immersion tends to be greater in virtual environments when the user is isolated from the physical environment.

Nevertheless, some authors argue that the feeling of being immersed in a virtual environment is not solely dependent on technical devices (Witmer and Singer, 1998). A virtual environment, despite being mediated by screens, has inherent characteristics that facilitate and amplify immersion into the narrative (Domínguez, 2010, 2013; Mielniczuk et al., 2015; Murray, 1997). One of the concepts of immersion that is closest to a holistic definition of immersion comes from virtual reality pioneer Janet Murray (1997): [Immersion is] 'the sensation of being surrounded by a completely other reality (…) that takes over all our attention, our whole perceptual apparatus' (99).

Deconstructing the concept of immersion

To zoom in into how immersion has been defined and characterised by immersive journalism research in the last decade, we categorised and quantified the data collected with a focus only on the concept of immersion. The Scopus database was again used to collect a sample of publications (in English and within the scientific scope of Journalism and Communication) that discuss the topic of immersive journalism which contained a conceptualization of the term *immersion*.

We first structured the concepts extracted from the texts and identified descriptive approaches to immersion. Then, a comparison of the contents of the collected samples was carried out, which offered a quantitative overview of the results. Based on the categorisation described in the methodology of this process, we performed subjective traceability from deductive categories. We ended up with 11 scientific publications published since 2016 in which definitions of immersion are centred on the following previously outlined categories (see Table 5.1).

We found that the definition of immersion, for the most part, was based upon its technological features and that it was argued that immersion was the result of technological effects. A second major conceptual tendency was to define immersion as enabled by affective and emotional dynamics triggered by a given immersive media story. In this case, immersion is triggered by the narrative itself, rather than by the direct result of isolation from the physical world and entering a virtual world through technology.

One might argue that a coherent characterization for immersion might encompass both previously mentioned perspectives, i.e. immersion, in essence, is the feeling of being inside a virtual world that depicts a given news story that results from the confluence of a user being technology-enabled through immersive media devices in tandem with 'affectively appropriating' the story itself.

TABLE 5.1 Number of scientific publications related to the wider conceptual categories of the term 'immersion'

Category	Number of publications
C1: Technical centred	4
C2: Emotionally centred	4
C3: Bodily centred	1
C4: Interactivity centred	2
C5: Psychologically centred	0
C6: Not assignable	0

Source: Own elaboration.

Older references are centred on defining immersion as the combination of given dynamics related to emotion and technicalities. Sentences such as 'feeling of actually being there' or 'as if you are there' being quite recurrent. Moreover, the higher the combined result of emotional impact and technological facilitation, the higher the level of immersion and the plausibility of a given immersive news story experience. Most research points out the direct relationship between employing certain technical features such as virtual reality accessories or given computational techniques as fundamental triggers to enable a state of emotional consciousness and therefore an affective connection with a virtual environment. The more technologically refined and deployed in a controlled environment the experience is, the more emotionally immersive it tends to become to the audience. It is argued that different devices generate different responses. Within the specific scope of immersive journalism and following the major tendencies identified in our study, immersion seems to be substantially linked to an ability to create, by technical means, a virtual environment that is similar and resonates with the physical world, an environment in which the user can psychologically and emotionally approach the story being told. This argument stresses the technological/affective dynamic as key to fully realise immersion.

Others argue that immersive journalism news stories enable the creation of a mental connection with their audience, making use of the unconscious desire that people must be living or experiencing a situation that emotionally connects them with given news facts, situations or scenarios. Citing Pavlik, Longhi (2017) talks about how immersion allows the audience to experience a fact in an intense way, depending on the various degrees of immersion produced by combining given technological devices and techniques in coherence with the potential of a given news narrative.

We summarise the consensus as follows:

> *Immersion is the ability to create an inclusive, vivid and interactive feeling of being inside a news story. This is a combined result of stimulation of a user's different senses through immersive media technology and the capacity of news story narratives to affectively engage the audience with the depicted stories.*

The concept of *presence*: The feeling of immediate departure from the physical world and arrival to the virtual world

In addition to immersion, presence is also central when discussing immersive media. Admittedly, the relationship between immersion and presence is yet to be fully clarified. In fact, there are different approaches that define immersion as a sub-area, a concomitant dynamic, or even an amplification of presence and vice versa (Cummings and Bailenson, 2016).

Despite the apparent intertwinement between immersion and presence, our data offers some insights on how the meaning of the concept of presence can become more tangible and distinct. On the one hand, presence can be defined based on technical reception experiences (Witmer and Singer, 1998). Here, the focus is on the technical requirements and devices that enable the audience to experience a sense of presence in the first place. Within this conceptualization, a specific emphasis is placed on the possibilities of immersive technologies *per se* and their ability to involve the audience more vividly in the reception process in comparison to previous media formats: 'immersive technologies can make it possible to have the immediate physical world disappear from the user's awareness (something that is referred to as inclusion)' (de Bruin et al., 2020: 484). On the other hand, the bodily perception in virtual spaces can also help define presence. Here, the so-called feeling of 'being there' is described as an essential part of presence (Slater and Wilbur, 1997) as perceiving a spatial surrounding, or identifying with a given avatar with which one might walk around in virtual environments (Yee and Bailenson, 2007). Presence becomes more about the psychological and interactive aspects. In fact, interactivity is often connected to the requirements of feeling presence in virtual spaces (Witmer and Singer, 1998). Both the possibilities to move within the virtual environments and elements with which the audience can interact are relevant to elicit presence (Witmer and Singer, 1998). Moreover, interactions with other avatars, either the ones controlled by humans or the ones triggered by artificial intelligence, are important for presence (Ma, 2019; Ahn et al., 2016). A further aspect is the psychological effects within the reception processes. Users' reactions to the virtual environments, both on a social level and in a bodily-reactive way, are therefore key aspects to distinguish between immersion and presence (Slater and Sanchez-Vives, 2016; Bailenson, 2018). Presence in the context of immersive media is very much related to an affective dimension and emotion is a recurrent keyword in our sample for the term presence. Emotion is nevertheless rarely found as an independent sub-area directly connected to the feeling of presence. It is often described only in relation to other presence-related factors (de Bruin et al., 2020; Kukkakorpi and Pantti, 2021). However, newer approaches define emotion as a central phenomenon for the perception of presence in immersive contexts (de Bruin et al., 2020).

Deconstructing the concept of presence

During the part-quantitative evaluation, the focus categories that are central to the texts were recorded for all articles contained in the sample ($n = 66$). This consisted

TABLE 5.2 Number of scientific publications related to the wider conceptual categories of the term 'presence'

Category	Number of publications
C1: Technical centred	13
C2: Emotionally centred	1
C3: Bodily centred	26
C4: Interactivity centred	10
C5: Psychologically centred	3
C6: Not assignable	0

Source: Own elaboration.

Note: Besides the presented categories in Table 5.2, a total of 13 texts did not include a definitional focus at all.

of a quantitative count of the individual coded categories (see Table 5.2). The three most common definition characteristics were examined in search for the thematic focal points in the individual texts. These were classified according to the total number of coded units outlined in the software MAXQDA. Within the complete sample, 507 codes were collected. We found a clear focus on bodily ($n = 170$), interactive ($n = 95$) and technically-centred aspects for the term 'presence'. The psychological ($n = 64$) and emotional ($n = 35$) descriptions of presence were less frequent.

In the evaluation of the coded units within the individual texts of the sample, a clear dominance of bodily-centred definition approaches is noticeable. These represent a sum of ($n = 45$) codes, which makes it the most common type of definition approach. Also, interactivity ($n = 21$) and technology ($n = 28$) are strongly represented. Because there is no necessary numerical weighting between the different focus categories of definitory focal points, no quantitative prediction can be drawn from the results. However, this provides some pointers for further qualitative discussion and analysis of the existing approaches to defining presence.

In addition to the frequent occurrence of bodily, interactive and technically-centred approaches, we noticed that when looking at the different focal points, different aspects are often thought of in combination. For example, interactivity and technology are often combined with the concept of bodily centrality. Also, the psychological aspects of presence are often related to bodily, technical or interactive centrality as an additional dimension or as a sub-area. Here, the 'psychologically-centred' category gave $n = 18$ records in total. Emotion was only coded for $n = 10$ records. Emotion seems therefore to play a rather subordinate role within the analysed approaches. A total of $n = 13$ records either (a) did not introduce any definitional approaches to presence or (b) did not refer to already existing characterisations in the literature.

In summary, only a few clear and self-contained definitions of presence were apparent in our sample. The existing definitions mainly refer to the feeling of bodily and spatial transportation into a virtual space (Slater and Wilbur, 1997). Definitions of presence were also based on the interactive possibilities in the virtual environments, which placed the interaction of the users at the centre (Witmer and Singer, 1998). Most of the texts within our sample did not describe or made their own attempts to create a definition or to at least establish what presence was in the context of their own research. References were made to existing approaches or presence was described from different perspectives without conclusively bringing the various perspectives together.

After examining the various definitions, we find that it is rather difficult to describe the term presence based upon just one determining factor. Rather, a combination of different elements is what ultimately leads to the feeling of virtual presence. A few specific elements were identified during the qualitative content analysis. Amongst these are technical elements. As argued in some studies (Green et al., 2020), the technological possibilities of immersive media open entirely new perspectives for the audience and result in a deeper feeling of presence within the content (Ahn et al., 2016; Bailenson, 2018). The immersive technology represents a central prerequisite as a 'gateway', also influencing the possible 'detachment' from one's own reality over into a virtual space through the properties of the hardware and the representational capacity of the software. The feeling of one's own bodily presence, however, does not seem to be an obligatory derivation from the technical possibilities and does not seem to depend on the level of interactivity within the virtual environments either. Rather, the concept of presence can be divided into different levels that have a mutual influence on the feeling of presence and its intensity, but these elements are not necessarily mutually dependent (Slater and Wilbur, 1997; Witmer and Singer, 1998). We suggest calling this the *technical level* of presence. This level can be seen as an access level that enables the recipient to 'merely' consume immersive media content. Compared to other media formats, the technical possibilities of immersive media productions offer more and stronger sensory impressions, which also enables further immersion in the content (Bailenson, 2018). However, a feeling of presence does not automatically arise from the availability and use of technical devices and techniques alone. The technical aspect of immersive presence, therefore, is a kind of 'gateway' towards fully realising virtual presence. Within this context, the literature primarily speaks of bodily perception in an immersive context. This bodily self-perception in an artificial digital environment serves as a connecting point for many of the other aspects that can be found both in academic debates and in the study hereby presented. It is precisely this bodily centrality of the reception experience that can be seen here as a *sine qua non* condition for the feeling of presence.

In addition to the prerequisite of the experience of presence as something enabled by immersive technology and bodily self-perception, we identified other aspects that represented influencing factors, rather than core prerequisites. In the literature, these influencing factors favour and intensify presence by opening additional levels of impact and experience for the audience. Depending on their specification, different sub-areas of the user experience are addressed. Interactivity (the degree of involvement) increases and might generate deeper engagement, thus affecting and reinforcing the feeling of presence (Kishore et al., 2018). Psychological effects and dynamics are another key component (e.g. an unconscious physical protective reaction to simulated earthquakes or other feared event will influence presence in the simulation, see Bailenson, 2018). Psychological factors can also trigger deepening processes in the aftermath of the reception (Sundar, Kang and Oprean, 2017), such as creating emotional bonds between audiences and subjects (Domínguez, 2010). It is argued that greater involvement and the perceived 'closeness' to the event have the potential to trigger a more subjective interpretation of news stories and this can be facilitated by immersive journalism. The concept of empathy, described as putting oneself in another person's situation or environment, is a recurrent theme when studying presence pre-, during and post-experience.

Presence is a complex and multidimensional concept. From our data, we find it can be divided into three different levels of meaning. The *access or technological level* enables the sensation of presence in an immersive context. This is directly connected to a technical dimension. The *bodily self-perception level* is the condition that makes presence possible in virtual spaces, thus representing the central level of the concept of presence. Finally, the *extension or psychological level* includes the psychological, interactive and emotional dimensions, which intensify the experience of presence, albeit without being crucial to achieving the feeling of presence.

Conclusion

Immersion and presence are complex and far-reaching concepts in immersive media and journalism. Different approaches to defining these concepts span from technically-centred ones to emotion-centred descriptions. Definitions seem to focus on completely different aspects, sometimes even contradicting each other. The concepts of immersion and presence still require further examination and scientific discussion – consensus has not been reached. We do find some commonalities; for example, a common interest in understanding the role of technical and affective components. However, we find that the field needs to establish more standardised notions. As a contribution to this, we outline how an integrative approach to the terms of immersion and presence can be achieved, by seeking common categories in which to group elements of definitions. From our exercise, we find the following consensus:

- The feeling of immersion depends on specific technical conditions. Both the technical conditions and the degree of computerization and control of the virtual environment have an impact on the recipient's ability to immerse themselves in what is shown. This also determines the intensity of the perceived presence in immersive content since immersion has a direct effect on the *access level* of presence.
- Immersion is both a 'gateway' and the realization of a feeling. It is a gateway to virtual environments where news stories are depicted or recreated making use of immersive media production techniques (e.g. 360° video cameras or

- computer-generated imagery) and where effective entrance is enabled by immersive media technologies (e.g. a virtual reality head-mounted displays or haptic suits). It is a realization of a feeling to the extent of how inclusive, vivid and engaging the narrative is, i.e. becoming immersed requires the audience to establish an affective, emotional connection to the news story. The capacity of the system to allow users to 'leave' the physical world through technical devices to connect with the immersive news stories progressively and emotionally is what defines the system's ability to create full immersion.
- Presence is also a 'gateway' and the realization of a feeling. Like immersion, it is a gateway to virtual environments enabled by immersive media technologies. The difference here is that presence is an almost instantaneous/simultaneous feeling of both departure and arrival to a virtual world – 'I was here in the physical world, but now I'm in the virtual world'. Conversely with immersion, the feeling may be: 'I'm here in the physical world, but now I'm in the process of becoming immersed in the virtual world'.
- Presence is also the realisation of a feeling, the feeling of self-perception within the virtual environment, which in combination with given psychological, interactive and emotional nuances pave the way towards full presence.

Immersion and presence are closely connected and in some areas are even mutually dependent. As always, new conceptual paradigms at the crossroads of media and journalism production, technology development and emergent ecosystems such as artificial intelligence or the Web 3.0 will require a constant reconfiguration of both these and other concepts. With the emergence of the idea of the metaverse and the continuous advancements of immersive media technology, immersion and presence will require a more nuanced conceptual and practical approach. We hope to have contributed to this task.

Discussion questions

- What do you see as the main differences between immersion and presence?
- Do you agree/disagree with any of the definitions provided in the literature? With which and why? Discuss with your peers.
- Are there other concepts that you think are more important for the study of immersive journalism? List some of these concepts and discuss with your peers.

Note

1 These include today's *metaverse* and its apparent potential for generating titanic alike virtual realities parallel to our 'real reality'. The metaverse is fuelled by intricate social experiences enabled by refined immersive media technologies, thus allowing for evermore complex and organic-like forms of digital embodiment and human-computer interactions (Mystakidis, 2022).

References

Ahn, S., Bostick, J., Ogle, E., Nowak, K., McGillicuddy, K. and Bailenson, J. (2016). Experiencing Nature: Embodying Animals in Immersive Virtual Environments Increases Inclusion of Nature in Self and Involvement with Nature, *Journal of Computer-Mediated Communication,* 21(6), pp. 399–419. DOI:10.1111/jcc4.12173

Baía Reis, A. and Castro Coelho, A. (2018). Virtual Reality and Journalism. A gateway to conceptualizing immersive journalism, *Digital Journalism,* 6(8), pp. 1090–1100. DOI:10.1080/21670811.2018.1502046

Bailenson, J. (2018). *Experience on Demand.* New York: W.W. Norton.

Biocca, F. (1997). Cyborg's Dilemma: Progressive Embodiment in Virtual Environments. *Journal of Computer Mediated-Communication,* 3(2). DOI:10.1111/j.1083-6101.1997.tb00070.x

Bösch, M., Gensch, S., and Rath-Wiggins, L. (2018). Immersive Journalism: How Virtual Reality Impacts Investigative Storytelling. In: O. Hahn and F. Stalph (eds.), *Digital Investigative Journalism: Data, Visual Analytics and Innovative Methodologies in International Reporting,* pp. 103–111. Cham: Palgrave Macmillan.

Cummings, J. and Bailenson, J. (2016). How Immersive Is Enough? A Meta-Analysis of the Effect of Immersive Technology on User Presence, *Media Psychology,* 19(2), pp. 272–309. DOI:10.1080/15213269.2015.1015740

Cruz-Neira, C., Sandin, D. J., DeFanti, T. A., Kenyon, R. V., and Hart, J. C. (1992). The CAVE: Audio Visual Experience Automatic Virtual Environment. *Communications of the ACM,* 35(6), 64–73.

de Bruin, K., de Haan, Y., Kruikemeier, S., Lecheler, S., and Goutier, N. (2020). A first-person promise? A content-analysis of immersive journalistic productions, *Journalism,* 23(2), pp. 479–498. DOI:10.1177/1464884920922006

De la Peña, N. Weil, P., Llobera, J., Giannopoulos, E., Pomés Freixa, A., Spanlang, B., Friedman, D., Sánchez-Vives, M.V., and Slater, M. (2010). Immersive Journalism: Immersive Virtual Reality for the First-Person Experience of News, *Presence Teleoperators & Virtual Environments,* 19(4), pp. 291–301.

Domínguez, E. (2010). The new immersive formats and their application in journalism. In: II International Congress on Cyberjournalism and Web 2.0, 10–12 November, Bilbao.

Grau, O. (2003). *Virtual Art: From Illusion to Immersion.* Cambridge, MA: The MIT Press (Leonardo Books).

Green, D., Rose, M., Bevan, C., Farmer, H., Cater, K., and Fraser, D. (2020). 'You Wouldn't Get That from Watching TV!': Exploring Audience Responses to Virtual Reality Non-fiction in the Home, *Convergence,* 27(3), pp. 805–829. DOI:10.1177/1354856520979966

Heim, M. (1993). The Essence of VR. In: M. Heim (ed.), *The Metaphysics of Virtual Reality.* New York: Oxford University Press, pp. 109–128.

Kishore, S., Navarro, X., Dominguez, E., de la Peña, N. and Slater, M. (2018). Beaming into the News: A System for and Case Study of Tele-Immersive Journalism, *IEEE Computer Graphics and Applications,* 38(2), pp. 89–101. DOI:10.1109/MCG.2017.2801407

Kukkakorpi, M. and Pantti, M. (2021). A Sense of Place: VR Journalism and Emotional Engagement, *Journalism Practice,* 15(6), pp. 785–802. DOI:10.1080/17512786.2020.1799237

Longhi, R. (2017). Jornalismo experiencial, pesquisa aplicada e o desafio da investigação em Realidade Virtual no ciberjornalismo [Experiential journalism, applied research and the challenge of investigating Virtual Reality in cyberjournalism]. In: 15° Encontro da SBPJOR, São Paulo, 2017.

Ma, Z. (2019). Effects of immersive stories on prosocial attitudes and willingness to help: testing psychological mechanisms, *Media Psychology*, 23(6), pp. 865–890. DOI:10.1080/15213269.2019.1651655

Mayring, P. (2015). *Qualitative Inhaltsanalyse. Grundlagen und Techniken* [Qualitative Content Analysis. Foundations and Techniques] (12th ed.). Weinheim: Beltz. DOI:10.1007/978-3-531-18939-0_38

Mielniczuk, L., Nolibos Baccin, A., Sousa, M., and Leão, C. (2015) A reportagem hipermídia em revistas digitais móveis [Hypermedia reporting in mobile digital magazines]. In: J. Canalvilhas and I. Satuf (eds.), *Jornalismo para Dispositivos Móveis: Produção, Distribuição e Consumo* (1st ed.) [Journalism for Mobile Devices: Production, Distribution and Consumption]. Covilhã: Livros Labcom, pp. 127–152.

Murray, J. (1997). *Hamlet on the Holodeck: The Future of Narrative in Cyberspace*. New York: Simon & Schuster.

Mystakidis, S. (2022). Metaverse. *Encyclopedia 2022*, 2(1), pp. 486–497. DOI:10.3390/encyclopedia2010031

Owen, T., Pitt, F., Aronson-Rath, R., and Milward, J. (2015). *Virtual Reality Journalism*. Tow Report, Tow Center for Digital Journalism at Columbia's Graduate School of Journalism. New York: Columbia Journalism Review. www.cjr.org/tow_center_reports/virtual_reality_journalism.php

Pavlik, J. (2019). *Journalism in the Age of Virtual Reality: How Experiential Media Are Transforming News*. New York: Columbia University Press.

Slater, M. and Sanchez-Vives, M. (2016). Enhancing Our Lives with Immersive Virtual Reality, *Frontiers in Robotic and AI*, 3(74). DOI:10.3389/frobt.2016.00074

Slater, M. and Wilbur, S. (1997). A framework for immersive virtual environments (FIVE): Speculations on the role of presence in virtual environments, *Presence: Teleoperators and Virtual Environments*, 6(6), pp. 603–616.

Sundar, S., Kang, J., and Oprean, D. (2017). Being There in the Midst of the Story: How Immersive Journalism Affects Our Perceptions and Cognitions, *Cyberpsychology, Behavior, and Social Networking*, 20(11), pp. 672–682. DOI:10.1089/cyber.2017.0271

Witmer, B. and Singer, M. (1998). Measuring Presence in Virtual Environments: A Presence Questionnaire. *Presence: Teleoperators and Virtual Environments*, 7(3), pp. 225–240.

Yee, N. and Bailenson, J. (2007). The Proteus Effect: The Effect of Transformed Self-Representation on Behavior, *Human Communication Research*, 33(3), pp. 271–290. DOI:10.1111/j.1468-2958.2007.00299.x

PART III
Critical views on immersive journalism

6
NORMATIVE QUESTIONS IN IMMERSIVE JOURNALISM

Tanja Aitamurto

Introduction

Immersive technologies have become more common platforms in journalistic storytelling in recent years. Newspapers publish reportages as virtual reality (VR) stories, whether as photorealistic 360° videos or as computer-generated imagery (CGI) simulations. Publications also visualize aspects of their articles with augmented reality (AR) visualizations, which can be shown in their own applications or as AR filters on other platforms, such as Instagram or Snapchat. Newspapers have also experimented with mixed reality (MR) productions, in which the boundary of AR and VR becomes more blurred. In mixed reality, features from both technologies are merged in journalistic storytelling (Speicher et al., 2019).

Immersive technologies were welcomed to journalism with a fair amount of optimism. Immersive journalism has been hoped to provide much needed enhanced audience engagement and thus increased revenue streams to newspapers that are struggling with shrinking resources. Both the informational and the engagement aspects are appealing to journalistic storytelling: Immersive technologies can provide more information with a more emotionally engaging manner to the viewer, compared to more traditional storytelling media.

As immersive technologies are permeating journalistic storytelling, it is increasingly important to understand how these technologies affect the normative boundaries in journalism. Journalistic norms include accuracy, objectivity/impartiality, transparency and autonomy, which create a framework for journalism practice. These norms define what is 'proper' professional journalism in the current time and they guide professional journalists' daily work in newsrooms and on the ground. Furthermore, journalistic norms are foundational building blocks for the credibility of journalism – the claim that journalism depicts the world accurately, autonomously and impartially; essentially, the claim that journalism tells the truth.

Paradoxically though, these norms are only aspirational ideals, which are rarely, if ever, fully reached in practice. For instance, reaching a fully neutral or objective reporting is practically impossible for any journalist – newspaper agendas, societal ideologies and practical decisions mould all journalistic output, even in the most independent and influence-free newspapers. However, despite their aspirational nature, journalistic norms set the ethical standards in professional journalism and differentiate journalism from other professional communication practices such as PR, advertising and propaganda. While these norms are particularly prevalent in the Anglo-Saxon normative framework, journalists pursue accurate, objective, autonomous and transparent reporting also in other parts of the world with mutual professional journalistic goals. Journalistic norms are the foundation for ethical codebooks published by associations for professional journalists, such as the Society of Professional Journalists (SPJ), in the United States. In addition, larger newsrooms and publications have their own, more detailed ethical code books, which are used as guidelines in the news operations.

In this book chapter, I discuss normative quandaries in immersive journalism. The questions that I address are the following: How do immersive technologies, when deployed in journalism, affect normative boundaries in journalism? What challenges and concerns do immersive technologies pose to journalistic norms? By undertaking these questions, I discuss how immersive technologies create pressure on journalistic norms and make journalism renegotiate its boundaries, pushing them and perhaps making new norms to emerge. New practices are forming in journalism always in parallel with the introduction and deployment of new technologies in journalism, including immersive media.

This chapter is structured into five parts, each of which discuss timely and foundational questions about normative boundaries in immersive journalism. In the first part I discuss the questions related to the journalistic norms of accuracy, objectivity and transparency in immersive journalism. To understand the current normative challenges in immersive journalism better, in the second part of this chapter, I review important historical developments in visual journalism and journalistic norms. That enables us to situate today's challenges on a continuum of questions about authenticity, accuracy and objectivity in visual journalism. In the third part, I visit questions about the affective dimensions in immersive journalism and journalists' responsibility to protect the viewers from harm. Then, in the fourth part, I discuss questions of journalistic autonomy and user privacy. Finally, in the fifth part, I close with a brief discussion about the future of normative questions in immersive journalism, including the implications of rising virtual environments such as the Metaverse.

Throughout this chapter, I use the SPJ ethical code as an example of the journalists' ethical code. SPJ is a national organization representing professional journalists in the United States. All Western countries have similar organizations with ethical code for journalists.

Questions of accuracy, objectivity and transparency in immersive journalism

Accuracy is a key norm guiding professional journalism practice. The norm of accuracy is supposed to ensure that journalism portrays the world as truthfully as possible (Kovach and Rosenstiel, 2007, Shapiro et al., 2013). Accuracy in journalism practice means that the journalist, ideally, always reports the events as accurately as possible. Journalists strive for maximizing accuracy by rigorous factchecking, using multiple information sources and triangulating sources. The goal is to gather, verify and report the relevant facts accurately. According to this norm, journalism should show the world as is and depict the world's events as they unfolded without journalists staging, altering, intervening or influencing the scene. Accuracy is also an important building block in journalists' self-identification and professional self-image (Bogart, 2004; Gladney, Shapiro and Castaldo, 2007). The drive for accuracy differentiates journalism from several other communication practices such as PR and advertising.

The importance of accuracy as the building block in professional journalism is also reflected in journalists' ethical codes. The first principle in SPJ ethical code states that 'The journalists' job is to 'seek truth and report it' (Society of Professional Journalists, 2014). More specifically, the SPJ code reminds journalists that 'Ethical journalism should be accurate and fair. Journalists should be honest and courageous in gathering, reporting and interpreting information' and that 'Remember that neither speed nor format excuses inaccuracy'. In journalism practice, accuracy is sought for in rigorous verification practices such as fact checking. Accuracy is such a fundamental norm in journalism, that journalism has been called as 'discipline of verification' to separate it from 'entertainment, propaganda, fiction, or art' (Kovach and Rosenstiel, 2007).

Alongside accuracy, objectivity, which is also commonly called as neutrality or impartiality, is another fundamental yet very conflicted norm in journalism. This norm guides journalism to maintain a neutral stance and avoid bias in reporting. The SPJ Code of Ethics emphasizes the importance of clear difference between advocacy, commentary and factual reporting by labelling the content accordingly in journalism. However, facts in journalism are socially constructed artefacts, cultural contracts about what is considered as a true, factual statement. Therefore, facts never portray reality completely accurately. As Michael Schudson (1978, 2001) posits, facts in journalism are consensually validated statements about the world rather than aspects of it.

Visual journalism serves in an important role in constructing the notion of truth in journalism and thus contributing to the claims of accuracy and objectivity in journalism. Photorealism in journalistic imagery is viewed as evidence of authenticity: A photograph of a news event in a newspaper is a claim, which states the details of the event. Visual journalism thus uses the verisimilitude of photographs as evidence of authentic and accurate storytelling. Consequently, documentary photography is an important part of 'the strategic ritual of objectivity' (Tuchman, 1972), which assists in the construction of objectivity and accuracy in visual journalism. The strategic rituals of objectivity mean the practices that journalists use to establish facts in their articles. An example of these practices is journalists using several sources for verifying the accuracy claims in their articles. Journalistic imagery is powerful in shaping the ideological interpretations of the events it captures because it claims to present visual evidence of the 'real world'.

A useful approach to understand the power of visual journalism is to view each visual having both denotative and connotative aspects. 'Denotative' refers to the factual elements and 'connotative' to the symbolic elements of the journalistic imagery. The claim that visual journalism shows the world 'as is' reflects the denotative aspect of the imagery, whereas its ability to depict the 'as if' represents the connotative and symbolic aspect of the imagery, as Barbie Zelizer (2010) has aptly stated. The denotative in the imagery thus represents the accuracy and objectivity claims of visual journalism, whereas the connotative, the 'as if' reflects the imaginary, illusionary possibilities of what could have happened, should have happened or might have happened. The 'as if' provides a connotative interpretation of reality, whereas the 'as is' is about portraying the world in a truthful, factual and accurate manner. Immersive technologies afford constructing new layers for representing the denotative and connotative in visual journalism. In these layers, immersive journalism blends the authentic with the unauthentic, the real with the unreal. That is, the connotative – the as if – what could be, what should be, what might be, becomes the stronger side of the imagery. The element of 'as is', which represents accuracy and objectivity in visual journalism, is overshadowed and overrun by the connotative, the symbolic, the imaginary aspects.

Let us look closer into what the blending of 'the real' and 'the unreal' and the authentic with unauthentic means in practice in immersive journalism. One type of VR journalism is based on computer-generated imagery (CGI). In CGI-based VR the visuals are computer-generated simulations developed on game-engines. Think about CGI imagery as a very advanced drawing, which is created with computers – a drawing, which can look so photorealistic that the viewer cannot decipher the difference between a realistic, authentic, photorealistic imagery and a drawing. Journalists tell stories and reconstruct events with CGI imagery similarly as they do with other types of video imagery. In CGI-based journalism, however, the imagery is constructed by humans, based on their ideas about how the visuals should look like. In contrast, another type of VR journalism, also called as 360° journalism, uses photorealistic, authentically captured imagery, which presents the same level of realism as traditional, flat video.

An example of a CGI-based journalistic storytelling is a CGI-based VR production about solitary confinement called *6x9*, which was published by the British newspaper the *Guardian*. The video provides a virtual experiment, in which the user can explore the experience of being in a solitary confinement cell in a prison. The imagery in the video looks very photorealistic and authentic, but the visuals are based on CGI. While the experience of watching the video about solitary confinement can provide a very realistic experience to the users, it also blurs the boundary between the authentic and unauthentic in journalistic storytelling. The viewer may not be able to differentiate the realistic, yet unauthentic imagery from photorealistic, authentic one. The video does not communicate to the user that the visuals are not photorealistic, but CGI. Thus, these visuals are provided to the user as authentic, photorealistic imagery. The viewer can hence easily assume that the visuals are authentic capture, based on the expectation created by the context of this video: It is published by a very credible journalistic publication (the *Guardian*) and the user is used to expect seeing photorealistic visuals in that context. Consequently, the users have indeed assumed that the *6x9* video represents photorealistic imagery (Aitamurto, 2019). However, even though the imagery is constructed using journalistic research into the topic, it is not photorealistic imagery. It is the journalist's creation of a cell about how the cell could look like, or should look like, rather than an authentic capture of a cell. The visuals are an imaginary representation developed on journalists' subjective interpretation about the object of visualization, thus amplifying the imaginary, connotative, the 'as if' in visual journalism and overshadowing the factual, the 'as is'.

The issue described above is about *journalists creating their version of a reality* with CGI visuals, a version of reality, which fits with the narrative they want to tell rather than the actual, authentic visual narrative. Another concern about the normative boundaries emerges when the journalists set to *alter or edit* photorealistic imagery. This is reflected in certain practices deployed in 360° video journalism. It is not uncommon to see journalistic 360° videos, in which items such as tripods or other distracting objects have been edited out from the videos in post-processing. In some cases, even people, such as the journalists conducting the interviews, have been removed from the scene in the post-processing of the video imagery (Aitamurto, 2019). Journalists have justified the manipulation with aesthetic and engagement reasons: Certain objects, in their reasoning, could distract the viewer and thus potentially compromise the viewing experience and, consequently, reduce the viewer's engagement with the visual content.

By altering the reality or by providing an unauthentic reality to the viewers and justifying it with better plausibility and engagement value, journalists compromise journalistic norms for plausibility and engagement, key goals of immersive technologies. The goal of immersive technologies is to create a high degree of plausibility in the immersive experience (Slater, 2009). VR journalism, for example, attempts to provide the user with experiences in which the user is transported into virtual spaces in such a plausible manner, that the user feels that they are experiencing the virtual environment as the real one. The feeling of being immersed in the virtual world is called sense of presence (Slater and Wilbur, 1997). The virtual environment and its events can thus represent a high degree of plausibility and realism to the user. These, in turn, can translate into deep audience engagement, a desirable result in journalism at the times where traditional business models are failing and newspapers have shrinking resources.

However, on its quest for maximising plausibility and engagement, journalists obscure the difference between the authentic and unauthentic imagery, the real and the unreal. By doing so, journalists abdicate the norm of accuracy, which instructs journalists to portray the world authentically, truthfully, as it is, rather than as it could be or should be. The manipulation of the imagery also risks compromising the norm of objectivity, which guides journalism not to take stances and remain as objective observers of events as possible. Furthermore, creating CGI experiences that the user cannot decipher from unauthentic imagery creates more space for subjectivity in journalism; subjective interpretation of the events, the situation and the space, instead of objective or neutral stance that authentic imagery could portray more strongly.

When using CGI imagery in journalism, it would be vitally important to label it clearly as such so that the viewer would not assume it is a photorealistic capture. Particularly important that would be when the degree of realism in the CGI visuals is very close to photorealistic. Consequently, it is hard for the user to decipher the difference. However, even though the difference between authentic, photorealistic imagery and the unauthentic one would not be great, to follow journalistic norms, unauthentic imagery should be clearly communicated to the user. Similarly, any photorealistic, 360° video content, which has been manipulated, for instance, by removing objects, should be labelled as such. This guideline is also clearly stated in journalists' ethical code. The American SPJ ethical code, for instance, outlines that 'Never deliberately distort facts or context, including visual information. Clearly label illustrations and re-enactments'.[1] When applied in practice, this ethical code means that any CGI-based visual imagery needs to be labelled so that the user understands that they are watching a non-photorealistic footage. Clear communication about the degree of authenticity would be important considering the journalistic norm of transparency, which guides journalists to communicate about their choices to the public as transparently as possible. As the SPJ Code of Ethics states: 'Ethical journalism means taking responsibility for one's work and explaining one's decisions to the public.'

Continuum of questions about authenticity in visual journalism

The difficulty of drawing the boundary between 'the real' and 'the unreal', however, is not a novel concern in journalism. Providing altered reality as a depiction of 'the real, authentic reality' is a familiar issue in the history of professional journalism. Looking at important developments relevant to photorealism and authenticity in the history of visual journalism will help us understand how. The first important thing to note is that the journalistic norms of accuracy and objectivity were not always the cornerstones of journalism. In the 1920s, for instance, newspapers commonly used a type of a visual called composograph to illustrate news events. Composographs were compiled of a mix of visualizations such as illustrations and photographs. These collages were the forerunner of modern photo manipulation; think about composographs as heavily photoshopped compilations of various types of visuals. The viewers could not decipher the original, authentic imagery from the manipulated one. This is a parallel situation to the visual manipulation practices we are witnessing in the current, digitized era in immersive journalism: Advanced computational image processing technologies can create such sophisticated visual manipulations that it is impossible to differentiate them from authentic imagery.

In the era of composographs, professional journalism had not established its normative boundaries the way they exist today. In the 1920s, the journalistic norms of objectivity, accuracy and transparency were not yet the prominent guidelines of journalism. That is why newspapers were able to use composographs in place of authentic photojournalism. Journalism was about gossip, scandals, as it was also about news and facts. Before the 1930s, journalists commonly and openly retouched, embellished and manipulated photographs (Barnhurst, 1991; Schwartz, 1992, 1999). It was only around World War II when the current day norms such as accuracy and objectivity became the guiding principles in certain journalistic publications and in professional journalistic practices (Barnhurst, 1991, Barnhurst and Nerone 1999).

Objectivity and accuracy became fundamental norms in professional journalism primarily because of two parallel developments. The first development was the rise of the importance of science and naturalism in society, which photography supported with its inherent verisimilitude. The second one was the development of journalism as an industry. Certain newspapers started to advertise themselves as 'truthtellers' – as unbiased and trustworthy sources of information. This was to distinguish their news product from other publications, which could not bolster about their credibility. Eventually, the goal was to sell the paper better and consequently to make more money. Truth was discovered as a money-making machine in journalism. The role of photography was notable in establishing journalism's role as truthteller in society and constructing journalistic authority. Documentary photography became an important part of constructing the objectivity and accuracy claims in visual journalism. Photojournalism was framed as a truthful depiction of the world; it was offered to the readers as evidence of the truthful reporting. Photography served as evidence to the readers, for instance, from the frontline in World War II. In a similar vein, when I am writing this chapter in the Spring of 2022, when Russia attacked Ukraine, news photography played an important role telling the horrific stories about civilian casualties and mass graves in the battlegrounds in Ukraine.

These developments illustrate how news photography began to play a vital role in constructing the illusions of accuracy and objectivity in professional journalism. News photography became a confirmation, a kind of a guarantee, that the newspaper was reporting the truth accurately and objectively, because it could show in images to verify its news. Gradually, the journalistic norms that we know today as a foundation for any credible professional journalism were then established in and scribed down in various ethical codebooks by professional journalist and editor associations and news outlets. These norms contributed to the legitimisation of journalists as truthtellers in society and built the foundation for journalism as a powerful authority that we know in the modern-day society.

Despite the importance of accuracy and objectivity as journalistic norms, they have also been and remain also today only constructed illusions in professional journalism. These norms are aspirational goals, which can never be fully accomplished or reached. To understand the illusionary nature of these norms, let us look at the norm of accuracy as an example. In visual journalism, the goal for journalists is to portray the world's events as accurately as possible. In that quest, journalistic photography serves as an eyewitness of the world. Photographs serve as evidence of the accuracy of the reporting. The accuracy of the imagery, however, is constrained by several factors. One key factor is journalistic practices: The routines and processes in which professional journalism is produced. Journalistic practices, often framed by the interpretation of news values, strongly influence the creation of visual journalism.

News values are one main factor determining the topics that are covered and the pictures that are taken and published. News values, also called as news criteria, determine the daily news agenda. News values include criteria such as relevance, significance and proximity (Galtung and Ruge, 1965) and they are deployed in everyday practices in newsrooms. News values determine what topics are covered and for which articles pictures are taken and published. News values are fundamentally important factors, which differentiate journalism from other informational and communication services, such as PR and advertising, that do not operate based on news values. The continuous selection and curation of topics creates the journalistic agenda and outlines the role of journalism as an agenda setter in society. Journalism, through mass media, affects greatly the topics people talk about and pay attention to. Visual journalism is a part of this agenda setting and carries a role of as an agenda-setter. With the claims of accuracy and objectivity, visual journalism contributes to constructing journalistic authority (Carlson, 2009, 2017).

The news values, however, are not objective criteria but they are rather subjectively constructed perceptions about the importance and priority of the almost endless amount of news topics. Various ideological, cultural and financial factors shape news values in every society and every publication. Visual journalism is never a fully unbiased, objective representation either.

Photographs, even if accurate in the details they portray, are only one selected picture or view of the event. That picture is one perspective of the event, leaving out everything else around it, everything else that does not fit into that specific, chosen frame. Furthermore, when the images are processed in the editing process, the photos are often cropped and framed to emphasize the main message and for aesthetic pleasure. As a result, even though the details in the imagery would be accurate, i.e., shown as is, it is never a full, comprehensive representation of the world.

Furthermore, when considering the normative quandaries in immersive journalism, it is important to recall that the history of visual journalism has always witnessed manipulations, staging and lack of transparency. Many of the iconic photographs witnessing the pivotal moments in world history have later been questioned, or have revealed to be manipulated, altered or staged. For example, Robert Capa, one of the most celebrated war photographers of all times, portrayed a man seemingly dying of a bullet in the Spanish Civil War in 1936 in his famous picture 'The Falling Soldier'.[2] The veracity of this photograph has since been questioned. It has been claimed that the picture was not taken where it was said to have been taken, raising questions about staging. Another well-known example is the iconic picture of American soldiers raising an American flag in Iwo Jima, Japan, at the end of World War II. The iconic picture was taken by a photographer and distributed in 1945 across the world and published in numerous news outlets. However, it has been later claimed that the photograph was staged.[3]

And there are numerous other instances too. These cases show that the concerns about manipulation and providing unauthentic imagery as authentic one in immersive journalism are not unprecedented in the history of visual journalism. The concerns have existed throughout the history of professional journalism and taken different forms in different times. Thus, the normative questions in immersive journalism fall on a long continuum of manipulation. In addition, there are continuous challenges with journalistic norms in daily journalism practices in newsrooms and beyond. With digital photo editing, there are more opportunities to alter the imagery in postprocessing. For instance, by altering lightning, brightness, contrast, editing out distracting objects and so on. Apart from the associations for professional journalists' guidelines for acceptable photo editing, news outlets have specific guidelines for acceptable practices, yet these guidelines are also violated (Maenpaa and Seppanen, 2010).

The challenges of normative boundaries in immersive journalism are similar as they have been throughout the history of visual journalism. When a journalist removes a tripod in post-processing in a 360° video to create a more aesthetically pleasing and engaging experience to the user, the process is the same as it has been in the history of visual journalism and particularly photojournalism: The journalist is compromising the journalistic norm of accuracy by altering the original imagery and providing a manipulated depiction of the world as an authentic one to the user, without communicating the difference to the audience.

In a similar vein, when CGI-based imagery is shown to the user, without communicating that it is CGI, not photorealistic, authentic capture, a similar violation of journalistic norms occurs. The viewer watches the visuals and is not able to necessarily to distinguish what is authentic capture versus what is illusionary imagery. With advanced postprocessing technologies, it is increasingly easy to blend authentic with a non-authentic imagery, making the boundary between real and unreal even more blurry.

This same dynamic applies to journalistic AR experiences. When viewing AR visualisations, the augmentations blend in with the 'real reality' and afford a sense of presence and transportation to the user (Aitamurto et al., 2020). When the user interacts with the AR content, more information in written text can appear, as the user walks around or taps the visuals. Users' interactions with the visualisations thus determine what the user sees in the AR visuals and thus composes their own understanding, their own storyline of the visualisations. However, by doing so, the user may miss some important elements in the AR content and thus receive a partial or even an inaccurate understanding of the news subject.

Despite the history of concerns about authenticity, objectivity and accuracy in visual journalism, one could argue that the challenges with normative boundaries are even greater now with certain types of immersive journalism than they were in the past. This is because the omnidirectional view in immersive journalism poses a promise of a more comprehensive and holistic picture of the world. In theory, in 360° video journalism, nothing is left out of the picture, because the camera captures everything around it. The unlimited field of view could be seen as a more accurate, objective and transparent depiction of the events. This promise, however, is just an illusion. It is an illusion, because what is captured and published, what is shown to the user versus what is cut off from the narrative, is still a result of editorial decision-making, based on news values and journalistic agenda-setting process.

This is called the paradox of accuracy. On one hand, the spherical view can create a more accurate picture of the covered topic compared to a video with a traditional, narrower field of view. On the other hand, however, journalism loses control over the viewer's gaze in the spherical view. The viewer can choose the field of view and they can thus compose their own storyline of the elements they happen to see. The viewers may miss important elements in the storyline, without being aware of it. Thus, they might get a distorted or biased understanding of the issue about the topic.

By offering altered imagery to the viewers as the real one, journalism betrays its audience: Journalism is not showing the world as it is, as it happened, with all the detail, the miniscule, trivial seeming detail such as tripod, but creating an alternative depiction of the world, an illusionary one, that could have happened, it could have looked like that, but it did not. This raises a justified question about the role of journalism. Is the role to create alternative realities, show how things could have been, or could be, or should be? Or is the role of journalism to show the world as is, to document, to evidence, to serve as an eyewitness to the public, to the audience?

To adhere to the journalistic norms of accuracy and transparency, professional journalism should bear its responsibility and clearly label altered, manipulated or CGI-based imagery. Otherwise, visual journalism will return to the age of composographs, to the 1920s, when portraying truth was not the foundational goal of journalism but providing entertainment and eye candy as a part of it, blending truth, real, with the illusionary, was more important than the factual basis of reporting as it is nowadays. This blurs the boundary between journalism and other forms of visual communication such as art, PR and advocacy.

Questions about the affective dimensions in immersive journalism

The affective dimension of immersive content poses more normative questions to immersive journalism. Decades of studies have shown that CGI-based VR can create a stronger emotional effect on people than more traditional forms of media (cf. Bailey et al., 2016). Similar effects were hypothesized when photorealistic 360° video was introduced in journalism. Empirical evidence shows a mixed bag: Some studies have found 360° video contributing to users' emotional effects, others have not found similar results. Consequently, VR is not considered anymore solely as an empathy machine (Barreda-Ángeles et al., 2020; Bollmer, 2017; Nakamura, 2020). Empirical studies have, however, consistently found that journalistic 360° video can make the users experience sense of presence, i.e., transporting them to the virtual environment. Sense of presence may lead to emotional engagement, empathy and attitude change when the viewers can embed themselves in the virtual experiences and others' perspectives.

Considering the potentially strong affective impact of immersive journalism, journalists should pay very close attention to the normative boundaries, which are aimed to protect the viewers from harm, including emotional distress. The second code in the SPJ code states that journalists should 'Balance the public's need for information against potential harm or discomfort.' This guideline states that every individual apart of the journalistic process should be treated with respect. It also calls for the protection of everyone involved, including the readers/viewers.

The affective dimensions of immersive journalism create new challenges for avoiding causing harm. Immersive journalism has the power to create emotionally effective and impactful experiences. The immersive elements, including sense of presence and body transfer – the user being able to embody the actors in immersive content – can intensify the emotional experience.

For instance, when a viewer watches a journalistic piece about solitary confinement and the experience situates the viewer in the authentic-looking cell in a prison, the viewer may feel that they really are sitting in the cell. This experience can cause emotional distress. Similarly, if the immersive journalism narrative places the viewer in an airplane doing air strikes over Berlin in World War II, the viewer may feel that they are sitting in the airplane. These experiences can create negative emotions and potentially even cause emotional flashbacks to negative situations in the viewers' lives. Adding to the need to protect the viewer, the impact of immersive journalism on the users can be hard to predict. VR users experience the videos based on their own preferences and needs (Shin and Biocca, 2018).

The immersive elements and the affective implications of immersive journalism create more responsibility to journalists in terms of choosing the story topics. Journalists need to decide, case by case, how ethical and responsible it is to transport the user to a potentially emotionally disturbing situation, like on the frontlines of war, or to the scene of an accident. These considerations, of course, have been present and dealt with in journalism even prior to immersive technologies. For instance, when television news channels are presenting disturbing content, they display a warning to the user. However, the novel dimension of immersive journalism is the intensified emotional aspects, presented in visuals with a high degree of realism and the feeling of presence, which can lead to greater plausibility than with traditional visuals. As a result, the viewer might be experiencing the narrative as a real-world experience.

Particularly careful journalists ought to be with superrealistic immersive content. Superrealistic means virtual imagery that has greater realness than what we have previously seen, for instance, with avatars that are virtual copies of real people (Slater et al., 2020). The fidelity of immersive content is improving and it is becoming more indistinguishable from the physical world. The emotional impact and, consequently, the harmful effects of negative immersive experiences can be exacerbated by the improvement in realness. One environment where superrealism will be prevalent is the metaverse, a network of immersive worlds. The metaverse will embed advanced forms of immersive technologies with a representation of superrealistic content, which can be emotionally very affective. Journalism will have an important role in the metaverse in creating journalistic content, distributing and experiencing it in immersive environments.

Questions of journalistic autonomy and user privacy

The journalistic norm of autonomy sets the foundation for independent, unbiased professional journalism. This norm guides journalism to serve the public as its highest and primary obligation. Professional journalism should be independent from external pressures and factors, which could compromise journalistic autonomy and lead to biased reporting, thus harming journalistic integrity. Compromising journalistic autonomy would thus lead to eroding of journalistic credibility and consequently to the legitimation of journalism as the truthteller in society. These factors, that could cause a conflict of interest, include influences of political, ideological and financial powers, among others. Autonomous professional journalism should be able to report about issues without letting these external factors bias the reporting or compromise the accuracy of the coverage in any way. Accordingly, the SPJ' ethical code instructs journalists to 'Avoid conflicts of interest, real or perceived. Disclose unavoidable conflicts.'[4] In addition, the ethical code guides journalists to resist internal and external pressure to influence coverage and gifts that may compromise integrity or impartiality, or damage credibility.

The execution of immersive journalistic projects, however, has raised questions about journalistic autonomy. Immersive journalism is a technology-heavy practice, but with the shrinking resources in newsrooms, news outlets have challenges producing immersive journalism without contributions from technology companies, such as Google and Samsung. These companies have supported immersive journalism production in newspapers such as *The New York Times*. For instance, *The New York Times* 'Daily 360°' was a series of 360° videos from all over the world. The videos were published daily on *The New York Times* and were produced in collaboration with Samsung. In a similar vein, the technology giant Google has allocated funding as grants for news organisations to experiment with immersive journalism technologies.

The support from technology companies is labelled as collaboration. The collaboration can, of course, be conducted in a manner, which allows the news outlet to maintain its journalistic integrity, while benefiting from the resources and knowledge derived from technology companies. However, these increasingly complex webs of collaborations, funding streams and other 'synergies' between journalistic actors and technology companies raise justified questions about journalistic norms and the control over journalistic autonomy and integrity. These questions include the following: How much do the technology actors get to influence the coverage? For instance, would a news outlet publish a VR video about questionable conduct in a Samsung VR gear factory, if the coverage was produced in collaboration with Samsung? And how much does the technology itself affect the coverage – i.e., the topics that are covered, the angles, the source selection and so on?

Another fundamental normative question related to autonomy in immersive journalism is about protecting the users' privacy. When the viewers view immersive journalism, they leave a trace of various types of data. Watching a journalistic VR video in a headset can capture rotational data, which can potentially be connected to individual users (Miller et al., 2020). In addition, biometric data such as iris or retina scans and voiceprints can be gathered through interactive experiences. Most immersive journalism is viewed and used on external, third-party platforms such as SnapChat and Instagram (Meta). The immersive journalistic content is produced by a journalistic publication but is delivered and consumed on these third-party applications. This raises questions about data ownership: Who owns the data in these cases? Who has access to the data? How much autonomy and independence does the journalistic actor have in deciding about the destiny of the data? How can the journalistic content producer protect the user data so that using the immersive application does not cause harm to the user, or compromise the user's privacy?

The location-based dimension in AR introduces another dimension to privacy issues in immersive journalism. AR is a location-based medium, and to activate the AR content, the user often scans the area around the user before projecting the AR visualisations onto the space. AR applications often request extensive access to the users' mobile phone, including camera, storage, GPS and Bluetooth. In addition, people use AR in private spaces such as their homes. While using AR, the users may be submitting a large amount of content to web servers, including pictures from inside of their house and other private areas. The use of user data gathered through AR applications can thus violate the user's physical privacy. Physical privacy is the use of geolocation technology and can be used to pinpoint someone's location (Christopoulos et al., 2021). Furthermore, new types of personal information can be collected through AR devices; such personal information includes biometric data such as facial features, reflexes, eyes and motor movement (kinetic fingerprint). Moreover, the developers of AR applications have a strong interest in gathering user data to learn about user behaviour with the technology. Developers may track users' behaviour and pass around that information, with a goal to develop new features and improve existing ones.

While user data can help customize the user experience and provide more personalized, interesting, engaging and relevant content to the user, the dissemination of this information can also compromise users' privacy. Particularly disconcerting the collection of user data in immersive journalism experiences is when considering the parallel advances in artificial intelligence (AI), which enable personal identification of anonymized, motion tracking recorded data with machine learning (ML) (Miller et al., 2020).

The concerns of data privacy are closely connected to the collaboration between journalism outlets with technology companies. Who owns that data and who has access to it? The immersive content is produced by the newspaper, yet it is published on a technology company's such as Meta-owned (former Facebook) Instagram. The same questions apply to privacy. How is the users' privacy protected when viewing journalistic content on those platforms, that are external to the newsroom, that are owned by technology giants, who are not adhering to journalistic norms? How do the news outlets navigate this maze and make decisions that enable maintaining journalistic integrity? And finally, how are those decisions communicated to the public, to the audience, whose interest – their right to know – journalism ought to serve?

These questions of privacy and data protection are germane not only to journalism, but also to all realms in which immersive technologies are used. For instance, the immensely popular AR game Pokémon Go requests extensive access to the users' mobile phone, including camera, storage, GPS, Bluetooth, contacts, among other information. However, in journalism, the questions connect back to journalistic norms. These norms make the essence of journalism function as its cornerstone and develop its credibility, its authority, which is based on users' trust. If the news outlets betray that trust, it will erode journalistic credibility and authority.

The future of normative questions in immersive journalism

In this chapter, I discussed several normative challenges in immersive journalism. These challenges include concerns about accuracy, objectivity and transparency. Immersive journalism has raised familiar questions about the role of authenticity in visual journalism, namely, about the role of accuracy and impartiality. This highlights the everlasting question of the normative boundaries in journalism: Where do the boundaries for accurate, impartial, transparent and ethical journalism lie? Furthermore, immersive journalism raises familiar questions in visual journalism about image manipulation: Can manipulated imagery be offered to the viewers in the name of accurate, truthful professional journalism? If not, how can we allow photographers and other visual journalists continuously stage and edit regular photographs and videos and publish them in the name of professional journalism? If yes, where is the boundary then – if CGI visuals can be shown to the viewer as accurate depictions of the world, why would visual journalists need to make extensive efforts to capture authentic imagery in the first place?

The importance of asking these questions will only intensify in the future as computational image processing advances. It is increasingly easy to produce more sophisticated CGI content and image manipulations. Consequently, it becomes more appealing for journalistic actors to use such technologies in the name of journalism. Moreover, it is easy for also other than journalistic actors to produce authentic looking, engaging immersive content under the label of journalism.

Another parallel development is the quick rise of immersive technologies in everyday communication. Several AR applications, such as various filters, have quickly become widely used, mainstream means of communication and media also for journalism. Metaverse, a network of immersive worlds, is gaining ground in the trading of digital assets and in avatar communication. Journalistic content will be part of the metaverse in multiple ways: Journalism will be produced, delivered and consumed in the metaverse.

These developments make it ever more important to discuss normative aspects in journalism, because these boundaries define the practice of professional journalism. What will the future generations perceive as acceptable, 'proper' journalism, that meets standards developed by the communities? Also, it raises questions about the essence of journalism: What is more important in journalism – to inform, or to engage people? Does one goal need to be compromised to reach another in immersive journalism? Could immersive journalism be as accurate, impartial and authentic as possible, yet at the same time, be engaging? Do engagement and informative goals need to be mutually exclusive?

Discussion questions

- What is the journalists' responsibility to communicate about publishing unauthentic material as journalism?
- Can storytelling based on CGI be called as journalism? Justify why, why not?
- How does the professional journalists' ethical code in your country guide journalism practice?

Notes

1 www.spj.org/ethicscode.asp
2 Larry Rohter, 2009: New Doubts Raised Over Famous War Photo. Published at *The New York Times*, August 17, 2009. Accessible at: www.nytimes.com/2009/08/18/arts/design/18capa.html; Richard Whelan, 2002: Proving that Robert Capa's Falling Soldier Is Genuine: A Detective Story. Published at PBS, May 26, 2006. Accessible at www.pbs.org/wnet/americanmasters/robert-capa-in-love-and-war/47/; Amanda Vaill, 2014: Did Robert Capa Fake "Falling Soldier"? Published at the Foreign Policy. Accessible at https://foreignpolicy.com/2014/04/22/did-robert-capa-fake-falling-soldier/
3 Bill Newcott, 2020. Was this iconic World War II photo staged? Here's the heroic true story. Published at National Geographic, February 21, 2020. Accessible at www.nationalgeographic.com/history/article/iconic-world-war-ii-photo-staged-heroic-true-story

Matthew Pressman and James Kimble, 2020. The Famous Iwo Jima Flag-Raising Photo Captured an Authentic Moment—But Gave Many Americans a False Impression. Published in *Time* magazine, February 21, 2020. Accessible at https://time.com/5788381/iwo-jima-photo/

Thom Patterson, 2013. The inside story of the famous Iwo Jima photo. Published at CNN, February 23, 2016. Accessible at www.cnn.com/2015/02/22/world/cnnphotos-iwo-jima/index.html
4 https://blogs.spjnetwork.org/ethicscode/?p=175

References

Aitamurto, T. (2019). Normative paradoxes in 360° journalism: Contested accuracy and objectivity. *New Media & Society*, 21(1), pp. 3–19. DOI:10.1177/1461444818785153

Aitamurto, T., Aymerich-Franch, L., Saldivar, J., Kircos, C., Sadeghi, Y., and Sakshuwong, S. (2020). Examining augmented reality in journalism: Presence, knowledge gain, and perceived visual authenticity. *New Media & Society*, 24(6), pp. 1281–1302. DOI:10.1177/1461444820951925

Bailey, J., Bailenson, Jeremy, N., and Casasanto, Daniel. (2016). When does virtual embodiment change our minds? *Presence: Teleoperators and Virtual Environments*, 25(3), pp. 222–233. DOI:10.1162/PRES_a_00263

Barnhurst, K. G. (1991). Journalism: The great American newspaper. *The American Scholar*, 60(1), pp. 106–112.

Barnhurst, K. and Nerone, J. (1999) The president is dead: American news photography and the new long journalism. In: B. Brennen and H. Hardt (eds.), *Picturing the past: Media, History, and Photography*. Chicago, IL: University of Illinois Press, pp. 60–92.

Barreda-Ángeles, M., Aleix-Guillaume, S., and Pereda-Baños, A. (2020). An "empathy machine" or a "just-for-the-fun-of-it" machine? Effects of immersion in nonfiction 360-video stories on empathy and enjoyment. *Cyberpsychology, Behavior, and Social Networking*, 23(10), 683–688.

Bogart, L. (2004). Reflections on content quality in newspapers. *Newspaper Research Journal*, 25(1), 40–53.

Bollmer, G. (2017). Empathy machines. *Media International Australia*, 165(1), 63–76.

Carlson, M. (2009). The reality of a fake image: News norms, photojournalistic craft and Brian Walski's fabricated photograph. *Journalism Practice*, 3(2), pp. 125–139. DOI:10.1080/17512780802681140

Carlson, M. (2017). *Journalistic Authority: Legitimating News in the Digital Era*. New York: Columbia University Press.

Christopoulos, A., Mystakidis, S., Pellas, N. and Laakso, M.-J. (2021). ARLEAN: An augmented reality learning analytics ethical framework. *Computers*, 10(8), 92. DOI:10.3390/computers10080092

Galtung, J. and Ruge, M. H. (1965). The structure of foreign news: The presentation of the Congo, Cuba and Cyprus crises in four Norwegian newspapers. *Journal of Peace Research*, 2(1), 64–90.

Gladney, G., Shapiro, I. and Castaldo J. (2007). Online editors rate web news quality criteria. *Newspaper Research Journal*, 28(1), 5569.

Kovach, B. and Rosenstiel, T. (2007). *The Elements of Journalism: What News People Should Know and the Public Should Expect*. New York: Three Rivers Press.

Maenpaa, J. and Seppanen, J. (2010). Imaginary darkroom: Digital photo editing as a strategic ritual. *Journalism Practice*, 4(4), pp. 454–475. DOI:10.1080/17512781003760501

Miller, M. R., Herrera, F., Jun, H., Landay, J. A. and Bailenson, J. N. (2020). Personal identifiability of user tracking data during observation of 360-degree VR video. *Scientific Reports*, 10(1), 17404. DOI:10.1038/s41598-020-74486-y

Nakamura, L. (2020). Feeling good about feeling bad: Virtuous virtual reality and the automation of racial empathy. *Journal of Visual Culture*, 19(1), 47–64.

Schudson, M. (1978). *Discovering the News: A Social History of American Newspapers*. New York: Basic Books.

Schudson, M. (2001). The objectivity norm in American journalism. *Journalism*, 2(2), pp. 149–170. DOI:10.1177/146488490100200201

Schwartz, D. (1992). To tell the truth: Codes of objectivity in photojournalism. *Communication*, 13(2), pp. 95–109.

Schwartz, D. (1999). Objective representation: Photographs as facts. In: Brennen, B. and Hardt, H. (eds.), *Picturing the Past: Media, History, and Photography*. Chicago, IL: University of Illinois Press, pp. 158–181.

Shapiro, I., Brin, C., Bédard-Brûlé, I. and Mychajlowycz, K. (2013). Verification as a strategic ritual. *Journalism Practice*, 7(6), pp. 657–673. DOI:10.1080/17512786.2013.765638

Shin, D. and Biocca, F. (2018). Exploring immersive experience in journalism. *New Media & Society*, 20(8), 2800–2823.

Slater, M. (2009). Place illusion and plausibility can lead to realistic behaviour in immersive virtual environments. *Philosophical Transactions of the Royal Society of London. Series B, Biological Sciences*, 364(1535), pp. 3549–3557. DOI:10.1098/rstb.2009.0138

Slater, M. and Wilbur, S. (1997). A framework for immersive virtual environments (FIVE): Speculations on the role of presence in virtual environments. *Presence: Teleoperators and Virtual Environments*, 6(6), pp. 603–616. DOI:10.1162/pres.1997.6.6.603

Slater, M., Gonzalez-Liencres, C., Haggard, P., Vinkers, C., Gregory-Clarke, R., Jelley, S. and Silver, J. (2020). The ethics of realism in virtual and augmented reality. *Frontiers in Virtual Reality*, 1(1). DOI:10.3389/frvir.2020.00001

Society of Professional Journalists. (2014). SPJ code of ethics. www.spj.org/ethicscode.asp (accessed 24 April 2022).

Speicher, M., Hall, B. D. and Nebeling, M. (2019). What is mixed reality? CHI '19: Proceedings of the 2019 CHI Conference on Human Factors in Computing Systems, May 2019, Glasgow, UK, Paper No. 537, pp. 1–15. DOI:10.1145/3290605.3300767

Tuchman, G. (1972). Objectivity as strategic ritual: An examination of newsmen's notions of objectivity. *American Journal of Sociology*, 77(4), pp. 660–679. www.jstor.org/stable/2776752

Zelizer, B. (2010). *About to Die: How News Images Move the Public*. Oxford: Oxford University Press.

7
PROMISES, PITFALLS AND POTENTIALS OF IMMERSIVE JOURNALISM

Holger Pötzsch

> 'VR Helped Me Grasp the Life of a Transgender Wheelchair User'
> Aron Souppouris, 2016

The citation above is in many ways illustrative of what is at stake in this chapter. It sums up much of what is presented as the promises of new immersive virtual reality (VR). It attests to the emotional access VR allegedly offered him into the life worlds of others. At the same time, Lisa Nakamura (2020) takes a critical stance towards these applications. Stating that 'pathos is VR's proof of concept', she alerts to the danger of emotional manipulation as an important feature of this technology. These two positions illustrative of what is at stake in this chapter. While the first sums up much of what is presented as the promises of new immersive VR, the second invites more critical perspectives on this technology's inherent pitfalls. Realistically assessing its genuine potentials, I will argue in this chapter, means to carefully take heed of the latter to enable a responsible realisation of the former.

Dependent on the context of reception and the person reading it, the quote by Aron Souppouris might be understood in three different ways: (1) as a genuine appreciation of a deeply felt vicarious experience of being someone else that was made possible by new immersive technologies, (2) as a naïve expression of a self-centred belief in the empathic powers of new commercial tech gadgets, or (3) as an intended pun where the author ironically combines politically correct identity markers to denounce uncritical appraisals of the largely assumed ethical effects of the latest technological hype. In the following, I will try to navigate such tensions and interrogate the often-false promises, the largely unacknowledged pitfalls and the usually difficult-to-realise potentials of immersive technology-use in non-fiction film making and journalism.

When reading the full article from which the first quote was taken (Souppouris 2016), it becomes clear rather quickly that the rendered experience is of the first kind. The author reflects upon the 'transformative' insights he gained from engaging the VR-driven interactive simulation *The Circle* designed by Manos Agianniotakis.[1] According to Souppouris, the Oculus Rift-based application enabled him co-presence in the body of a transgender person who became tied to a wheelchair after a traumatizing transphobic attack. Tapping into a discourse of 360° video and VR as 'empathy machines' – a term originally coined in a much-cited Ted Talk by tech guru Chris Milk (2015) – Souppouris claims that *The Circle* allowed him to enter an artificial world and 'embody the character Alex and understand her frustrations and feelings' offering him a profound 'educational experience' (n.p.).

The Circle is a game. It has an artificial setting, fictitious characters and a scripted storyline and it allows players to navigate the game-space in a manner that is deliberately designed to replicate a disadvantaged person's relation to the world and to other people. As such, it opens for important insights, but in principle also enables voyeuristic forms of engagement. Thereby, the example points to a series of aporia in much writing about the ethical potentials of empathy-inducing immersive technologies that, in essence, might be more about pathos and profit than about genuinely improving the lives of the many.

I see the following issues in need of further interrogation before any conclusions regarding the possible pro-social effects of VR can be reached: (1) making someone feel something does not necessarily imply understanding or political conscientisation and mobilisation, (2) if feelings are pre-rationally induced by means of technology, the subject is not convinced into reacting in a certain manner, but simply manipulated into doing so, (3) empathy-inducing VR is focused on the isolated individual and built on the presumption that politics is mainly about changing individual behaviour and finally, (4) if the emotion of empathy can be technologically induced in a long-term attitude and behaviour-changing manner, so can other less progressive emotions such as hate or despair.

When moving the discussion from VR-based interactive fiction to non-fiction genres such as immersive journalism, other issues of critical concern come to the fore that need to be taken seriously before jumping on the bandwagon of the next big-tech driven 'revolution': (1) how can the informants (or, indeed, the objects) of the immersive experiences implied by 360° journalism be adequately protected and how can they be properly included in the projects realised in their life worlds? (2) which implicit understandings of realism are underlying the widespread presumption of VR-promoters to be able to offer unmitigated access to the lives of others? (3) is the triggering of emotional reactions really a task for journalists? If yes, what are the wider implications of this for the journalistic profession? Finally, (4) how can audiences be sufficiently made aware of the manipulative nature, constructed frames and potentially disturbing effects of the simulations they are immersed in?

Promises, premises and pretensions: Immersive journalism and its discontents

In their study on *Governing Affects,* Otto Penz and Birgit Sauer (2020: 1) assert that today, in politics, culture, society and even the economy 'affect, emotion and feeling flourish like never before'. In line with this development, the authors argue, affective regulation and amplification of individuals and populations by means of new technologies and procedures of management become key elements of contemporary apparatuses of power. Jodi Dean (2009) argues in a similar direction when she connects current neoliberal forms of governance with technology and an elicitation of feelings for political purposes. According to her, communicative capitalism brings together consumerism, excessive individualism and an embrace of victimisation and combines these elements with new technologies of mediation and exchange. This constellation, Dean continues, has grave implications for politics and society as it tends to reduce political engagement to a self-centred registration of opinions and an exhibitionist expression of feeling that leads to a privileging of emotionality over a rational exchange of arguments. Drawing upon the work of Jacques Lacan, she concludes that ideological formations 'work as economies of enjoyment (i.e., affective intensities) to forbid, permit, direct and command' (50). It is my contention in this chapter that VR-based immersive technologies constitute powerful tools for governing through affects under conditions of communicative capitalism. Therefore, these tools merit our critical attention.

Ana Luisa Sánchez Laws (2020a) opens her investigation of theory, practices and challenges of immersive journalism by reiterating 'the promise' of this new technology of news production in terms of affective engagement. VR-based reporting, she writes, enables viewers to be 'virtually at the location' and 'feel present with the subjects of the news' (2), a setting that induces empathy, thereby increasing 'our understanding of a situation in ways traditional formats cannot' (2). As she acknowledges a few pages later, however, this approach 'poses profound ethical challenges' (6) and, as I would like to add, epistemological and political ones as well. To be able to critically interrogate the promise of immersive journalism and the challenges this technique implies, I will have to take a closer look at some of the most salient premises underpinning a contemporary discourse of innovation, disruption and affective amplification that currently emanates from the higher echelons of a technology-focused business world.

The idea of using immersive technologies such as VR or 360° video to induce emotions and thereby move media experiences 'to the next level' have been common in environments working with game development and experimental film making since the 1980s (Rose 2018; Sánchez Laws 2020a; Nakamura 2020). Head-mounted displays, sensor-covered suits or gloves, as well as specially designed rooms (e.g., CAVE) should enable a spatial presence somewhere else and often as someone else, that was meant to be so immersing that it could elicit responses-as-if-real (Laws 2020a: 24–5). These ideas of tech-induced real experiences in virtual worlds were readily disseminated through advertising and popular sales events aimed at gathering venture capital for the development of 'the next big thing' in entertainment technologies – with Zuckerberg's metaverse as the so far latest addition to this commercialised and surveillance-driven media 'ecology'.

The transfer from the field of fictional media to uses in factual news reporting gradually started already in the 1990s (see for instance Boczkowski 2005) but gained momentum with an important study conducted by Nonny de la Peña and colleagues (2010) who used the term 'immersive journalism' in conjunction with their experiments about news dissemination in and through navigable 3D virtual environments. Developer Chris Milk (2015) later branded the high-tech tools behind immersive journalism and other VR-based non-fiction formats as an 'empathy machine'. According to his postulates, this new technology-enabled co-presence and therefore emotional engagement with the otherwise inaccessible other thus facilitating compassionate and therefore progressive real-world responses. As among others Ruberg (2020) and Andrejevic and Volcic (2020) have pointed out, in such claims about technologies' potentials to incite pro-social effects, the term 'empathy' often remains undefined, thus, making it difficult to criticise sweeping assertions and test hypotheses (see also Sánchez Laws, 2020b).

The discussion about possibilities and pitfalls of immersive journalism is essentially a debate about media specificity, i.e., the question of how exactly 360° videos or VR-environments can be seen to impact upon audiences and how different this is compared to traditional media such as television news casts or documentary films. De la Peña et al. (2010), for instance, argue that three factors distinguish immersive technologies from other forms of mediation: 'plausibility', 'place illusion' and 'body ownership'. The authors claim that these three aspects, when brought together in the right manner, can elicit responses-as-if-real that have the capacity 'to transform not only people's sensation of place and reality but also themselves' (295). They allege further that, because of this, immersive technologies hold considerable ethical potentials (see also Reis, Vasconcelos and Coelho, 2018). However, the connection made by de la Peña and colleagues between a technologically induced *potential* for specific media effects and a contingent actualisation of these potentials in concrete contexts of reception remains rather weak. Ultimately, the authors base their conclusions on a dataset that is limited to a small number of participants who self-report certain effects of VR-based experiences that are interpreted as being pro-social by the authors of the study.

However, certain prosocial effects of 360° video have recently been confirmed in (among others) a study by Pimentel and colleagues (2021) who empirically connect a certain increase in the exhibited willingness to give donations with exposure to an empathy-enhancing non-fictional immersive experience (for applications in conflict resolution, see Hasler et al. 2021). It is important to note, however, that studies confirming pro-social effects of immersive technologies usually do so with reference to VR-based scenarios where the content that is exhibited was designed to precisely support such effects from the outset. In other words, in most of these studies the supreme importance of technological immersion for the elicited pro-social effects remains an assumption.

In his study on VR-based immersive technologies, McRoberts (2018) introduces four aspects that according to him are crucial for a realisation of a sense of presence and 'being there' (114). The key factors he identifies are (1) immersion, (2) positionality (or situatedness) of the user, (3) a degree of interactivity and (4) narrative agency. In his article, McRoberts creates a check list of elements for both design and critical evaluation of immersive film making based on both technical aspects and storytelling devices. It is in this case interesting to note that he merely explains how an increased sense of presence can be invited but refrains from assuming a success of such attempts with every audience. Neither does he premise a necessarily pro-social impact of the induced emotions. Arguing in a similar direction as McRoberts, Jones (2017) has shown the significance of actual interactivity and, thus, real audience influence on what to focus on and which perspective to adopt for a truly immersive experience without connecting her findings to presumed ethical effects. According to her, techniques such as VR-based journalism in essence serve to renew news production with the aim of reaching 'a disengaged audience' (182). In the cases referred here, ethical effects are not simply assumed, but treated as contingent upon form, content and reception of each specific journalistic product.

Discourses about allegedly unharnessed potentials of the most recent technological hype often emanate from marketing and are aimed at increasing sales or attracting investments (see for instance Boczkowski 2005). Statements about the unrealised ethical possibilities of immersive journalism are no exception to this rule. At a time, as Rose notes,

> when the dark potential of digital has been brought into view, it is remarkable to see the same techno-utopianism that was pervasive in relation to the development of the internet at play around a new generation of technology … that carries significant risks of harm.
>
> *2018: 147*

Nakamura (2020: 48–49) makes a similar point in her scathing criticism of immersive non-fiction when she asserts that 'the idea of VR as an empathy machine … is part and parcel of Big Tech's attempt to rebrand'. Virtuous VR, she continues in implicit agreement with Dean (2009), 'is a cultural alibi for a digital media culture that has taken a wrong turn, towards distraction, detachment and misinformation'. Mind that both Rose and Nakamura wrote these lines prior to Zuckerberg announcing his newest and for me rather dystopic vision of his metaverse.

Today, the question is not any longer if VR-based immersive technologies enable experiences of presence, embodiment and agency (De la Peña, 2010; Reis, Vasconcelos and Coelho, 2018). Several empirical studies have attested to the fact that such experiences are indeed generated in encounters with immersive technologies (Pimentel et al., 2021; Hasler et al., 2021). The question that remains unanswered, however, pertains to the implications of these experiences in wider political and societal contexts and to the new ethical obligations for journalists and spectators these imply (Sánchez Laws and Utne 2019). And here serious doubts regarding often-alleged pro-social effects abound.

Forced empathy, toxic embodiment and the power to manipulate: The unavoidable politics of immersive journalism

The claim to be able to elicit emotional responses in audiences in a manner apparently unfettered by mediation is crucial for the postulate of pro-social political effects of factual immersive media. Nakamura (2020) summarises the most central epistemological premises held in what she terms 'the co-presence for good movement' (56) by showing how claims to truth are directly connected with claims to elicit true feelings. 'Virtuous VR', she writes, 'fills a very special niche: as the medium that not only needs to be felt to be believed, but cannot be doubted once it is felt' (53). Pathos, she concludes 'is VR's proof of concept'. Eliciting emotions seems to help us avoid messy detours through representation. Rather than arguing about the politics and ideologies of mediation we seem empowered to directly access the truth itself that reveals itself in our unquestionable emotional and bodily experiences.

The evocation of affective responses for political purposes by means of powerful media technologies should indeed be a cause of concern (Penz and Sauer, 2020; Dean, 2009). Audiences are not convinced by ways of rational arguments that balance different perspectives and include backgrounds and contexts of what is shown. Instead, they are meant to bodily experience without filters or frames a suffering other and build political positions and actions based on these allegedly pre-cognitive and pre-ideological sensations (Schlembach and Clewer 2021). This, of course, does not really sound like a description of the function of journalism in contemporary democracies, but reminds more of insidious subliminal practices familiar from fields such as advertising, PR and propaganda (e.g., Bernays, 1928.).

And, indeed, one of the most cited examples of the use of immersive factual VR for good, Emblematic Group's *Project Syria* (2014), was commissioned for presentation at the World Economic Forum in Davos by Klaus Schwab with the explicit purpose of making world leaders act. However, the nature of the induced action, the context of the presented events, and their possible causes remained beyond the scope of the presentation that merely aimed at making the horrors of Aleppo[2] experienced by a little girl vicariously tangible to world leaders in an embodied manner who were then assumed to retain a willingness *to act* in an unspecified way using unspecified means. According to Laws (2020a: 84–85), this approach 'poses ethical concerns' and reveals that, rather than a tool for political enlightenment, *Project Syria* is first and foremost a 'campaigning product for a humanitarian agency' – or, as I would contend, for imperial practices disguised as liberal humanitarian interventionism.

Based on considerations such as the ones presented above, Schlembach and Clewer (2021: 828) propose the term 'forced empathy' to grasp the technologically facilitated manufacturing of emotions for specific political or other purposes that, according to the authors, is 'highly unethical and manipulative'. Again, Schlembach and Clewer do not doubt the capacity of VR to elicit emotions with the aim to support progressive projects but merely show that this 'power is not politically unidirectional' (832). They illustrate this position by showing how the fast-food chain McDonalds uses immersive VR in an advertising campaign aimed at emotionally charging the idea of their products as healthy and ecologically sustainable. Pro-social, it seems, can mean very different things to many different people and, as such, can include military interventionism and selling more burgers as well as increased humanitarian aid or genuine de-colonisation. An awareness of such contingencies is largely absent among proponents of the pro-social effects of immersive VR.

In her review of the VR-based immersive product *Across the Line*, Robertson (2016) alerts to similar problems. *Across the Line* allows the user to step into the shoes of young woman trying to reach an abortion clinic passing through an angry mob of pro-life demonstrators. She summarises his experience of anger with the following words of cautioning that *Across the Line*

> is an inversion of what empathy VR is supposed to do for the world – a connection that aligns you with one person and makes another a monster. This may be what makes me suspicious of changing the world by provoking emotions: emotions are not inherently good, and they're not inherently helpful. Hate is one of the purest emotions of all.
>
> *cited in Laws 2020a: 56–57*

It seems that Milk's empathy machine should rather have been termed an emotion machine that can induce both pro-social and toxic affective responses.

But then, maybe emotional VR is not really about politics, the 'other', or political action but about *you*? Among others, Penz and Sauer (2020), Dean (2009), Pedwell (2014), Nakamura (2020), and Schlembach and Clewer (2021) have shown that there is an uncanny connection between a rhetoric of emotion, new immersive technologies, and neoliberal subjectification. This focus taps into questions of self-indulgence, pleasure-seeking spectacle, voyeurism, and an instrumentalisation as well as cannibalisation of the suffering other.

Nakamura (2020: 51), for instance, asserts that VR technologies often give rise to what she terms 'toxic embodiment' – a practice that allows people who can afford the latest technological gadgets to temporarily enter and vicariously experience the sufferings of people 'who might not even own their own body' while blissfully ignoring the various forms of suffering taking place in their immediate neighbourhood such as homelessness. Rightfully alerting to the severe power imbalances involved in the production and dissemination of immersive VR, she warns against a new form of identity tourism that temporarily opts into the lives of marginalised others and thus confuses 'immersive viewing with access to the actual experience' (54). This, she continues, is 'not only a profound insult to those who live with challenges that cannot be simulated, but also a clear indication to the limits of VR-based immersion and the artificial empathy it hopes to manufacture' (54).

Attempts to make individuals feel rather than convincing them to engage in rational deliberation carries additional challenges. In recent scholarship the fragmenting and atomizing tendencies of focusing on individual emotional impacts rather than intersubjective understanding and collective action have been amply foregrounded (Dean, 2009). According to Schlembach and Clewer (2021: 838), for instance, immersive VR reporting individualises responses to mediated suffering and privileges 'victimhood over historical agency'. In Nakamura's (2020: 59) terms, 'empathy machines' frame challenges as 'problems with head-mounted solutions, rather than as a set of structural relations that require structural solutions'. The depoliticising tendencies of a neoliberal post-democratic moment (Crouch, 2004) seem to have found their representational technology of choice.

Much writing about the supposedly beneficial impacts of empathy-inducing VR technologies sets up a false dichotomy between rationality and emotion as a conceptual framework to support their claims. This thinking often starts with a critique of what is seen as a one-sided focus on reason that, as is argued, not least since Kant has dominated Western thinking at the detriment of emotion and embodiment (for an overview, see Laws 2020a, chapter 3). A critique of a certain over-reliance on Kant and rationality in Western philosophy is certainly valid and has productively been pursued by many thinkers. However, in undermining rationality per se, many proponents of non-fiction VR as prime tool to achieve pro-social goals, in essence, throw out the child with the bathwater. As Laws (2020a: 91) concludes, 'emotional embodiment can … be coupled to our rational thinking about the situation we find ourselves in, to thus attain a holistic view of what happened'. Apparently, a viable approach to political engagement is not about emotion or not. Rather, the question must be exactly which emotions should be mobilised by which means to achieve precisely which objectives. In such endeavours, emotional engagement needs to be coupled with rational arguments to incite reflected collective political action.

The last issue to be addressed on VR's manipulative potentials as an empathy machine is the idea that immersion in a setting as someone else somehow can successfully go beyond representation, 'remove the frame' (Milk, cited in Laws, 2020a: 52), and offer direct unmediated access to the event as such. To achieve this, it is argued, technology must aid us with becoming the other, so we can empathise and then make the right choices based on this affective positioning by the socio-technical apparatus of contemporary immersive VR. Mandy Rose (2018: 137) connects this thinking to an ongoing 'human fascination with creating mimetic representations of our world' stretching from André Bazin's 'myth of total cinema' (Bazin and Gray 1971; cited in ibid.), via initial expectations connected to the invention of hand-held cameras and up to the most recent brand of techno-utopianism promising a 'unique power of VR' in terms of immersion for beneficial goals (Bailenson, 2018, cited in Rose, 2018: 138).

Removing the frame of representation, however, has again and again proven to be difficult. Ever more convincing immersive technologies often base their claims to authenticity and unmitigated access on a form of surface realism that mistakes an increase in technologically achieved verisimilitude for an increase in truth-value (Pötzsch, 2012). In particular when approaching the limits of representation, as is the case with attempts to make accessible the current or past sufferings of others (Saltzmann, 2000; Dauphinée, 2007), these ideas lead to two opposing strategies of mediation: either attempts are made to increase the transparency of the medium until a feeling of supposedly total immersion and, therefore, a direct access to an presupposed truth is reached, or the viewer can be made aware of the medial apparatus and the with necessity always partial and contingent nature of representation. In such approaches, explicit images can be avoided altogether and techniques such as allusion can be used to incite a re-imagination of what defies outright representation. Both cases are strategies of mediation and even though the former purports to offer direct access to the event as such, also here a medial frame that tacitly predisposes experiences remains in place and needs to be taken seriously (Nash, 2018; Rose, 2018; Schlembach and Clewer, 2021).

Let's consider the previously mentioned *Project Syria* as an example. Even though the user might feel as if present in Aleppo as the child, someone made the decision to place cameras and microphones in such a manner that they can replicate this child's perspective and not another one's. In addition, the decision has been made to follow a girl in Eastern as opposed to Western Aleppo. These two simple facts make clear that claims to a frameless direct access to an event rendered through an empathy-inducing embodiment of the other that supposedly remains outside ideology and therefore politics are mere pretensions. As Judith Butler (2009: 70) writes, even the 'most transparent of documentary image is framed, and framed for a purpose, carrying that purpose within its frame and implementing it through the frame'. Though VR may enable you to embody others and explore their worlds, what you can perceive and experience, remains determined by someone's choices. And these choices are always ideologically inflected and, therefore, political.

Looking back to the future: The implications of seeing, speaking and feeling *for*, *as* or *with* the other in 'old' and 'new' media

This section interrogates earlier writings about potentials and pitfalls of mediated witnessing of others' pain. As is often the case in debates about affordances and effects of 'new' media technologies, we will see that what is currently discussed in relation the supposed pro-social effects of VR-based immersive journalism, has already been taken up earlier with reference to other once 'new' technologies (Rose, 2018). As such, proponents of the unharnessed powers of empathy-inducing machines such as Chris Milk would have been wise to engage with the works of such scholars as Susan Sontag, Elizabeth Dauphinée and Judith Butler.

Susan Sontag, for instance, has critically inquired into the ethics of photography for more than three decades. The results are summarised in her seminal book *Regarding the Pain of Others* (2003) – a reflection on the necessary ambivalences and unpredictable discursive and political effects of mediation. Her work, I contend, can productively inform thinking about other media technologies currently coming to the fore. Sontag poses a series of questions to photography that retain their validity, and indeed their urgency, also in relation to the technologies of mediation behind immersive journalism.

First, Sontag warns against uncritical assumptions of pro-social effects through a mediated elicitation of emotions. Mirroring later warnings against manipulation through immersive VR (e.g., Schlembach and Clewer, 2021: Robertson cited in Laws, 2020a), she warns that photographs of an atrocity 'may give rise to opposing responses ... a call for peace. A cry for revenge. Or simply the bemused awareness

… that terrible things happen' (11–12). Again, we see that mediation – of whatever type – is not a politically speaking unidirectional process with necessarily progressive outcomes. The inevitable contingencies of reception need to be adequately considered – in photography as much as elsewhere.

Second, Sontag also problematises the alleged truth-value of photography that, through its indexical nature, apparently merely records the world as it is in a quasi-objective mechanical fashion. She shows that photographs can indeed serve as important documentation to prove certain facts. At the same time, however, she acknowledges the limitations of a medium riddled with contingencies. To problematise the truth-value of photography, Sontag initially points to the importance of not only focusing on what is made visible, but also asking 'what pictures, whose cruelties, whose deaths are not being shown' (12) as such alerting to the necessary blank spots implied in all forms of mediation. Later, she asserts that photographs 'always had, necessarily, a point of view … they are both objective record and personal testimony' (23) thereby highlighting the subjective framing function of the invisible photographer behind every image.

Furthermore, Sontag addresses the problem of voyeurism and desensitisation. When repeatedly being exposed to images of others' suffering, shock effects will wear off and fade, or the images might induce passivity, despair, or even a usually disavowed form of perverse pleasure (107). Finally, she directs attention to the interdependences between photography and other media in processes of meaning-making and asserts that 'all photographs wait to be explained or falsified by their captions' (9). Every image is received in a variety of medial and other contexts and these contexts matter for the meaning taken from them. I contend that all these aspects taken up by Sontag in relation to photography retain their validity also when looking at the ethical prospects and problems of immersive journalism.

Can the suffering other be experienced in an ethically sustainable manner? Contemplating the representation of violent abuse drawing upon the notorious Abu Ghraib images, Elizabeth Dauphinée (2007) warns against a fetishisation of the body of the other in pain. She asks the question whether, the images of the Abu Ghraib torture scandal should be published and concludes that this 'produces an irresolvable ethical dilemma' (153). On the one hand, a publication is required to provide documentation of officially sanctioned deeply repulsive practices of the US military in occupied Iraq. On the other hand, Dauphinée is acutely aware of the treacherous ethical terrains an instrumentalizing of deeply traumatic and humiliating experiences of others for political purposes leads to. She warns that such well-meaning and politically progressive media practices quickly can lead to a 'double-betrayal' (153) of the victims by their supposed advocates. She writes that 'images do not speak for themselves – they are made to speak for, by and about *us*. We are asking these bodies to do political work for us that, however "right", also works to reduce them to representative examples of their plight' (153; emphasis in original).

Cassandra Falke (2019: 80) concludes a text about framing embodiment in violent narratives in a similar manner writing that when the material body becomes the focus, the problem arises that what is seen and experienced are 'bodies ... instead of people'. The relation between the exposed other and us as producers and consumers of their mediated sufferings interrogated by Dauphinée and Falke remains the same regardless of whether representation in form of still images or in form of an embodying simulation by means of latest immersive technologies are concerned. Both scholars' conclusions about the severe ethical challenges implied by attempts to represent the suffering other should be heeded carefully by the various proponents of virtuous VR-productions for good such as *Clouds Over Sidra* or *Project Syria*.

In her books *Precarious Life* (2004) and *Frames of War* (2009), Judith Butler investigates the institutional infrastructures and cultural frames that condition a scaling of forms of life in public discourses about war and the other. She writes that the public sphere

> is constituted in part by what can appear, and the regulation of the sphere of appearance is one way ... of establishing whose lives can be marked as lives, and whose deaths will count as deaths. Our capacity to feel and to apprehend hangs in the balance.
>
> *2004: xx–xxi*

Butler traces the scopic regimes behind the reality-constructs that tacitly predispose public opinion and political decision-making in the US-initiated global war on terror. In her works, she investigates how specific 'normative schemes of intelligibility' are established by powerful state interests to regulate 'what will and will not be human, what will be a livable life, what will be a grievable death' (146). Her studies identify three ways of framing life and the other through mediation in current war culture: (1) idolisation as either hero or victim, (2) demonisation as less than human and imminent threat, or (3) invisibilisation by 'providing no image, no name, no narrative, so that there never was a life, and there never was a death' (2004: 146). Taken together, these strategies are realised by means of a powerful medial apparatus that is an integral component of every nation's war effort – including those using immersive VR.

The scopic regimes of war identified by Butler (2004, 2009) oscillate the mediated other between hyper-visibility and invisibility. Either the other becomes a constant object of mediation effort as a mere monster or pure victim, or it is effectively hidden from view and not mediated at all and therefore becomes marginalised and disposable ungrievable life. Drawing upon the ethics of Immanuel Levinas, Butler (2009) argues that both hypervisibility and invisibility constitute a defacing of others that in essence will preclude our ability to ethically respond to their suffering despite a shared condition of precarity and vulnerability. All these strategies of framing others as monsters, victims, or non-life are salient and need to be engaged with in a critical manner regardless of whether the medium under scrutiny photography, television, film or VR-based empathy-enhancing immersive technologies.

In all cases, a response to the question of how to ethically represent a suffering other and thereby achieve a form of mediation that entails pro-social effects, implies attention to the socio-technical apparatuses and power-laden practices of media production and consumption. It implies that we, in Butler's (2007: 966) words, 'rebuff our visual consumerism' and 'learn to see the frame that blinds us to what we see'. After all, she concludes in her study, this 'not seeing in the midst of seeing, this not-seeing that is the condition of seeing, has become the visual norm' in current war culture. In a similar manner, as I would like to add, *a not-feeling in the midst of feeling, a not-feeling that is the condition of feeling* in current war culture needs to be critically addressed as an implicitly normative frame implied by current attempts to use affective immersive technologies for the sake of advancing human interests and peace.

When discussing Susan Sontag's writings about the Aby Ghraib images, Butler (2007: 966) engages with the politics implied by mediated witnessing. She asserts that what is outrageous about the visual representations of torture published in connection to the scandal is not only their content documenting the systematic harrowing and illegal practices of US occupation forces in Iraq, but also a lack of instruction on 'how to transfer ... affect into effective political action'. As such, she continues, the torture photograph 'enrages without directing the rage, and so excites moral sentiments at the same time that it confirms our political paralysis'. A similar disjoint between affective engagement and reflected collective political action becomes palpable when asking if, and how, VR-based journalism can be enlisted for the purpose of a progressive and pro-social politics of nonviolence.

Estrangement and participation: Doing immersive journalism with Brecht and Boal

Sontag, Dauphinée, and Butler are at their strongest when critiquing dominant scopic regimes of war and when throwing light upon the various ambiguities and pitfalls inherent in attempts to represent the suffering of others. Their works are less detailed when concrete instructions about how to create the conditions for ethical practices of mediation and witnessing are concerned. How exactly could a 'disobedient act of seeing' (Butler 2009: 72) be invited and which technologies could afford the creation of what Kozol (2014: 166) terms 'sceptical documents' that connect emotion, reasoning, and critical self-reflection in a productive and progressive manner to facilitate sustainable collective political mobilisation?

I contend that, to achieve reflected long-term political mobilisation, emotional immersion must be balanced by rational arguments and deliberation based on accessible facts. Here, a form of mediation is required that raises awareness for the with necessity partial and partisan nature of any form of representation, and that acknowledges the suffering other as more than an object of a cannibalistic or voyeuristic gaze, but as an autonomous agent in charge of determining its own images and fates. This is not easily achieved even under circumstances where one has the latest technologies for immersive VR-based film making at one's disposal. Bertolt

Brecht's and Augusto Boal's theories of the stage can give inspiration that might prove useful for facilitating such endeavours.

Bertolt Brecht's (1957) theories and practical guidelines for the stage are characterised by a deep distrust of immersion. According to him, a too seamlessly transparent theatrical apparatus offers pleasurable distraction rather than productive challenges and, therefore, facilitates an escapism into fantasy worlds that pacifies audiences and blinds them to their true political situations and collective interests. Brecht develops his epic theatre in dialogue with and in contrast to Aristotle's then dominating ideas of the stage. He argues that the main problem with an Aristotelian notion of catharsis – the pleasurable release of emotional energies when the main conflict of a play is resolved – is that it is temporally and conceptually limited to the stage. In Aristotelian theory of the drama, catharsis, and the affective engagement it enables, never points beyond the borders of the stage, and thus remains without relevance for audiences' attempts to gain an understanding of the contradictions in their actual lives. It pacifies more than it enlightens. According to Brecht, this, together with anagnorisis, the understanding acquired by a tragic hero at the end of a play that earlier attempts to change a world determined by higher powers always must be in vain, makes the Aristotelian tragedy a conservative art form bent on stabilizing and reproducing a received status quo.

In contrast to this, Brecht develops his own theory of an epic theatre based on Marxist thought that retains the emotional and intellectual engagement of audiences also after the play is finished and directs them towards real-world political struggles. This normative directing of drama is achieved by means of both content and form of presentation. In terms of content, Brecht argues that the stage is an arena where political positions, ideas and insights can be disseminated, explained and critiqued. A play can (1) convey facts about actual political situations, it can (2) try and test possible individual and collective actions in a safe setting, or it can (3) use allegories where narratives set in different times or places bring universal structures and relationships of oppression to the attention of audiences and contextualise these with reference to current political challenges. By these and other means the audience is treated as a political body that is both correctly informed and emotionally engaged, rather than a group of pleasure-seeking consumers in search for distraction.

In terms of form, Brecht explicitly directs the theatrical apparatus against emotional immersion. Acknowledging the importance of emotion for motivating political engagement, he argues that emotion alone will not lead to self-determination and collective mobilisation as it remains without direction and shared understanding of the contexts of a given challenge and possible solutions to it (reflecting some of Butler's arguments introduced above). As a solution, Brecht devises a series of concrete instructions of how audience immersion can be broken throughout the play to re-engage reason and explicitly connect the staged events to collective real-world struggles showing concrete options for action. The so-called *Verfremdungseffekt*, or V-effect, precisely serves this purpose.

On Brecht's stage actors can suddenly turn on spectators and comment their (lack of) reactions. Alternatively, giant posters can be set up without warning that break the illusion and draw explicit connections between diegetic events and real-world issues, or background choirs can be used to alert to inconsistencies and omissions in the staged story. By such means, the V-effect positions audiences as at once immersed in a story-world and its characters, and at the same time at a distance and constantly forced to reflect upon the artificial nature of the staged settings and their connection to actual life-worlds and political struggles. Both content and form of Brecht's theatre, thus, make the stage an instrument of class struggle bent toward facilitating pro-social goals such as more just and less oppressive societies.

The significance of Brecht's thinking for attempts of using VR-based immersion to facilitate progressive political struggles can hardly be overestimated and can serve as inspiration for possible improvements.[3] To fulfil its promise of mobilizing viewers for prosocial goals, VR-based journalism needs to address both rational thought and emotion and must engage spectators both as individuals and as embedded in various collective structures. To achieve this, it needs to oscillate between immersion and emersion – between a direct elicitation of feelings for a certain issue and a rational contemplation about this issue and the tactics and strategies required to collectively mobilise on behalf of identified shared goals. In this, a Brechtian V-effect can prove beneficial as it can repeatedly draw viewers out of a merely experiential state and thereby instigate critical reflection about the implied purpose of the evoked feelings, the wider socio-political context of the events these feelings are directed at, and the technical apparatus eliciting these feelings.

Applying Brecht to immersive journalism, enables a breaking of the illusion and a critical contemplation of the politics behind affective engagement for certain causes. In his thinking, however, the audience remains somewhat passive – an entity in need of education and guidance to see through the structures blinding them to their genuine interests. In the next paragraphs, I will turn to ways of thinking about the stage that not only position audiences as political subjects enlightened by conscientious playwrights and directors, but – paralleling VR-based immersive environments – also as active participants in the very same staged settings. Here the thought by Augusto Boal will prove useful.

In Augusto Boal's (1979, 2004) theory of the theatre, the audience is central not only as a target for politically relevant interventions via a Brechtian V-effect, but also as a co-constitutive component of the play itself and of the theatrical apparatus sustaining it. Boal coins the term *spect-actor* (2002: 243) to grasp this form of active participation by audiences that become simultaneously spectators and actors. He devises the setting of the *forum theatre* (ibid.: 242) to show how such a participatory stage-work can be realised and how it can serve progressive political objectives. In essence, forum theatre and spect-actor recalibrate the relation between playwright, director, stage and audience. Rather than merely taking down the fourth wall in Brechtian move of estrangement that reveals the medial apparatus and its in-built politics offering concrete instructions for activism, Boal dissolves the distinction between a play and its audience entirely. As spect-actors, audiences not only watch but become a constitutive component of the play actively changing its content and the way this content is presented. This way of thinking has relevance for ideas and practices of immersive journalism and film making.

In a forum theatre, the playwright, director and actors merely initiate a story based on a few rudimentary instructions. Once the scene is set and the play begins, members of the audience can at any moment raise and intervene in the play either by suggesting a different course of action, by questioning performances, or by themselves entering the stage as participants. According to Boal, neither the written play nor the staged drama is the most significant element determining the political potentials of theatre. Rather, he deems an active process of participatory reception and the various debates and practices of deliberation these entail as most salient for political conscientisation and mobilisation. Therefore, the act of collectively staging events and of debating about why and how these should, or should not, be staged in a particular manner becomes formative of political subjectivities. Boal moves thinking about the political nature of theatre from decoding, interpreting and contextualizing set staged events to a participatory interactive performance and a collective negotiation of acts of staging while these take place. This way politics is transformed from something represented or enacted somewhere else by others to something happening among the audience while collectively engaging with the representation, its apparatus, form and content.

From these ideas, I believe, genuine benefits can be drawn for the practice of immersive journalism that, so far, has directed too much attention to total immersion aimed at inducing merely behavioural changes at the level of the isolated individual (Nakamura, 2020; Schlembach and Clewer, 2021). When seeing immersive empathy machines in the light of Boal's ideas, the role of the experientially invaded other and their interests and stakes in specific cases of 360° VR-filmmaking can productively be addressed.

In a Boal-inspired immersive form of immersive mediation, audiences can be enabled to, firstly, vicariously witness and bodily experience the world of the other to then retract and critically reflect about what they lived through. This reflection can take place in similar virtual settings that, this time, facilitate encounters not with the other but among the spectators. In such a virtual version of a forum theatre ways of engaging and embodying others can be thematised and both emotional appeal and political content of the presentation can be collectively interrogated and questioned including both form, content, and the medial apparatus behind it. This can facilitate a deliberation among audiences about their own position vis-á-vis this apparatus and its inherent relations of power, dangers of instrumentalisation, and possibilities for exploitation.

In addition, VR-based immersive experiences should be rendered in a reciprocal fashion by default. This means that for instance 'Westerners' stepping into the shoes of suffering people in the global south must be willing to accept equal vicarious experiencing of their own lives by the witnessed other. To enable an estranging, truly participatory, mutually beneficial, and genuinely inclusive form of immersive journalism and filmmaking that productively activates the ideas of both Brecht and Boal, small-scale experiments need to be conducted over time on a series of preconceived locations that are all both witnessed and witnessing on an equal measure and scale. This would equally distribute the means of representation among the different locations and would enable all participants to become both object and subject of the process of mediation thus empowering them and raising awareness for the contextual and deeply political aspects of vicariously becoming someone else.

In this alternative, the most crucial element is not the relation between the witness and the object of immersive co-presence, but between various subject-objects, or spectators, of the same VR-based simulation – both 'here' and 'there' – deliberating about its conditions, frames and impacts. Thereby, users cease to be isolated subjects that are made to feel something for a given purpose through manipulative technologies. Instead, they are led to conceive of themselves as both producers and receivers embedded in communal structures that motivate a critical interrogation and possibly change of the very medial frames. The ability to engage in collective deliberation about difficult political questions and about the medial apparatuses predisposing our access to them, thus, moves centre stage and becomes the core of ethical potentials of immersive technologies. This solution would also enforce a radical opening-up of physical technologies and code through which an event or setting is experienced (open access, open data, open code, and open technology). Thereby, an immersive journalism based on Brechtian Verfremdung and Boalian forum theatre would also radically undermine the business models and return-of-investment logics currently structuring much of the field of VR-based film making.

Conclusion

In this chapter, I have engaged with the premises, promises and pitfalls of immersive journalism. Moving from hype and hope to a critique of this new technique of emotion-focused film making and reporting, I have summarised a series of severe reservations and warning against a premature belief in the alleged pro-social powers of an 'empathy machine' (Milk 2015) claiming to be able to automate progressive political change. Drawing upon the works by Nakamura (2020), Schlembach and Clewer (2021), Rose (2018) and Nash (2018) among others, I showed that scepticism against emotional manipulation by means of commercial high-tech products is on the rise. Furthermore, by adding a historical dimension, I argued that the ambiguous ethics and varying political stakes of remotely witnessing the suffering of others have been treated in a profound manner earlier by among others Susan Sontag (2003), Elizabeth Dauphinée (2007) and Judith Butler (2004, 2009). Their works on photography, film and medial as well as discursive frames of war retain much of their validity also for a cautioning against pretensions of the latest 'new' technology for ethical and pro-social vicarious witnessing. Finally, enlisting the theories and practical guidelines for the stage by Bertolt Brecht (1957) and Augusto Boal (1979, 2002), I advanced concrete ideas for how a focus on artistic estrangement (V-effect) and collective participatory engagement of audiences not only with content, but also with the immersive apparatus of mediation as such (forum theatre), might facilitate the development of truly pro-social technologies of reciprocal and truly participatory, remote witnessing.

Unfortunately, Zuckerberg's metaverse is currently promising the exact opposite – a seamless, imposed-from-above, and comprehensively commercialised alternative world that has been less augmented than tacitly tampered with to serve his and his company's particular interests. This chapter is also a rallying cry demanding not only critique, but concrete resistance against Zuckerberg's and other tech-guru's pretensions at being able to save humanity by making ever more money by selling in, ultimately unnecessary, new gadgets and devices.

Discussion questions

- How can the informants of supposedly immersive experiences created by 360° video journalism be adequately protected?
- How can informants be properly included in projects realised in their own life worlds?
- Which implicit understandings of realism are underlying the widespread presumption of VR-promoters to be able to offer unmitigated access to the lives of others?
- Is the triggering of emotional reactions a task for journalists? If yes, what are the wider implications of this for the journalistic profession?
- How can audiences be sufficiently made aware of the potential manipulative nature, constructed frames or disturbing effects of the simulations they are immersed in?
- What are the exact problems that should be solved by new immersive technologies? Who is shouldering the costs and who will reap the economic and political benefits?

Notes

1 More information on *The Circle* can be accessed here: https://igf.com/circle
2 Given the political bias of the producers and intended audience of *Project Syria*, the girl portrayed in the VR piece must be assumed to live in Eastern Aleppo, an area that was besieged by the Syrian Arab Army at the given time. The sufferings inflicted upon the population of Western Aleppo by US-, Turkish- and Saudi-backed militant groups at roughly the same time in history seem not to be worthy of similar attempts to arouse the empathy of key audiences. This implicit political positioning raises serious doubts concerning the 'actions' world leaders should take in response to the emotions evoked by the VR piece. In this light, *Project Syria's* condemnation of one bombing campaign might just as well have contributed to justifying another major bombing campaign against Syria. The affective value of little girls is apparently a variable dependent upon the political factions causing their sufferings. Project Syria is a plain example for the insidious instrumentalization of the suffering of others for partisan political purposes.
3 For an earlier application of Brecht's theory of estrangement on VR-based technologies, see Dare (2020).

References

Andrejevic, M. and Volcic, Z. (2020). Virtual Empathy. *Communication, Culture & Critique*, 13(3), pp. 295–310. DOI: 10.1093/CCC/TCZ035

Baía Reis, A., Vasconcelos A.F. and Coelho, C.C. (2018). Virtual Reality Journalism: A Gateway to Conceptualizing Immersive Journalism. *Digital Journalism*, 6(8), pp. 1090–1100. DOI: 10.1080/21670811.2018.1502046

Bailenson, J.N. (2018). *Experience on Demand: What Virtual Reality Is, How It Works, and What It Can Do*. New York: W.W. Norton.

Bazin, A. and Gray, H. (1971). *What is Cinema? Vol. 2*. Berkeley, CA: University of California Press.

Bernays, E. (1928). *Propaganda*. New York: H. Liveright.

Boal, A. (1979). *Theatre of the Oppressed*. London: Pluto Press.

Boal, A. (2002). *Games for Actors and Non-Actors* (2nd ed.). London: Routledge.

Boczkowski, P.J. (2005). *Digitizing the News: Innovation in Online Newspapers*. Cambridge: MIT Press.

Brecht, B. (1957). *Schriften zum Theater: Über eine nicht-aristotelische Dramatik*. [Writings on theatre: about a non-Aristotelian drama]. Frankfurt: Suhrkamp Verlag.

Butler, J. (2004). *Precarious Life: The Powers of Mourning and Violence*. London: Verso.

Butler, J. (2007). Torture and the Ethics of Photography. *EPD: Society & Space* 25(6), pp. 951–966. DOI:10.1068/d2506jb

Butler, J. (2009). *Frames of War: When Is Life Grievable?* London: Verso.

Crouch, C. (2004). *Post-Democracy: A Sociological Introduction*. London: Polity Press.

Dare, E. (2020). Diffracting Virtual Realities: Towards an A-Effected VR. *Performance Research*, 25(5), pp. 101–106. DOI: 10.1080/13528165.2020.1868851

Dauphinée, E. (2007). The Politics of the Body in Pain: Reading the Ethics of Imagery. *Security Dialogue*, 38(2), pp. 139–155. DOI: 10.1177/0967010607078529

Dean, J. (2009). *Democracy and Other Neoliberal Fantasies*. Durham: Duke University Press.

De la Peña, N., Weil, P., Llobera, J., Giannopoulos, E., Pomés, A., Spanlang, B., Friedman, D., Sanchez-Vives, M. and Slater, M. (2010). Immersive Journalism: Immersive Virtual Reality for the First-Person Experience of News. *Presence*, 19, pp. 291–301. DOI:10.1162/PRES_a_00005

Falke, C. (2019). Framing Embodiment in Violent Narratives. In: E. Dahl, C. Falke and T.E. Eriksen (eds.), *Phenomenology of the Broken Body*, pp. 66–82. Abingdon, Oxon: Routledge.

Hasler, B.S., Landau, D.H., Hasson, Y., Schori-Eyal, N., Giron, J., Levy, J. ... and Friedman, D. (2021). Virtual Reality-Based Conflict Resolution: The Impact of Immersive 360° Video on Changing View Points and Moral Judgment in the Context of Violent Intergroup Conflict. *New Media & Society*, 23(8), pp. 2255–2278. DOI:10.1177/1461444821993133

Jones, S. (2017). Disrupting the Narrative: Immersive Journalism in Virtual Reality. *Journal of Media Practice*, 18(2–3), pp. 171–185. DOI: 10.1080/14682753.2017.1374677

Kozol, W. (2014). *Distant Wars Visible: The Ambivalence of Witnessing*. Minneapolis: University of Minnesota Press.

McRoberts, J. (2018). Are We There Yet? Media Content and Sense of Presence in Non-Fiction Virtual Reality. *Studies in Documentary Film*, 12(2), pp. 101–118. DOI: 10.1080/17503280.2017.1344924

Milk, C. (2015). How Virtual Reality Can Create the Ultimate Empathy Machine. *TED Talks* (April 22). www.youtube.com/watch?v=iXHil1TPxvA

Nakamura, L. (2020). Feeling Good about Feeling Bad: Virtuous Virtual Reality and the Automation of Racial Empathy. *Journal of Visual Culture*, 19(1), pp. 47–64. DOI: 10.1177/1470412920906259

Nash, K. (2018). Virtual Reality Witness: Exploring the Ethics of Mediated Presence. *Studies in Documentary Film*, 12(2), pp. 119–131. DOI: 10.1080/17503280.2017.1340796

Pedwell, C. (2014). *Affective Relations: The Transnational Politics of Empathy*. Basingstoke: Palgrave Macmillan.

Penz, O. and Sauer, B. (2020). *Governing Affects: Neoliberalism, Neo-Bureaucracies, and Service Work*. Abingdon, Oxon: Routledge.

Pimentel, D., Kalyanaraman, S., Lee, Y.H. and Halan, S. (2021). Voices of the Unsung: The Role of Social Presence and Interactivity in Building Empathy in 360° Video. *New Media & Society*, 23(8), pp. 2230–2254. DOI: 10.1177/1461444821993124

Pötzsch, H. (2012). Imag(in)ing Painful Pasts: Mimetic and Poetic Style in War Films. In: A. Grønstad and H. Gustafsson (eds.), *Ethics and Images of Pain*. London: Routledge, pp. 251–278.

Robertson, A. (2016). The virtual reality of Sundance, Day 2: hate is the purest emotion. *The Verge* [Online]. 25th of January. www.theverge.com/2016/1/24/10820778/sundance-2016-virtual-reality-immersive-journalism-experiences

Rose, M. (2018). The Immersive Turn: Hype and Hope in the Emergence of Virtual Reality as a Nonfiction Platform. *Studies in Documentary Film*, 12(2), pp. 132–149.

Ruberg, B. (2020). Empathy and Its Alternatives: Deconstructing the Rhetoric of 'Empathy' in Video Games. *Communication, Culture & Critique*, 13(1), pp. 54–71.

Salzmann, L. (2000). *Anselm Kiefer and Art after Auschwitz*. Cambridge: Cambridge University Press.

Sánchez Laws, A.L. (2020a). *Conceptualising Immersive Journalism*. Abingdon, Oxon: Routledge.

Sánchez Laws, A.L. (2020b). Can Immersive Journalism Enhance Empathy? *Digital Journalism*, 8(2), pp. 213–228.

Sánchez Laws, A.L. and Utne, T. (2019). Ethics Guidelines for Immersive Journalism. *Frontiers in Robotics and AI*, 6(28), pp. 1–13. DOI:10.3389/frobt.2019.00028

Schlembach, R. and Clewer, N. (2021). 'Forced Empathy': Manipulation, Trauma, and Affect in Virtual Reality Film. *International Journal of Cultural Studies*, 24(5), pp. 827–843.

Sontag, Susan (2003). *Regarding the Pain of Others*. London: Penguin Books.

Souppouris, A. (2016). VR Helped Me Grasp the Life of a Transgender Wheelchair User: 'The Circle' Uses VR's Strengths and Weaknesses to Help You Be Someone Else. *Engadget*, 17th of October. www.engadget.com/2016-10-17-the-circle-vr-manos-agianniotakis-nfts-games.html?guccounter=1.

8
JOURNALISM, TECHNOLOGY AND TRUTH IN THE AGE OF DIGITAL

Robert Hassan

A new immersivity

Mark Zuckerberg, the primary force behind the creation of the Meta platform, wagered the success of this new entity on the concept of digital immersivity. Launched in 2021, he dubbed his bold venture the 'metaverse'; a term drawn from Neal Stephenson's 1992 sci-fi novel *Snow Crash*, to describe a hyper-realistic immersive experience. In Zuckerberg's projected manifestation, advanced computation will construct digital representations of life that will be hardly distinguishable from physical reality; and through immersivity, the metaverse will parallel with the physical world and will eventually merge seamlessly with it. This was a combination of high-finance risk and technological hubris that was reported widely at the time (e.g., Chen, 2022). This soon dissipated, however, as the Meta CEO showed his determination by characteristically going his own way with a corporation that he largely controls anyway. Nonetheless, the success or otherwise of Meta depends upon the Zuckerbergian expectation that immersivity is an idea that is both practicable and whose time has come.

However, there is more than the future of Meta riding on the bet. Much of platform capitalism is also heavily invested, in their different ways, in a future where a digitally created and highly absorbing user experience can bring continuing profitability to the corporate bottom line. And of course, there is more again at stake than simply profit or loss for the platforms. The digital future they are building involves us all. The future is irreversibly digital and so the form it takes matters deeply for the kind of worlds it creates. At one level, the issues before us are those of political choice, technological feasibility and economic viability—choices which at present are in the possession of a global elite who are disinclined to give much of a say to the rest of us (Miller, 2018). But there are also the deeper philosophical issues emerging from the construction of a virtual world, such as the nature of the 'real'; what constitutes 'knowledge'; what is the status of a 'fact' and how do these questions impinge upon the construction of a society, civil and political, a world that is (or can be) democratic, inclusive and connected to the material and physical realities of nature, the problems of climate change and how we communicate with our fellow humans.

The user experience of immersivity has been ably critiqued in these pages and elsewhere and from a wide diversity of perspectives. There is no point in echoing the perceptive accounts offered here. What this chapter will do is to take a rather different view. It is one that has journalism at its core, but it goes to the techno-logical and social roots of the problem of immersivity. And in the specific context of journalism, it argues that the historical, philosophical, political and technological traditions of the profession are being choked-off by digitality. This means that what journalism has contributed to modernity and the modern world is being left to decline and degenerate (into what is labelled 'legacy' media) within a post-modernity characterised by the propelling force of a late-capitalist rationalisation of the world through the logic of digital.

The idea that 'Facebook is killing journalism and democracy' (Atkins, 2021) is a common one today. However, much of the criticism directed towards the platforms—from policymakers, the media and from the academy—is focused (often quite rightly) at the level of political economy, which identifies the main danger as being the immense power of these new monopolies in that most crucial of spheres, the public sphere. This essay does not avoid the political economy approach, far from it. However, the problem of immersivity and journalism is guided by deeper concerns (and wider perspectives) that draw from a synthesis of *philosophical anthropology*, which is deals with the human relationship with technology and an adapted *critical media theory* that holds the 'promise' of technology up to the light of Enlightenment reason.

This approach also rests upon the idea, developed from computer and technology studies, that analogue and digital are fundamentally two *different categories of technology*, meaning that each has different logics, and each affect the world and the human interaction with technology in very different ways (Hassan, 2020). This approach further argues that *humans themselves* are analogue and so essentially incompatible with the more instrumental and mathematical logic of digital and the worlds it brings into being. Digital immersivity, therefore, is argued to be an estranging and abstract world that corresponds more to the needs of a rationalizing late-capitalism, than to the analogue worlds and analogue technologies (and the analogue human) that gave rise to journalism in the early modern period.

The essay has two parts: first it will describe the techno-logic of digital and how the adoption of ubiquitous computing has been the largely unwitting embrace of a 'category error' in our relationship with technology. We failed to follow the maxim of Australian media theorist Chris Cheshire, who wrote that at the vital ontological level we must understand that 'The distinction between digital and analogue representation is philosophical before it is technical' (1997, 40). And so, in the words of Caleb Madison in his critique of digital immersion, we blithely operate under the category error of mistaking 'abstraction for transcendence' (2022). This lack of philosophical reflection means that over the last 30 years we have rapidly constructed a world now dominated by digital – a digitality that functions as an alien sphere for humans in much of their endeavours due to the logic of digital itself, which is oriented towards the abstraction of the human subject from the material worlds from where humans originated and evolved as analogue beings. Second, the essay will devote the bulk of the analysis to an elaboration of our analogue essence, to show how, through our deep and mutually shaping interaction with analogue technologies, created an *analogue immersive reality* based upon a material subjectivity. Journalism, of course, emerged from this world and this culture and as we shall see, this was based upon the irreducibly analogue communication tools, the 'means of production' that is writing and reading—analogue technologies that we will compare with their digital equivalents, especially in the realm of immersive virtual reality (VR). Let us begin, however, with an analysis with the essence of the new immersivity, digital logic.

Digital and digitality

When the behavioural scientist R.W. Gerard defined analogue logic as being 'continuous' and digital as 'discontinuous' he helpfully illustrated it in the following way:

> The prototype of the analogue is the slide rule, where a number is represented as a distance and there is continuity between greater distance and greater number. The prototype (of the digital) is the abacus, where the bead on one half of the wire is not counted at all, while that on the other half is counted as a full unit. … In the analogical system there are continuity relations; in the digital, discontinuity relations.
>
> 1953: 172

Gerard was describing his part in the Macy Cybernetics Conference series that ran from 1946 to 1953. The 1950 event was titled 'Some of the Problems Concerning Digital Notions in the Central Nervous System'. A group of prominent philosophers and scientists convened to try to understand the nature of digital logic as it pertained to psychology, computing and other fields. However, little conceptual headway was made beyond a reinforcing of the assumption that the human body was compatible with digital logic and that the digital computer would someday be sophisticated enough to replicate the functioning of the brain. The more philosophically reflexive aspects of the question were hardly discussed. The Cold War was just beginning, and geopolitical pressures meant that digital computing's capacities would be seen through a particularly narrow lens. Consequently, massive US military-industrial complex research funding programs into digital's supposed superiority over analogue in terms of speed, efficiency and flexibility, ensured its future as preferred computational mode. The assumptions about digital being able to imitate the human brain persisted and developed in tandem. Indeed, the assumption dominates still, with research into artificial intelligence at the leading edge of computer science.

Organisational management theorists François-Xavier de Vaujany and Natalie Mitev reviewed the 1950 conference and saw it as marking a turning-point in computer history. For them it helped establish the techno-ideology of the 'philosophy of the digital' which set in stone the concept of the brain as computer. The conference also helped generate the growth in influence of so-called representational philosophy within the field of computer science—a concept that argues that the world and its objects can be signified and 'manipulated according to logical rules to become "computable" symbols'. Physical reality, in other words, can be faithfully represented by computer code. Imprecise and 'incomputable' human characteristics such as 'emotions, sense-making and embodiment' were considered too subjective and so 'not part of the design or description of…information processes' (2017: 380). Such a view has important consequences, because, as we will see, the philosophy of the digital *in practice* inserted a disconnect between human and tool that follows from the 'discontinuous' logic of digital—and this has implications for the craft of the journalist.

The failure of digital to embody the subjective consciousness of humans is one thing, but its inability to represent also became evident within human communication—a process at the very centre of our digital age. In 1967, Paul Watzlawick published a highly original work in the psychology of communication titled, *The Pragmatics of Human Communication*. The book's central claim is startling when considered in the context of the hegemony of digital communication today. Watzlawick argues that the 'quantizing' or 'discrete' logic of digital (as compared with analogue) cannot dependably reproduce human verbal and non-verbal communication. He writes:

> In digital computers both data and instructions are processed in the form of numbers so that often … there is only an arbitrary correspondence between the particular piece of information and its digital expression.
>
> *41–42*

The book goes on to argue that where human communication has a 'content and relationship aspect' and where 'relationship is the central issue in communication', then 'digital language is almost meaningless' (44–45). What digital lacks is an 'adequate vocabulary' for the infinite possibilities that exist within human communication; and so 'not only can there be no translation from the digital into the analogic mode without great loss of information … but the opposite is extraordinarily difficult' (ibid.).

The discontinuity that governs digital representation thus produces interstices in the reproduction process, leading to what can only be called 'missing information'. This was noticed at the subjective level by the environmentalist Bill McKibben who, in a 1992 book titled *The Age of Missing Information*, reasoned that the 'information explosion' of the computer age produced a communication system that disrupts and disconnects as much as it connects, creating numerous cracks and voids in our knowledge of 'who we are' (1992: 9). Moreover, he argues that 'missing information' is not simply ignorance of certain knowledge or facts that may have slipped through the gaps in our communication via digital, but the beginnings of an analogue-level *withdrawal* from each other, from nature and from 'most of our physical sense of the world' (1992: 34).

It's possible to see that the 'missing information' coming from digital's inability to reproduce analogue communication with fidelity leads to another problem—that of the 'recognition' (or lack of it) that the anthropologist Silvia Estévez argues to be a key element of the human–digital relationship (2009: 401). We will look at Estévez's important work shortly. Moving forward, the logic of digital is so alien, so different from our evolved relationship with technology, that we cannot easily understand or recognise its functioning as technology. Even complex analogue technologies we can recognise readily because we can apprehend their functioning in our bodies or in nature. For example, in the early 20th century, people might have been astonished at the sight of the airplane in the sky, but they could nonetheless 'grasp' the logic of its action. And in 1969, people may have been thrilled by the satellite signals that beamed grainy television pictures back from the surface moon, but they could understand how this was done. However, the digital computer, the omnipresent mobile phone, the networks that give them existence and for our purposes, the VR immersive experience, are extremely difficult to comprehend in a 'way that allow us to grasp the link between a movement and its effect, the process, the continuity.' The 'black box' proprietary logic of the devices that surround us is only one aspect of our lack of 'recognition' of digital devices. The entire system is beyond the understanding of any of us and there's little or nothing in our history or in our relationship with technology that can give us the cultural bearings or technological coordinates to be able to recognise and follow the logic that drives a 'movement and its effects' within a virtual time and space that digital compresses into a real-time instant.

McLuhan's 'extension' thesis is a serviceable way to understand what the disconnect that digital has inserted between humans and the world has done. With digital we extend differently from the analogue extension where, as McLuhan puts, it the '…Indian (sic) is the servomechanism (extension) of his canoe, as the cowboy of his horse or the executive of his clock' (1964: 55). Digital extension is *cognitive* extension into *virtual* time and space. There has been nothing like this before; it is literally unrecognizable to us, yet we do it freely and largely accept, consciously or unconsciously, digital's technological predicates. And following the logic of digital, the extension constitutes a profound cognitive disconnection. When online we exist virtually and physically at the same time, with the latter being subsumed by the former. As we gaze at the VR display, for example, we cross into the liminal space of virtuality, leaving the physical and material world behind. This disengagement is something McLuhan sensed in his 'extension' theory when he said that it was also a form of 'narcosis', a kind of 'numbness', or as he put it more graphically, an 'autoamputation' from the analogue world (1964: Ch. 4). In my reading, digital 'autoamputation' is also a form of alienation, one more radical than McLuhan's, or even that of Marx in his writings on the subject. It takes two forms. First, we are alienated from the technology itself, from the computer and its workings and capacities and digital representations that are inherently alien and unrecognisable to us as analogue creatures. Second, we are alienated by the virtual worlds that digital creates—and of which we a part, but not. This is a generalised alienation stemming from the cognitive-virtual experience that Leonardo Impett (2018) terms 'the alienation of the technological everyday'. Digitality thus provides for a *double-alienation* from both technology and material world.

This is a different relationship with technology. For Rahel Jaeggi, who has written a ground-breaking book on the subject, alienation has achieved a new level of completeness in a world where connection and meaning have become free-floating and virtualised through digital automation. Automation has been a core capacity of digital that has attracted capitalism and the military to it. And digitality has inserted automation into much of our post-modern existence. From the factory and office to leisure and education, automation infiltrates increasing registers of production and consumption across all social, cultural and economic life. Automation *appropriates* us by creating contexts for us which determine much of how we produce and consume, live and work. Digital automation doesn't alienate in a way that suggests a total severing of our connections; it's more a relation of domination, but in a special context. Jaeggi called it heteronomy, a lack of mastery over ourselves and our individual contexts and as 'having one's properties determined by another…the complete absence of essential properties or substances'. It is a virtuality-generated vacuum that creates the absence of a relation with the technology and the skills of using and comprehending it in ways that correspond with our evolutionary analogue essence. As Jaeggi puts it: 'Alienation is a relation of relationlessness' and '…is a failure to apprehend and a halting of, the movement of appropriation' (2014: 1).

The physics of digital and analogue suggest a profound differentiation in their respective logics. At the micro-level they express as 'discontinuous' and 'continuous', respectively. This matters when scaled up to the level of machine technology and especially when implemented to be vectors for human communication. The difference when seen from the perspective comparison of human use is a fundamental disconnect between digital processes and analogue humans. In the social realm of experience of and interaction with technology the rise to dominance of digital thus renders us suspended within the void of the loss of a relationship: a 'relation of relationlessness' with which we have analogically evolved and with what we have become in a mere few decades in our self- re-creation through digital.

A reflexive philosophical understanding of what constitutes digital has, in our breakneck adoption of computation in almost every register of life, been sidelined—sacrificed on the capitalist altar of efficiency and productivity. Along the way, the loss of a material-analogue connection with technology has meant, in the words of Jacques Ellul, that we operate, in our alienated state, or the basis of 'reflex' instead of 'reflection' (1992). This occurs everywhere, from education, to the political process and to the practice of journalism.

To the second part of the essay and to reflect upon journalism—a defence of journalism—as an essentially analogue technology-based profession; a skilled craft that is (or was) founded upon one of our most monumental human achievements—the technology of writing and what writing enabled in the describing and recording of the 'reality' of things in the social world.

Technology, truth and the story

A certain concept of truth-telling has been central to journalism since its early-modern beginnings. For much of its history it was an ethic or ideal rooted in the soil of Enlightenment metaphysics; an acceptance of the idea of the truth-value, where truth existed in opposition to falsehood. This idea of truth was given weight of legitimacy and concreteness by the relatively swift evolution of a journalistic writing profession, or craft, which carved out its own distinctive space in the emerging mass societies of Europe and North America. Journalism held itself to a different standard from other writing activities. It was different from the search for the truth of the 'laws' of nature that was the domain of the scientist; different from the search for meaning pursued by the philosopher; different from the alternative realities in the imagined worlds of the novelist; and different from the hack writing of Grub Street. Of course, all these forms overlapped within journalism and writers historically made a living where they could in what was always a fundamentally commercial occupation.

Nonetheless, this journalistic truth, in its high-idealistic sense, the kind that sought to 'speak truth to power' has, again since early modern times, been contained within the protective layers of technology and politics. Suitably equipped journalism was the means to an end that was supposed to be a written *fact*, a storied *accuracy and a* published *true account* of what the Uruguayan journalist Eduardo Galeano called the 'realities of the world' (cited in Younge, 2013). Truth-seeking presupposed the existence of its object, something to be found and held up for the world to see (and to recognise) to be a fact.

Speaking truth to power was always risky business. At least 2297 journalists were killed between 1990 and 2015, according to the International Federation of Journalists (IFJ.org, 2016). It invited opprobrium, imprisonment, exile or death from those exposed unfavourably by truth. Journalism provokes reaction like no other profession. The ideal-typical journalist thus required not only personal bravery, but also an imbued sense of Kantian-inspired duty to a moral principle whose 'value' was contained in the ethical structuring of the method. There was a 'right' thing to do, or way to act, one based on the conviction that one's position is based upon an objective fact, upon a truth to be revealed and narrated and made public and thereby given the stamp of legitimacy; an objective truth. We see an early example in the work of Tom Paine, author of the revolutionary anti–monarchical *Common Sense* of 1776. A counterblast to authority and its abuses, it stands as representative of the journalistic craft emerging through the relatively new media technology of mechanical print. In it, Paine wrote that 'We have it in our power to begin the world over again' (1982[1776]: 119). And through the printed word, he believed, 'we see with other eyes; we hear with other ears; and think with other thoughts, than those we formerly used.' The printed word not only foregrounded truth through written declarations but could also transform how the reader saw the world.

The world may not necessarily have begun again, as Paine had hoped, but it has certainly changed, through mass media and its public spheres. The contemporary journalist's technique, shaped by the hand and mind of writers such as George Orwell, John Hersey, Bob Woodward and Carl Bernstein and more latterly, Barbara Ehrenreich, Marie Colvin and Anna Politkovskaya, to name just some, brought idealism, dedication and ethical commitment to realms as diverse (and connected) as ideology, corruption and conflict. And these were often influenced by politics, either those of the journalist or their object of investigation and often shaped by the integration of both. In important ways, journalists wrote the first and sometimes the final draft of history, enabling the world to be seen anew in positive or negative ways, depending on the nature of the truths they revealed.

The printed word gave truth cognitive reality and the truth-claim a trustworthiness. Purported facts took on the quality of truth simply because they were written down. Literacy was the key to the door of truth; and knowledge of truth was an immense advantage in early modern societies where the ability to read and write was limited. Importantly, journalism gave access to knowledge through a mode already familiar to peoples and cultures. The ancient practice of *storytelling* was imported into it and this gave a readily understood narrative coherence to the journalist's arrangements of facts and truth-claims. This has been part of the communicative power of writing since its invention. Journalism therefore uses writing and print in the same way that the Greek philosophers speculated about the world, in the same ways that Confucius wrote the *Four Books* and *Five Classics* (see Nylan, 2001) and in the same ways that the various chroniclers of the life and sayings of Jesus and Mohammed did to create the 'revealed truths' that exist as cognitive reality for billions to this day.

It follows that any purported fact or truth must be documented – must be written down – else they reside only as phantasms in the head of the individual or group; or, like the sound of the tree falling in an unpeopled forest, it did not happen for all human intents and purposes. In journalism, the technology, the truth and the story have combined over that past 300 years to bring a documented version of reality that has been completely dependent upon its constituent parts: the technology as the fundamental generative element; truth as the metaphysical concept given reality or correspondence to the 'way things actually are' by the technology; and the narrating of the story as the way the technology unfolds its logic.

All this is to say that *words matter* – and printed ones most particularly. For example, the facts surrounding the killing of George Floyd by police officers in May 2020, a death recorded for its entire eight minutes and forty-six seconds duration, was made 'real' not by the supremely graphic video on its own, which cannot speak for itself, but by how the video was interpreted: in the streets as a printed slogan, in the media, through social and mainstream reporting and commentary, by written witness testimony and by a state-appointed jury directed by legal and forensic experts in the trial of Derek Michael Chauvin. The truth arises and stabilises through words, spoken and especially written. Walter Ong, echoing Tom Paine, described the power of the written word entering the heads of people. He wrote that 'Writing is a technology that restructures thought' (1986: 23). It places truth in a different position to subjective perception. To write is to claim a truth and to place it 'out there' in the public sphere; to read it is to *internalise* the truth so to accept or reject it. This is an insight we can conceptually enrich using the rather more dialectically inclined Marshall McLuhan who argued that we make tools (writing) and in their turn tools (writing) remake us (Culkin, 1967).

These interactions are shaped also by ideology, a truth backed by power and the means to disseminate itself. And when certain ideologies become dominant, even for a short time, then journalistic truths and therefore social facts can take almost any form. Accordingly, the journalistic weapon of truth pitted against power has a mixed historical record. In the West during the 19th and 20th centuries, tabloid and broadsheet could be both toxic and fearless in their gathering and interpretating of truth and fact. There existed an ideologically inflected mass media spectrum, where truth and fact could range from hate speech and propaganda (*Der Stürmer* in Nazi Germany and *Pravda* in the Soviet Union) to bland conservativism (*Le Figaro* in France) to liberal democratic (*New York Times*)—and everything else in between. Moreover, if we accept, even partially, the Noam Chomsky 'agenda setting' thesis, then ideology and its means of expression emanate, at root, from media's commercial foundations. This is so even if journalists may view themselves as personally ethical. And so, technology, truth and story are connected by and potentially compromised with, the logic of the marketplace. The journalist's handling of truths and facts are necessarily assembled and distributed through what Régis Debray termed 'the communication networks that enable thought to have social existence' – and these networks have traditionally been devoted to money-making (2007: 5). Through such an inherently business-based process, truth morphed from being an 18th-century aspiration of the *philosophes*, something underlying and universal to be sought and found, to eventually reveal itself a commodity, something to be bought and sold and always contingent upon the flux of market forces. The commodification that underlies journalism has always been a truth that does not readily speak its name.

Nevertheless, the truth-seeking ideals of journalism still shine like beacons of light from its Enlightenment-era philosophy. However, human timber is crooked, as Kant (1784) maintained, and imperfection is the essence of the species. Ideals are abstract standards and life is messy. But journalism deals in a *special* commodity, which is truth, as conveyed through its special means of production – which is the technology of writing and its narrative construction.

Technology, truth and story thus encompass the idealised constituent parts of my theorisation of journalism. These are indissolubly connected parts. The connections between them throw critical light onto the immersive, VR-generated technology that is claimed to be a new literacy, a 'new journalistic tool' that will open the door to the 'frontlines' of experience where truth or reality no longer needs to be storied or revealed in words but rendered digitally and virtually through 'a new storytelling medium' that can 'fundamentally change journalism' (VICE News, 2015). Moving along, we want to reveal those connections through why we have seen as my understanding of the relatively unassuming (and endangered) term *analogue*. This is analogue acting as both *technological and human quality*. And the analogue connections will show the futuristic claims for digital immersivity and for a digital journalism as a form of technological progress and therefore a richer relationship with objective truths—are deeply problematic.

So let us consider the connections.

Analogue, writing and the journalist

Writing and reading is both cause and effect of what the journalist does. Journalist writes, reader reads. Truth is claimed and truth is (sometimes) recognised. Writing and reading are also technological in that they are capacities created through what anthropologist Arnold Gehlen termed 'replacement techniques', tools which act as auxiliary for capacities not inherently possessed by humans (1980: 49). The technology of reading and writing, moreover, is analogue. The crucial addendum to this uncontroversial claim is that as writing and reading are analogical, so also are we. Humans, in other words, are analogue creatures.

That we are analogue is a question, a realisation, that has become conceivable only in the present age of digital. For most of the history of human thought, the question 'are we analogue?' did not readily suggest itself. At most, tools were understood as extensions: the hammer the extension of the hand, the telescope the extension of the eye, etc. This is what McLuhan and others argued a long time ago. However, the more fruitful idea that the analogue tool is not simply an extension, something 'apart' from us, but is *integral* to an evolved species being, was not something we tended to ask. This absence of curiosity is understandable because there was nothing to contrast and compare analogue tools with, nothing that would make salient the analogue nature of the tool and so bring into question our relationship with it.

The arrival of digital technology changed this. Digital tools represent another category of tool, a different logic with different foundations, objectives and effects. A useful way to think about the difference was in R.W. Gerard's distinction (noted above) that analogue processes are 'continuous' whereas digital are 'discontinuous'. The continuity–discontinuity paradigm is at the source of the analogue–digital distinction. To consider more fully the distinction, however, we draw from both classical and contemporary anthropology. In the 1940s, Arnold Gehlen helped create the field of 'philosophical anthropology', where the science-based approach of the latter was fused with reflective and speculative method of the former. His book *Man in the Age of Technology* analysed the evolutionary process of human–technology interaction. For Gehlen, *Homo Sapiens* are born 'unfinished' and could not have survived without the long and tortuous evolutionary drift towards tool making – the single most important metamorphosis that enabled us to cling to life instead of suffering extinction. From our earliest prehistory, tool use was interactive and generated by materials drawn from our immediate natural surroundings, such as wood, stone, flint and workable metals. Gehlen called this process the 'circle of action' where, as he put it, the association with technology 'goes through object, eye and hand and which in returning to the object conclude(s) itself and begins anew' (1980: 19). He continues:

> ...the analogous process of the external world bespeaks a 'resonance' which conveys to man an intimate feeling for his very nature, by focusing on what echoes his nature in the external world. And if we today still speak of the 'course' of the stars and of the 'running of machines', the similarities thus evoked are not in the least superficial; they convey to men certain distinctive conceptions of their own essential traits based on 'resonance'. Through these similarities man interprets the world after his own image and vice-versa, himself after his image of the world
>
> 14

The 'circle of action' and the 'resonance' that it stimulates with both the tool and the action upon the world it enables, signified a oneness with technology. It endowed a capacity that enabled survival within the context of the chaos of random forces that assailed all of nature. This interaction was cognitive as well as physical and it allowed humans to innovate and develop tools to shape their world according to the diversity of social and environmental contexts that confronted them.

More recently, anthropology has reflected on our analogue nature from the perspective of digital technology functioning as *another category* of technology. Silvia Estévez, whose work we touched on briefly, noticed the dissonance that digital brings. In her fieldwork on Ecuadoran migrant workers and their mobile phone use, she concludes that we are 'analogue human beings' who are very different from computers and do not interact very well with them (2009: 393–410). Our relationship with analogue machines is ancient and resonant in the ways that Gehlen describes. But she argues that our association has another characteristic that makes the contrast with digital tools even more stark. Analogue machines, even complex ones such as automobiles or airplanes, are resonant with us and our physical world, because they have operations that 'simulate processes that people had seen before in nature and in their own bodies' (402). In other words, we intuitively *recognise* what they do and how they do it. Estévez continues, analogue technology's activity '... crosses time and space in a visible way that allow us to grasp the link between a movement and its effect, the process, the continuity' (401).

Note the word 'continuity'. Also note the term 'recognition'. Both speak to the intimate connection, physical and cognitive, that humans have with analogue technology. The process goes deep into our essential nature as technological creatures; beings who cannot survive without technology but did because of the evolutionary drift that made us as one with the tools we invented.

Writing

Writing, or the 'technologizing of the word' as Walter Ong (1982) termed it, has a special place in human history. Not only did it transform language, the most profound and consequential of human achievements, but it also changed *consciousness* and what it meant to be human. Around 3500 BCE, the oral cultures that rose from language saw the symbols of their imminent annihilation with the appearance of the written word. A new way of thinking, a new way of seeing and most importantly, a new way of communicating was to change profoundly the course of human affairs. So deep was the transformation, indeed, that its significance is difficult to put into words. We get a sense of it only when one tries to imagine an alternative path that our species might have taken without writing... something almost impossible to imagine.

A principal effect of writing was that the interiority of consciousness that triggered the sound that uttered the spoken word through language, became exteriorised. And with print, the aeons-old culture of primary orality, of physical speech and of mental thought, could now almost magically, exist 'out there' in time and space in a form detached and autonomous from their author. This 'independent' discourse contained an immense social and cultural power. As Ong puts it:

> Like the oracle or the prophet, the (book) relays an utterance from a source, the one who really 'said' or wrote the book. The author might be challenged if only he or she could be reached, but the author cannot be reached in any book. There is no way to directly refute a text. ... This is one reason why 'the book says' is popularly tantamount to 'it is true'.
>
> 77

'It is written' says the Bible in various places, meaning that which is written is true. This vatic quality has attached itself to most writing forms and to serious journalism, especially. What gave the printed word the appearance of truth is that the words themselves, the information, the meaning that exists and springs up from a page when it is read, are given the power of actuality by the very fact of their being on a page. For Ong this is the power of 'closure'. Printed words, especially in cultures where literacy was minimally spread and a privilege, contained an 'aura' of authority, presenting to the reader as true and 'uninvolved with all else...somehow self-contained, complete' (129). Being 'complete' meant there was nothing else to be said. It is written and so seemingly objective, existing in splendid isolation and therefore authoritative and true.

Writing drew from oral culture in that the method of communication was narrativised. Writing told a story in the same way that oral cultures had done for millennia. They stored, organised and communicated through the narrative markers that functioned as *aides-memoire*. From the Bible to the Quran and from Marx's *Capital* to Freud's *Civilization and its Discontents*, the last two chosen at random, the major texts, the writings that had great influence on humankind, told stories in the same narrativised format that had allowed pre-literate cultures to absorb mythic tales of gods and ghosts and monsters and heroes from their shaman.

The Enlightenment and the print culture it spawned, created ideas and discourses in number and variety as never seen before. The *philosophes*, the pamphleteers, the natural scientists, the economist, the lawmaker, the journalist and the public, debated and polemicised within this new 'republic of letters', to create a world effervescing with new ways of seeing and being. To 'dare to know!' is how Kant described what modernity and Enlightenment were about (Fleischacker, 2013: 13) and through reason the 'hidden truths' of the world that had been obscured by religion, superstition, monarchy and illiteracy were brought out into the light. Truth was thus placed at the centre of the project of Enlightenment and the modern era that it inaugurated. Truth in the search for the 'laws' of the natural world though science; truth through the implementation of reason in the pursuit of knowledge about the world; truth as the authority of the 'given word' as expressed in law and constitutions ('We hold these truths to be self-evident'); and truth disseminated throughout society by means of print media acting as society's self-reflection, by means of the technology of writing and literacy, as articulating the heights of human achievement.

Journalism

Such are the principled, ambitious and ideal-typical roots of journalism and once established its rhizome spread to become the pre-eminent engine of the public sphere. Journalism also developed an inherently political character. Tom Paine's call for 'power to begin the world again' (see Paine 1774–1779) placed journalism and its truth seeking squarely in the realm of politics and political systems. Political ideas, political strategies and political criteria were thus always at the core of its practice.

Paine was in fact relatively late to the scene of political journalism and its project to change the world as well as report on it. We see this in the literary-inflected advocacy and pamphleteering of someone like Jonathan Swift. As editor of *The Examiner*, a Tory Party-supporting newspaper (1710–1714) he would attack the policies of the ruling Whig Party and especially its failure to end the war with France. Pamphlet wars had been carried on in Britain since Tudor times but growing literacy and newspaper circulation in the late 17th and 18th century meant that the public sphere had journalism as its technological and informational centre. Moreover, as part of its truth-seeking mission, journalism adopted an investigative ethos. In the late-19th century, for example, Elizabeth Cochran, using the pen name Nellie Bly, practically invented the undercover investigative procedure. Simulating mental illness, Bly got admitted into the Women's Lunatic Asylum in New York and later published sensational accounts for the *New York World*, that led to sweeping reforms. It was a practise taken up rather more famously by George Orwell and Joan Didion who each in their own ways and for their own generations, sought to discover the truth of class and culture through a politics of ethics and justice by immersing themselves physically into the lives and realms of their subjects. Again, the reporting of such journalists could make a difference through the power of their storytelling to influence, inspire, motivate and change the consciousness of readers and society more broadly.

The journalists' tools of writing and the readers' mediated connection through words on paper created something special, something specific to humans and their relationships with technology and knowledge. The vatic aura of ink on paper generated something strongly akin to the anthropological 'resonance' that Gehlen speaks of in human tool use. We see too the 'recognition' involved in the analogue relationship where through the stories that journalists put 'out there' in time and space, readers can 'empathise' or not with what is being depicted. And this recognition establishes a connection, or the 'continuity' that is also a key feature of the human–analogue relation. McLuhan (1964) told us that the medium is the message, meaning what is important in a media form is not what it conveys – but what it enables. But if we consider writing and the craft of journalism, we can say also that the *message is the medium*. It is the information, the story, the narrative that has been embedded in the technology of writing since its invention. This is why writing is so extraordinary. However, because it transformed our consciousness long ago, such that we became what McLuhan (1962) called 'Typographic Man' (sic), we take the amazing qualities of writing and our relationship with it, for granted. We have forgotten that writing is a technology, forgotten that it is analogue. And we have barely begun to think that we are analogue beings who are deeply implicated with a technology that enables us to exteriorise our thoughts and words and so to extend ourselves into time and space and to inhabit that time-space in a way and with effects that are possible only with the affordances that writing allows.

Ethos, pathos, logos

We need to remember, or perhaps just to realise, that no newspaper or magazine or journal ever went online because its owners and editors dreamed that it would enhance the sibylline and truth-telling qualities of the storied and printed and narrative. The migration from print to digital was undertaken as a forced march towards economic survival within a late-capitalism powered by neoliberal ideology, one possessed by the conceit of profit via efficiency-through-automation in every sector of production in the economy—even in news. Readers were already moving *en masse* in search of 'free' news content and newspapers and journalists had to follow them and adopt the risky, digital-based business model of the platform to capture an ever-rising number of eyeballs.

In 1996 Mark Weiser predicted a future of 'ubiquitous computing' where people would be able to 'live through their practices and tacit knowledge so that the most powerful things are those that are effectively invisible in use' (in Gritzalis, et. al 2006, 2). We live that future now. The Internet of things, the mobile phone as extension for every brain, digital systems of production and consumption, education, entertainment, warfare and news media. Ubiquity became invisibility and the context for a 'relation of relationlessness' with the world and with each other. Immersivity is the positive-sounding, digitally rendered axiom through which we know, or think we know, or are persuaded to know by VR industry propaganda, the coming metaverse and its attendant technologies. But where is truth in a world where our 'practices and tacit knowledge' are formed not predominantly by the analogue tools that shaped us and expressed what we are, but by algorithms whose codes are a commercial secret, logics we are unable to scrutinise and therefore learn to recognise with, at least at some level?

What we are, was what we knew a very long time ago. And what we knew came to us through the ways that we expressed our truths in writing and stories. Aristotle told us in his *Rhetoric* that the techniques of persuasion: *ethos*, *pathos* and *logos* are what communicate the proof of something and therefore the truth of something. For Aristotle, persuasion was achieved through speech and writing (see Bartlett, 2019). And writing, for the journalist, is the means to proof and the vector of truth. Writing took on the mantle of the speaker, as we saw, but gave it a revolutionary twist. In the act of writing the story became detached from its author to become independent and fixed in time and space upon the printed page. Truth spoke for itself, for all time. *Ethos*—or the appeal to authority, was contained in the aura of the printed word. Truth was contained in the ethical code of journalism, in the reputation of the journalist and in the prestige of the publication. This was an analogue chain of recognition and a grasp of processes of getting to truth developed over 300 years of print culture and fourth estate politics. *Ethos* created a place, a space for truth through what Richard Rorty called the 'contingency of language', a process where 'truth is made rather than found', a truth held in place by the vatic aura of writing until a more persuasively written truth replaces it (1989: 3).

With digital visualisation, nothing is 'made', truth or otherwise, because words and images consist of nanoscopic points of light, pixels, discrete (discontinuous) and always on the verge of change, contingent upon code, upon the feedback loop that they respond to as part of their cybernetic control and upon a vast infrastructural network that has no centre and no source in time and space. This point is important, because, to quote Régis Debray the 'material forms and processes through which ideas were transmitted—the communication networks that enable thought to have social existence', are no longer material but virtual. Human thought and the truths it sought and held within the written text, now have a vast and virtual social existence that floods the networks as torrents of light. The effect upon the material craft of the journalist as truth-teller is drastic. The journalist Peter Pomerantsev:

> The grand vessels of old media—books, television, newspapers and radio—that had contained and controlled identity and meaning, who we were and how we talked with one another, how we explained the world to our children, talked about our past, defined war and peace, news and opinion, satire and seriousness, right and left, right and wrong, true, false, realm unreal—these vessels have cracked and burst, breaking up the old architecture of what relates to whom, who speaks to whom and how, magnifying, shrinking,

> distorting all proportions, sending us in disorienting spirals where words lose shared meaning.
>
> 2019: 177

The covenant between analogue writer and reader, one based upon *Ethos*, is thus weakened within the digital context. Immersive communication networks expose the contingency of language and reveal the difficulty in assuming any straight transference of the ancient powers of the word from analogue to digital without considerable loss in fidelity.

Pathos, or the appeal to emotion, is a persuasive element that can move the consciousness of the reader. This has always been at the heart of the journalist's writing craft, either to give illusion of truth to the falsehood, or to raise a truth or fact to the status of conviction. Or something in between. Injustice, outrage, joy and sadness are just some of the myriad emotions the journalist can elicit. Historical and contemporary examples are numerous. But to take just one: Charles Dickens as journalist. His most famous writings such as *The Pickwick Papers* and *Oliver Twist* were serialised longform pieces before they were published as books (Dickens 1836, 1838). They were popular sensations and drew public attention to the horrors of the workhouse system and widespread social deprivation in industrial Britain (see Badinjki, 2016; Kryger, 2012). It's fair to say that his stories helped create a climate of opinion against the exploitative excesses of industrialisation and for the passage of the reforms of the second half of the 19th century. My point is that the evocation of emotion, a key element of the journalist's writing skill, needs time; it needs the development of a relationship between the writer and reader, over months and years and generations to regularise the emotion and build it into the social consciousness. Otherwise, emotion is evanescent and weak. Just like the emotion of fanaticism, as ideologies like Nazism to Communism show, *Pathos* requires the persistent and consistent communication of stories and slogans and ideas to keep the ideology alive and potent. The analogue form—through its inherent features of continuity and the emotional connection that comes through the process of recognition—can do this in ways that digital immersion cannot.

Digital media does of course generate emotion within news. But it does so mostly in a negative and distorting form that is intentionally coded into its applications. Jaron Lanier, early Silicon Valley computer scientist and coiner of the term 'virtual reality', tells how algorithms in Twitter and Facebook create a 'manipulation engine'. They are programmed through rapid binary measurement in social media newsfeed and comments to 'catch the negativity and amplify it' (Lanier, 2018). Growing user engagement, in other words, is achieved by promoting conflict and fear as opposed to cooperation and deliberation and the business model is about user engagement by any means. Through algorithmic manipulation, users are corralled into their topic-based silos of dread and outrage and feed off each other's negative emotions to create a psychological atmosphere for greater negativity, conspiracy stories and paranoia, all of which are recycled continually through the platform's networks in an ongoing feedback loop. Professional journalists are not immune to this negativity.

Research suggests that the normalisation of Twitter, for example, has augmented homophily or groupthink amongst journalists, concentrating and amplifying *pathos as partisanship*, especially at election times (Hanusch and Nölleke, 2019: 28). Related research suggests that Twitter generates an 'emotional valence' and a 'tendency for individuals to interact with those expressing similar (negative) valence', especially on the conservative side of politics (Himelboim, et. al, 2016: 1383). Much of the partisanship in politics today is a digitally mediated emotion, generated by Lanier's 'manipulation engine' which draws journalism and civil society into a vortex of negative and destructive sentiment—and does so as an unanticipated consequence of the main game which is the production and harvesting of user data.

Zuckerberg's metaverse and sundry other VR ventures seem destined only to provide yet more scope for the platform's unchanging business model. Moreover, the application of infinite connections and stupendously more powerful computing power based on innovations in quantum and chemical computing processing will enlarge the model exponentially. According to Shaan Puri, tech entrepreneur and ex-CEO of the early social networking site, Bebo, the metaverse will become that '…moment in time where our digital life is worth more to us than our physical (sic) life.' (Puri, 2021). It may well be a 'moment in time' but it is a particular form of time. It will be governed by a 'network time' (Hassan, 2003) one that functions to erase the subjective-phenomenological times of experience and the objective time of the clock. And the supervening time of the network, as Lanier has argued, is engineered, as is most Internet-based applications, for the control and manipulation of the user. Moreover, the metaverse is also to be a moment in space, a virtual space of immersion where the senses respond to the awesome visual and aural digital representations; but no matter how powerful and awe-inspiring the experience at the level of superficiality, the irreducibly 'physical' user can never escape gravity and where the only form of human recognition is the incipient gnaw of hunger after a time and then the inescapable need to piss and shit.

In Aristotle's triad, *Logos*, or logic, is argument based upon reason. It is a vital journalistic instrument. Walter Ong reminds us that 'formal logic is the invention of Greek culture after it had interiorised the technology of alphabetic writing' producing 'the kind of thinking that alphabetic writing makes possible' (1982: 51). Comparative research supports this idea. Fieldwork conducted in the 1930s in remote Uzbekistan on illiterate (i.e., oral) cultures by Alexander Luria suggests that his subjects 'seemed not to operate with formal deductive reasoning' and their orally grounded logic would not fit into the formal logic that comes from alphabetic writing (in Ong 1982: 49). Literate cultures think in a different way from oral ones. The invention of writing set humanity upon a specific path, one governed by formal logic and reasoning. And with the scientific revolution logic became increasingly receptive to the 'certainties' of mathematics as evidence of the correctness of the approach. Alphabetised logic led not only to science but to the technological revolution of the 17th century and to the capitalist revolution which created the social relations based on production and consumption that dominate still.

Journalism entered the flow of these historical evolutions equipped with the certainties regarding truth and logic. However, as capitalism and the technological revolution caused 'all that is solid to melt into air', as Marx phrased it and as literate, modern societies became more instrumentally oriented, journalism clung its original ethos, with its original tools of storied writing and truth-telling. And as pamphlet wars gave way to the age of mass media, as mass media became the electronic global village and as media technology 'progress' continued right up unto the digital age, then analogue journalism's relevance in the lives of people as the vector for social consciousness and social change became attenuated as the volume and diversity of digital forms burgeoned. And in that burgeoning the function of *Logos* struggled to hold on to its audience. The 'grand vessel of old media', with journalism at the helm, today resembles more a directionless ghost ship, blown by the winds of markets powered by the logic of Silicon Valley's algorithms.

All this digital has left journalism and most of the rest of us, with an alienated connection to analogue legacies and institutions—the public sphere being one of them. The tremendous productive capacity of digital news media, in respect of content, takes us to where the logic of efficient production is no longer logical. Logic cannot easily be discerned and followed in story or argument when the virtual world heaves with information overload and content is classified and arranged according to code. The new logic ensures that the object of the 'manipulation engine' sees what the engine wants them to see, and the partial view of VR begins to stand in for a whole worldview. Using digital tools to tell stories and break news and furnish truth means that a digital journalism only amplifies an illogicality and deepens the immersive experience of it.

Postscript for a vanishing craft

Digitality and its VR applications are perhaps the greatest challenge to its purpose that journalism has ever faced. Indeed, it is a watershed for all of us as members of a public sphere and civil society. That the threat is largely invisible makes it all the more insidious. The immersive computing that is the growing element of economy, polity and society, is the immersive ideology of neoliberal late capitalism. The leap from analogue to digital in the name of connectivity and efficiency in the economy has consummated capitalism's global project. More by accident than design it has also created a vulgar and chaotic social media and Internet. These are where the externalities of economic globalisation have had their effect and like global warming, they are not easy to see. The transformation of our relationship with print strikes at the heart of the journalistic craft and ethos. Craft, because digital constitutes a different tool with which to work; and ethos, because the quality of truth has been drastically undermined. And without writing and without truth, journalism is nothing much beyond hack work. This is the danger, and this is the future if we do nothing. What's left of the fourth estate struggles to remain solvent by moving online and using digital methods as much as possible. Some of these methods may prove amenable to the digital native and therefore signal what the future may look like for a journalism of reason and truth. Longform journalism about important matters such as climate change, the reversal of aspects of globalisation, alt-right politics, China's rise, illiberalism in Europe, etc., are relatively cheap 'content' for the digital flux and these can be voiced by the author and repacked as a podcast and sent to a place where undivided attention and thus reflection are possible. But atomised journalist and atomised listener does not compare with an active public sphere.

Today digital atomisation continues apace. If 360° immersive goggle-wearing technology is advertised as a futuristic solution that will 'fundamentally change journalism', so too, then, are more recognisable forms such as the app/blog Substack whose inventors claim it to be how journalism can best adapt to the digital ecology. Here, underemployed journalists, or journalists who see the digital writing on the wall, can take to the Substack blog to write for whomever they can attract and will pay a fee. Critics see it as an endeavour not unlike Uber, where you are on your own by force of economic circumstance, with nothing but a writing skill which the app will distribute for you, for a ten per cent cut. With only the app as companion, you become wholly subject to the impulses of market forces. And so lacking infrastructures of support, editorial input and a developed readership, the Substack journalist must sink or swim by reading market signals and hope that the roulette odds favour them with every article. Truth and ethics can easily become a secondary consideration when writing into the vast unknown in search of scattered particles of readership.

But journalism is not dead yet. And analogue technology and the analogue process are not dead either. Both are of the lineage that gave the world literacy and a politically literate civic and civil society. And both still inform politics at the lowest and highest levels. The problem, fundamentally, is one of what might be called reflexive recognition. What digital journalism does to the craft needs to be seen for what it is—a different category of technology being used for an analogue process it cannot replicate. To recognise this would be the gaining of knowledge about ourselves and our world. But it would also be the acquisition of much needed political wisdom—for journalism, for the public and for the political class. Political will can emerge from this getting of wisdom: the will to recognise and change the unintended relationship we have with digital and not see computers as a solution in search of a problem, but as a tool whose limits and capacities we must understand and control.

Whilst writing the previous paragraph, an email arrived from a former publisher, the University of Westminster Press, informing of a new open access book titled: *The Public Service Media and Public Service Internet Manifesto*. It was eerily synchronous. The blurb read:

> The Internet and the media landscape are broken. The dominant commercial Internet platforms endanger democracy. They have created a communications landscape overwhelmed by surveillance, advertising, fake news, hate speech, conspiracy theories and algorithmic politics. Commercial Internet platforms have harmed citizens, users, everyday life and society. Democracy and digital democracy require Public Service Media. A democracy-enhancing Internet

requires Public Service Media becoming Public Service Internet platforms – an Internet of the public, by the public and for the public; an Internet that advances instead of threatens democracy and the public sphere. The Public Service Internet is based on Internet platforms operated by a variety of Public Service Media, taking the public service remit into the digital age. The Public Service Internet provides opportunities for public debate, participation and the advancement of social cohesion.

Digital technology in the hands of a democratic public? That would be new. And that would be exciting. The *Manifesto* was signed by Jürgen Habermas, Noam Chomsky, the International Federation of Journalists and many, many others. You can find the free book here:

http://doi.org/10.16997/book60

And so, late on in the penning of this chapter, traditional journalism intervened via cyberspace to remind me that its original aims and ethos are still alive and that Tom Paine's injunction that 'We have it in our power to begin the world over again' is as compelling today than it ever was. We can begin the process of beginning by recognising that the original purpose of digital technology—instrumental efficiency in the quest for private profit—cannot be sustained. To begin again therefore requires a resetting of the system, from a logic based upon user manipulation and exploitation by the platforms, to one based on social needs, social objectives and social cohesion. And the technology of writing, the ethos of truth and the stories by which journalism persuades us, all need to be part of a more collective analogue-digital future where digital is seen as complement to what it means to be analogue. Immersive VR as a journalistic tool, one with authentic journalistic ends, may even have a positive society-enhancing future. However, to let things run as they are, to be constantly pressed into service as extras for every new project of the platforms, means that we become increasingly subservient to a logic that does not reflect us or the analogue form of truth and truth-telling that journalism established a long time ago.

Discussion questions

- What differences does the author argue exist between analogue and digital technologies for journalism?
- How do these differences affect the practice (and goals) of immersive journalism?
- According to the author, how should digital technologies be used by immersive journalists? Do you agree with the author's suggestions? If yes/no, why?

References

Atkins, D. (2021) 'How Facebook Is Killing Journalism and Democracy' Washington Monthly, 13th of March. https://washingtonmonthly.com/2021/03/13/facebook-is-killing-journalism-and-democracy-we-should-do-something-about-it/

Badinjki, T. (2016). Dickens's Dichotomous Formula for Social Reform in Oliver Twist, *International Journal of Applied Linguistics & English Literature.* 5(7), pp. 209–212. DOI:10.7575/aiac.ijalel.v.5n.7p.209

Bartlett, R.C. (2019). *Aristotle' Art of Rhetoric*, Translation with an Interpretive Essay. Chicago: University of Chicago Press.

Chen, B. (2022). 'What's All the Hype About the Metaverse? *New York Times,* 18th of January. www.nytimes.com/2022/01/18/technology/personaltech/metaverse-gaming-definition.html

Cheshire, C. (1997). 'The Ontology of Digital Domains' in D. Holmes (ed.), *Virtual Politics: Community and Identity in Cyberspace.* pp 79–92. London: Sage.

Culkin, J. (1967). 'A Schoolman's Guide to Marshall McLuhan', *The Saturday Review,* 18th of March, pp. 51–53. www.unz.org/Pub/SaturdayRev-1967mar18-00051

Debray, R. (2007). 'Socialism: A Life-Cycle', *New Left Review,* 46 (July–August), pp. 5–17.

de Vaujany, F.-X. and Mitev, N. (2017). 'The Post-Macy Paradox, Information Management and Organizing: Good Intentions and a Road to Hell?', *Culture & Organization,* 23(5), pp. 379–407.

Dickens, C. (1836). *The posthumous papers of the Pickwick Club.* London: Chapman and Hall. Published in serial form.

Dickens, C. (1838). *Oliver Twist.* London: Richard Bentley

Ellul, J. (1992). 'The Betrayal of Technology' Documentary from Holland. https://topdocumentaryfilms.com/betrayal-technology-portrait-jacques-ellul/

Estévez, S. (2009). 'Is Nostalgia Becoming Digital?' *Social Identities,* 15(3), pp. 393–410.

Fleischacker, S. (2013). *What Is Enlightenment?* London: Routledge.

Gehlen, A. (1980). *Man in the Age of Technology.* New York: Columbia University Press.

Gerard, R.W. (1953). 'Some of the Problems Concerning Digital Notions in the Central Nervous System', *Eighth Macy Conference,* pp.171–202. http://pcp.vub.ac.be/books/gerard.pdf

Gritzalis, D., Theoharidou, M., Dritsas, S. and Marias, G. (2006). *Ambient Intelligence: The Promise, the Price and the Social Disruption,* Review Report Series No.1. https://citeseerx.ist.psu.edu/viewdoc/download?doi=10.1.1.723.3329&rep=rep1&type=pdf.

Hanusch, F. and Nölleke, D. (2019). 'Journalistic Homophily on Social Media: Exploring Journalists' interactions with each other on Twitter', *Digital Journalism* 7(1), pp. 22–44.

Hassan, R. (2003). 'Network Time and the New Knowledge Epoch', *Time and Society,* 12(2/3), pp. 225–241.

Hassan, R. (2020). *The Condition of Digitality: A Post-Modern Marxism for the Practice of Digital Life.* London: The University of Westminster Press.

Himelboim, I., Sweetser, K.D., Tinkham, S.F., Cameron, K., Danelo, M. and West, K. (2016) Valence-based homophily on Twitter: Network Analysis of Emotions and Political Talk in the 2012 Presidential Election. *New Media & Society,* 18(7), pp. 1382–1400.

Impett, L. (2018). 'Prometheus Wired'. *New Left Review,* (111), pp. 151.

International Federation of Journalists. (2016). 'At least 2297 Journalists and Media Staff Have been Killed since 1990: IFJ Report'. www.ifj.org/media-centre/news/detail/category/safety/article/at-least-2297-journalists-and-media-staff-have-been-killed-since-1990-ifj-report-2.html

Jaeggi, R. (2014). *Alienation.* New York: Columbia University Press.

Kant, I. (1784). Idea for a Universal History from a Cosmopolitan Point of View. In: L. White Beck (ed.) (1963). *Immanuel Kant: On History.* Indianapolis: The Bobbs-Merrill Co.

Kryger, M. (2012). Charles Dickens: Impact on Medicine and Society. *Journal of Clinical Sleep Medicine, JCSM: Official Publication of the American Academy of Sleep Medicine,* 8(3), pp. 333–338. DOI:10.5664/jcsm.1930

Lanier, J. (2018) 'How Social Media Ruins Your Life' Interview, Channel 4. www.youtube.com/watch?v=kc_Jq42Og7Q&t=1016s

Madison, C. (2022). '*Meta Doesn't Mean What You Think It Does*', *The Atlantic Monthly*, 7th of June. www.theatlantic.com/newsletters/archive/2022/06/meta-origin-irony/661191

McKibben, B. (1992). *The Age of Missing Information*. New York: Penguin.

McLuhan, M. (1962). *The Gutenberg Galaxy: The Making of Typographic Man*. Toronto: University of Toronto Press.

McLuhan, M. (1964). *Understanding Media: The Extensions of Man*. New York: McGraw-Hill.

Miller, D. (2018). *The Death of the Gods: The New Global Power Grab*. London: Heinemann.

Nylan, M. (2001). The Five "Confucian" Classics. New Haven: Yale University Press. www.jstor.org/stable/j.ctt1nq7hj

Ong, W.J. (1982). *Orality and Literacy: The Technologizing of the Word*. New York: Routledge.

Ong, W.J. (1986) 'Writing Is a Technology that Restructures Thought.' In: Baumann. G. (ed.) *The Written Word: Literacy in Transition*. pp. 23–50. New York: Oxford UP.

Paine, T. (1774–1779). The Writings of Thomas Paine, Vol. I (1774–1779). New York: G. P. Putnam's Sons.

Paine, T. (1982 [1775–1776]) *Common Sense*. London: Penguin Classics.

Pomerantsev, P. (2019). *This Is Not Propaganda: Adventures in the War Against Reality*. New York: Hachette.

Puri, S (2021). Tweet on 30th of October. https://twitter.com/ShaanVP/status/1454151237650112512

Rorty, R. (1989). *Contingency, Irony, and Solidarity*. New York: Cambridge University Press.

VICE News. (2015). 'Chris Milk, Spike Jonze and VICE News Bring the First-Ever Virtual Reality Newscast to Sundance', 23rd of January. https://news.vice.com/article/chris-milk-spike-jonze-and-vice-news-bring-the-first-ever-virtual-reality-newscast-to-sundance

Watzlawick, P., Beavin-Bavelas, J. and Jackson, D. (1967). *Some Tentative Axioms of Communication. In Pragmatics of Human Communication: A Study of Interactional Patterns, Pathologies and Paradoxes*. New York: W. W. Norton.

Younge, G. (2013). 'Eduardo Galeano: "My Greatest Fear Is that We Are All Suffering from Amnesia"', *The Guardian*, 24th of July. www.theguardian.com/books/2013/jul/23/eduardo-galeano-children-days-interview

INDEX

6x9 110–111
360° video: critiques 125–127, 161; expert interviews 18, 23–25, 28–32; normative issues 110–112, 115–118; production 61–64, 67; researching 78, 94; screenplay writing 50–54

abstraction 144–145
Abu Ghraib 133, 135
accessibility 2, 26
accuracy 107–110, 112–116, 118, 120, 149
Across the Line 130
advertising 129, 161
affect 96–98, 116–118, 125–126, 129–131, 135–137; *see also* emotion
Agianniotakis, M. 125
Aitamurto, T. 8, 107–121
algorithms 158, 160
alienation 147–148, 160
anagnorisis 136
analogue 144–148, 152–153, 156–158, 160–162
Andrejevic, M. 127
anthropology 144, 147, 152–153, 156
Aristotle 136, 157, 159
artificial intelligence (AI) 119–120, 145
attention 47, 54–55, 78–79, 96
audience 28–29, 33, 35–36, 78; engagement 47, 55, 107, 111; as spect-actors 137–138
audio, spatial 18
augmented reality (AR) 67–68, 87, 115, 119–121
Ausserhofer, J. 76

authenticity 109–113, 115–117, 120–121, 131
authority 113–114, 120, 154–155, 157
autoamputation 147
automation 148, 156
autonomy 107–108, 118–119
avatars 95, 98, 118

Baía-Reis, A. 6, 21, 23–24, 26–29, 34, 36, 39–41, 92–102
Barbosa, S. 21, 24, 26–27
Bard, M.T. 55
Bartnett, R. 60
Bazin, A. 131
BBC 51–52
behavioural studies 87, 145
Benítez de Gracia, M.J. 1, 17–43
beta mode 36
bias 53–56, 109, 116, 118
Bible 154
bibliometrics 76, 79–88
Biocca, F. 95
Blein, J.-E. 21, 23–25, 27–28, 30–31, 34–35, 38
blogging 161
Bloom, P. 53
Bly, N. 155
Boal, A. 9, 136–139
body *see* embodiment
brain 145–146
Brasil, A. 7
Brecht, B. 136–139
Bristol 63

Bujic, M. 70
Butler, J. 132, 134–136

Capa, R. 114
capitalism 126, 143, 159–160
category errors 144–145
catharsis 136
CAVE 95, 126
Cheshire, C. 144
Chomsky, N. 151, 162
The Circle 125
Clewer, N. 129–130
Clouds Over Sidra 134
Cochran, E. 155
code cracking 69
coding 93–94, 99
Cold War 145
collaboration 62–67, 118–120
Coloma, J. 22, 26–27, 31, 37, 39
Colussi, J. 75, 78
commodification 151
communication 47, 121, 146–148, 151, 154, 157–158
composography 112–113, 116
computer-generated imagery (CGI) 110–112, 115–116, 120
computing 145–148; ubiquitous 156
conferences 17, 63, 145–146
conflicts of interest 118
Confucius 150
connotation 110–111
Conover, T. 3
consciousness 154, 156
content analysis 93
Covid-19 19
credibility 25, 82–88, 107, 118, 120
Cronkite, W. 93
cybernetics 145–146

Da Costa, L. G. 7
Dahle, M. B. 66
Damas, S. H. 1, 17–43
Darsø, L. 64
data 34, 40–41, 119–120
Dauphinée, E. 132–135
Davos 129
de Bruin, K. 48–49
De la Peña, N. 3, 6, 17, 22, 27, 32–34, 37, 39–41, 46, 92–93, 95, 126–127
de Vaujany, F.-X. 146
Dean, J. 126, 128, 130
death 134
Debray, R. 151, 157
deliberation 135, 138–139

Dell'Orto, G. 46
denotation 110
Deuze, M. 49
Dickens, C. 158
Didion, J. 155
digital, *v.* analogue 143–149, 151–163
disability 124–125
The Displaced 54
distribution 32
dizziness 31–32
documentary 2, 4–5, 113; expert interviews 29–31; research 87–88; screenplay writing 50–54; teaching 61–66, 69–70
Domínguez, E. 7, 21, 23–24, 28, 33, 35–36, 38–40
drama 136–138

editing 47–48, 54–55, 111, 115–116, 120
education 37, 41, 60–70
Ekström, M. 47
Ellul, J. 148
Emblematic Group 51, 129
embodiment 48–54, 98–100, 117, 128–134, 138; bodily self-perception 100–101; body ownership 127; toxic 130
emersion 137
emotion 70, 93–94, 96–98; analogue *v.* digital 146, 158–159; expert interviews 24–25, 27; normative issues 116–118; politics of 124–132, 135–139; screenplay writing 53–55
empathy 24, 70, 78, 101, 117; forced 128–129; politics of immersion 124–125, 127–132, 138–139; screenplay writing 53–54
engagement 47, 55, 107, 111, 121
Enlightenment 144, 149, 151, 155
epistemology 66, 126, 129
Estévez, S. 147, 153
estrangement 135–140, 144
ethics 64, 108–121; accuracy/objectivity/transparency 109–112; affective dimensions 116–118; analogue *v.* digital 149–151, 157; authenticity 112–116; autonomy/privacy 118–120; expert interviews 27, 32–33; politics of immersion 124–129, 133–135; screenplay writing 52–53, 56
ethos 157–158, 160, 162
experimentation 30, 36
extension 101, 147, 152

Facebook 17, 34, 39–40, 52, 87, 143–144, 158

Index **167**

facts 109, 149–151
fakeness 55–56
Falke, C. 133–134
'Falling Soldier' 115
Fallujah 50, 52
Ferrando, I. 17, 22, 24, 29–31, 34, 37, 39
first person 3
Floyd, G. 150
focus group 19–20
forced empathy 129
Fortnite 40
forum theatre 137–138
framing 131–134
Frontline 51

Galeano, E. 149
gaming 67–68, 86–87, 95, 120, 125–126
Geerds, J. 18
Gehlen, A. 152–153, 156
Gellhorn, M. 46, 93
Gerard, R. W. 145, 152
Google 61, 63, 118
GoPro 18, 66
governance 125–126
Guardian 110–111

Habermas, J. 162
Harbers, F. 49
harm 117–119, 128
Hasler, B. S. 53–54
Hassan, R. 10–11, 143–162
headsets 34, 77–78, 119
Helland Urke, E. 63
Hernández, R. 1–2, 17, 22–23, 28–29, 32–34, 39–40
heteronomy 148
Hidden 67
history: of journalism 112–116, 155–156; of writing 152–155
Hobbs, R. 55
Hololens 67
humanity 144–149, 151–159
humility 30, 35, 42–43, 153–154
Hunger in L.A. 51

ideology 4, 11, 126, 129, 132, 151, 158
immersion: critiques 8–11, 124–140, 143–162; definitions 6–7, 92–98, 101–102; emotional impact *see* emotion; expert interviews 23–43; keyword frequency 77–78, 83, 87; narrative characteristics *see* narrative
impartiality *see* objectivity
Impett, L. 148

innovation, pedagogy of 64–66
Instagram 36, 107, 119–120
integrity 118–120
interactivity 24, 94, 98–100, 127–128
interdisciplinarity 6–7, 62–66
International Federation of Journalists 149, 162
interoperability 41
interviews 19–20
Iraq 50, 133, 135
ISIS 50
Iwo Jima 115

Jaeggi, R. 148
Jones, S. 49, 128

Kang, S. 6–7, 75–88
Kant, I. 131, 149, 151, 155
Kayes, A. B. 63
keywords 80–88
Kick, L. 6, 92–102
Kirchhoff, S. 60
Kolb, D. A. 63
Kozol, W. 135

Lacan, J. 126
language 88, 154; contingency of 157–158
Lanier, J. 158–159
learning outcomes, measuring 68–69
LeBlanc, A. N. 3
Lee, W. S. 78
Levinas, I. 134
Lima, L. 21, 24
literacy 150–151, 154–155, 159, 161
literary journalism 46
logic 144–146; *logos* 157, 159–160
Longhi, R. 97
López-García, C. 48
Los Angeles 51
Luckey, P. 17
Luria, A. 159

Mabrook, R. 78
McDonalds 129
machine learning 120
McKibben, B. 146
McLuhan, M. 147, 151–152, 156
McRoberts, J. 49, 127–128
Madison, M. 144
magazines 63, 156
Mahood, C. 78
manipulation 11; analogue *v.* digital 158–160; normative issues 111–115, 120;

Index

politics of immersion 124–125, 128–132, 139; screenplay writing 48, 53–56
market 26, 33, 151, 160–161
marketing 39, 128
Marx, K. 136, 147, 160
Maschio, T. 49
Mayring, P. 93
mediation 128–129, 131–135, 138–140
memory 54–55, 79, 87
Meta 26, 39–40, 43, 119–120, 143
meta-analysis 80
metaverse 102, 143, 159; expert interviews 33, 38–41, 43; normative issues 118, 121; politics of 126, 128, 140
Metzinger, T. 7
Microsoft 67
migration 51–52
Milk, C. 53, 125, 127, 130, 132
missing information 146–147
Mitev, N. 146
Moore, K. 51
mountaineers 66
Murray, J. 7, 96
museums 38, 67–68

Nakamura, L. 124, 128–130
narrative 69, 154–155; non-linear 62–63; *see also* storytelling
negativity 158–159
neoliberalism 126, 130–131, 156
network time 159
neutrality *see* objectivity
New York 155
New York Times 18, 50, 54, 118, 151
news values 49, 114, 116
non-linear narrative 62–63
norms of journalism 107–109, 111–121
Norway 61–69

objectivity 4, 8; analogue *v.* digital 149–151; normative issues 107–116, 120; screenplay writing 47, 49, 56
O'Brien, E. 78
Oculus 17, 34, 125
Oliveto, M. 6, 92–102
Ong, W. 151, 154, 159
oral culture 154, 159
Orwell, G. 46, 150, 155

pain 132–133
Paine, T. 149–151, 155, 162
Paíno Ambrosio, A. 48
pathos 124–125, 129, 157–159
Pavlik, J. 97

PBS 51
pedagogy 60, 63, 66–67, 70; *see also* education
Pedwell, C. 130
Penz, O. 125–126, 130
Pérez-Seijo, S. 21, 23, 26, 28–29, 31, 39, 48
Perrin, D. 47
persona, user as 64
persuasion 53–54, 56–57, 157–158
philosophical anthropology 144, 152
philosophy 143–146, 150–151
photography 54, 109–115, 120, 132–135
physiology 78–79
Pimentel, D. 127
platforms 34–36, 40, 119, 143–144, 161–162
plausibility 111, 127
point of view 18, 31
Pokémon Go 120
politics 46, 54, 126; analogue *v.* digital 150, 155, 159, 161; emotional manipulation 128–132; estrangement/participation 135–139
Pomerantsev, P. 157–158
post-processing 111, 115
Pötzsch, H. 8–10, 124–140
power 126, 129–130, 134–136, 138, 151; of narrative 27, 50; speaking truth to 149
Prat, C. 22–23, 30, 32, 34, 38, 41
presence 6–7, 87, 92–94, 98–102; critical views 117, 127–128; expert interviews 19, 23, 30; screenplay writing 53–55
print culture 149–150, 154–157
prisons 50–51, 110, 117
privacy 118–120
production 60
Project Syria 129, 132, 134
propaganda 50, 54–56, 129, 151
psychology 6–7, 27, 32; cybernetic 145–146, 158; immersion/presence 94–99, 101; research 86–87
Public Relations (PR) 62, 108–109, 114, 116, 129
Public Service Media 161–162
Puri, S. 159

quality 28, 39

rationality 130–131, 135–137, 159
Raya, L. 22, 24–25, 30–32, 34, 40–41
reading 152
realism 109–112, 117–118, 125, 131
reality 144, 146, 149
reason 130–131, 135–137, 159

recognition 147, 153, 156–159, 161
reflection-in-action 66
refugees 50–52, 54
Reis, T. A. 75, 78
religion 154–155
replacement techniques 152
representation 114, 131–132, 135; representational philosophy 146
resonance 153, 156
Ressa, M. 26
rhetoric 156–160
Robertson, A. 130
Rodríguez Fidalgo, M. I. 48
Roeh, I. 4, 47
Rogers, E. 77
Rojas, D. 22, 24, 30, 39–40
Rorty, R. 157
Rose, M. 128, 131
Ruberg, B. 127

Samsung 118–119
Sánchez Laws, A. L. 1–11, 21, 26, 30, 32–33, 35, 38, 41, 54, 126, 129, 131
Sauer, B. 125–126, 130
Schlembach, R. 129–130
Schön, D. A. 66
Schudson, M. 4, 109
Schwab, K. 129
scientometrics 76, 79–88
Scopus 93, 96
screenplay 31, 46–56
sensory hyper-saturation 26
sexual harassment 52–53
Sidorenko, P. 21, 24–25, 27–29, 32, 35, 38
Silicon Valley 61, 158, 160
Singer, J. B. 78
smartphones 37, 39
Snapchat 107, 119
sociability 34–35
social media 83, 86–87, 158–160
social networks 33, 39–41, 43
Society of Professional Journalists (SPJ) 108–109, 112, 117–118
solitary confinement 51, 110, 117
Solomon, B. C. 50
Sontag, S. 132–133, 135
Sony Ericsson 18
Souppouris, A. 124–125
Space Explorers 23
Spain 19
spatial 24, 28–31; audio 18; storytelling 37, 77–78
spect-actor 137
spherical media 17–18, 60–61, 64, 116

staging 54, 114–115, 136–138
Steinfeld, N. 2–4, 9, 46–56
Stephenson, N. 143
storyliving 49, 53, 55, 77
storytelling 51–54, 150–152; journalism as 46–48; spatial 77–78; spherical 60–61; *see also* narrative
subjectivity 101, 111–112, 130, 145–146
Substack 161
Sullivan, M. 54
Sundance Independent Film Festival 17
superrealistic content 117–118
Swift, J. 155
Syria 51–52, 129, 132

Teknisk Ukeblad 63
theatre 136–138
tool making 152–153
torture 133, 135
toxic embodiment 130
transdisciplinarity 6–7, 62–66
transgender people 124–125
transparency: norms of 107–109, 112–114, 116, 120; politics of 131–132, 136
truth 108–110, 113, 116; analogue *v.* digital 149–152, 154–162; politics of immersion 129, 131, 133; without trauma 32
Tukachinsky, R. 80
Twitter 158–159
Typographic Man 156

Uber 161
ubiquitous computing 156
Ukraine 113
United Kingdom 61, 155, 158
United States of America 61, 108, 115, 133–135, 145
universities 37
University of Bergen 67
University of Southern California 17
University of Westminster Press 161
User Experience (UX) 48, 63–64
Utne, T. 5, 54, 60–70

V-effect (*Verfremdung*) 136–137, 139
Vikings 67
Villarreal, A. 78
Virtual Buddy 68
virtual reality (VR): critiques 8–11, 124–140, 143–162; emotional impact *see* emotion; expert interviews 23–43; immersion *see* immersion; keyword frequency 82–86; normative issues

see norms of journalism; screenplay *see* screenplay; teaching *see* education
visual journalism 108–116, 120
Viti-Sunnmøre Museum 67
Volcic, Z. 127
Volda University College (VUC) 61–69
VOSviewer 76, 80–82
voyeurism 125, 133, 135

Walter, N. 80
Walters, P. 3
war 29, 113–115, 117, 133–135, 145
Watzlawick, P. 146
We Wait 51, 53
Web of Science (WoS) 76, 80–82, 88

Weiser, M. 156
Wenger, E. 63
Witschge, T. 49
workplace harassment 52–53
World Economic Forum 129
World War II 113, 117
wow effect 24
writing 149–152, 154, 156–162

YouTube 28, 30, 34

Zampa, M. 47
Zelizer, B. 110
Zuckerberg, M. 38, 40, 126, 128, 140, 143, 159

For Product Safety Concerns and Information please contact our EU
representative GPSR@taylorandfrancis.com
Taylor & Francis Verlag GmbH, Kaufingerstraße 24, 80331 München, Germany

www.ingramcontent.com/pod-product-compliance
Lightning Source LLC
Chambersburg PA
CBHW051359290426
44108CB00015B/2087